D1600918

John Woo

John Woo
The Films

by Kenneth E. Hall

McFarland & Company, Inc., Publishers
Jefferson, North Carolina, and London

Frontispiece: John Woo in 1997. (Photograph by Stephen Vaughan; courtesy John Woo.)

Library of Congress Cataloguing-in-Publication Data

Hall, Kenneth E., 1954–
    John Woo: the films / by Kenneth E. Hall
        p.   cm.
    Filmography: p.
    Includes bibliographical references and index.
    ISBN 0-7864-0619-4 (library binding : 50# alkaline paper) ∞
    1. Woo, John, 1948–   —Criticism and interpretation.
  I. Title.
  PN1998.3.W655H36   1999   99-25445
  791.43'0233'092—dc21   CIP

British Library Cataloguing-in-Publication data are available

Manufactured in the United States of America

McFarland & Company, Inc., Publishers
  Box 611, Jefferson, North Carolina 28640
    www.mcfarlandpub.com

To Carla,
with love

Acknowledgments

This book would not have been possible without the unstinting cooperation of John Woo, whose graciousness and generosity are much appreciated. Besides agreeing to my numerous requests for interviews and information, he provided me with the opportunity to visit Vancouver in 1996 to watch him shoot *Once a Thief.* I simply cannot say enough, either, about the help given me by Terence Chang, who not only agreed to repeated interviews but assisted me in numerous other ways. Special thanks go as well to Lori Tilkin, Terence Chang's assistant, for her seemingly endless patience with my questions and also for her help with translations. Laurence Walsh, John Woo's assistant, has also been very helpful, as was David Chute, publicist for *Hard Target*, who provided me with access to his personal collection of videotapes.

My colleague at the University of North Dakota, Gene DuBois, inspired me to start the project and gave me helpful advice and feedback. Jane Berne, another colleague at UND, also encouraged and advised me, as did Michael Anderegg, who read a draft and contributed comments. Tony Williams of Southern Illinois University has been a highly valued e-mail correspondent and has supported me throughout in my efforts. I would also like to thank Calvin Young, owner of New World Video in Winnipeg, Manitoba, for his assistance in searching his collection for videos for me. Win Lee of Wake Forest University assisted me with translations. Amy Chin, from Hong Kong, helped me to find addresses for Hong Kong film figures. Thanks also to Bob Murawski and Faith Conroy for their assistance with the chapter on *Hard Target*. John Ettling, then dean of the College of Arts and Sciences at the University of North Dakota, and the university's Office of Research and Program Development provided funds for research and film purchases.

I also wish to thank all who agreed to answer questions for me for the book, whether in person, by telephone, or by fax. Their many contributions have considerably enriched the project.

I would never have finished this work without the patient encouragement, support, and urging of my wife, Carla, to whom the book is dedicated.

Contents

Introduction: Painting the True Colors of the Hero

Many heroes lived before Agamemnon; but all are
unknown and unwept, extinguished in everlasting night,
because they have no spirited chronicler.
—Horace,
Odes, Book 4, Ode 9, Stanza 7

Heroism feels and never reasons, and therefore is always right.
—Ralph Waldo Emerson,
Essays (First Series, 1841), "Heroism"

The greatest obstacle to being heroic is the doubt whether
one may not be going to prove one's self a fool; the truest
heroism is to resist the doubt; and the profoundest wisdom,
to know when it ought to be resisted, and when it be obeyed.
—Nathaniel Hawthorne,
The Blithedale Romance (1852), chapter 2[1]

John Woo, the now-famous director from Hong Kong, has spent most of his career celebrating the heroic. Woo is well known for his choreographed, kinetic action films with their capable yet vulnerable heroes. And although he made several comedies in Hong Kong and Taiwan, even the large majority of these can be seen as mock-heroic. Woo attained great celebrity in Hong Kong in 1986 when he directed a remake of a black-and-white Hong Kong film called *True Colors of a Hero*.[2] This remake became the astonishingly popular gangster movie *A Better Tomorrow*.[3] Woo soon developed into a master craftsman of action films. But his films were action movies with a difference. They focused on soulful, reluctant heroes with the integrity of samurai warriors or Chinese knights. Frequently they were outlaw figures, but that fact was peripheral to their basic self-consistency and their chivalrous conduct toward others.

This book will examine Woo's revival of the heroic as a legitimate mode of artistic discourse. In these pages the reader will see how such an apparently outmoded, romantic concept can become "truly colorful" once again in the hands of a director who genuinely believes in the hero figure as a standard-bearer of honor, integrity and ethical values, often in a familial context.

The heroic in Woo's films is typically expressed through self-sacrificial action. As Woo has commented:

> A real knight should come and go like an autumn leaf. He does not look for recognition. It is unimportant to him that those around know of him. Only his actions are important. He will sacrifice everything, even his life, for justice, loyalty, for love and his country. His life is like a cloud, it could disappear in an instant. I think there is something beautiful about this. Even if there is only one beautiful moment in life—it is worth it just for that moment [Woo, Interview by Jillian Sandell, 39].

All the heroes[4] of Woo's mature work are self-sacrificing in one way or another. Ho, his brother Kit, and especially Ho's friend Mark in *A Better Tomorrow* are self-sacrificial figures who nevertheless succeed in their heroism because the evil Shing is destroyed and Ho and Kit are reconciled. The outcome in *A Better Tomorrow II* (1987) is murkier because heroes Ken, Ho and Lung (Dean Shek) are treated rather comically, at least once Kit has been killed; still, the heroic trio is successful in avenging the wrongs done to Lung and Kit. *The Killer* (1989) is unique among Woo's work in that heroism is frustrated; although the evil is rooted out, the girl goes unsaved, and the heroes either die or see all their friends die. *Bullet in the Head* (1990) is conspicuous in having no true heroes, a point made by Woo himself (personal interview, November 8, 1995). *Once a Thief* (1991)[5] is a comic, light treatment of the heroic motif, with an admixture of love rivalry and three-way friendship. *Hard Boiled* (1992), like *A Better Tomorrow*, is a more traditional hero-villain story; the script tries to introduce the idea of heroes shading into villains, but this theme is not emphasized, and the viewer really does not question the essential heroism of the policemen Tequila (Chow Yun-fat) and Tony[6] (Tony Leung Chiu-wai)[7] by the end of the film.

In Woo's American movies, the heroic element is more muted but still in evidence. Even Chance (Jean-Claude Van Damme) in *Hard Target* (1993) is self-sacrificing in the sense that he voluntarily protects the heroine Natasha (Yancy Butler)—the $217 she is to pay him seems a mere plot device. Hale (Christian Slater) in *Broken Arrow* (1996) is a throwback to Hollywood heroes of an earlier period.

Woo is unabashed in his admiration of such heroic figures. Perhaps his favorite film is David Lean's *Lawrence of Arabia* (1962), which features just such a soulful and nearly masochistic hero, played by Peter O'Toole. He also identifies strongly with the persona of sixties icon Steve McQueen, who played frustrated or sacrificed heroes (in films such as *Hell Is for Heroes* [1962], *The Great Escape* [1963], and *Bullitt* [1968]), of the type that soon came to be called antihero. Going even further along the heroic (or antiheroic) spectrum, Woo admires the antihero Pike Bishop (William Holden) in Sam Peckinpah's *The Wild Bunch* (1969) as well as the seemingly unheroic character played by Warren Oates in Peckinpah's *Bring Me the Head of Alfredo Garcia* (1974). Woo spoke of his admiration for the self-sacrificing hero, referring to an incident from Chinese history that should seem familiar in spirit to anyone who has seen Japanese director Masaki Kobayashi's *Hara-kiri* (1962) or *Rebellion* (1967), in which the samurai heroes "win" precisely by dying for principle:[8]

> There was a pretty famous Chinese story, about four great assassins. One of the assassins [Ching K'o] tried to kill the king. Somehow it didn't work and he was ambushed by hundreds of people. And he fought so hard—and he got cut. When he got cut, he still stood still, and he got cut here and there, he fought, and cut, and he killed some people, and then he got cut again, and then at the end he put a knife on his belly and took the guts out and was holding them and still fighting. It was *real*.[9]

Woo brought his celebration of the heroic to the United States and is now securely established as a leading filmmaker here. He made his first Hollywood film, *Hard Target*, in 1993. Most of the attention to the film was attracted by its kickboxing star, Jean-Claude Van Damme. But Woo was already well known to numerous film critics and to enthusiastic Hong Kong audiences. Beginning with *A Better Tomorrow* (1986), Woo had left the relative obscurity of his earlier career and entered the phase of his filmmaking that has caused him to gain publicity as an "action painter" (McDonagh 46), to be compared, not always accurately, with Sam Peckinpah, and to acquire a fervent cult following in the United States and elsewhere.

Woo is indeed an "action painter," but his appeal rests only partially upon his frenetic yet superbly controlled action sequences. Watching a Woo film is a unique experience, one difficult to fix and explain. As Maitland McDonagh writes, critics are uncomfortable with Woo's work because it escapes their usual aesthetic categories (47). Genre films that mix genres, homages to movies that seem more like quotations in a surreal context, his films appear to violate some cherished rules, yet fortuitously end by making their own. Woo borrows freely from the modernist film tradition, creating a postmodern mix that nevertheless escapes the archness of postmodern exercises: Woo's work, technically dazzling, does not apologize for its lapses into sentimentality, its sometimes crude humor, or any of the other rough spots on its glittering surface.[10] A self-professed religious moralist ("Woo in Interview," 25), Woo naturally draws upon directors such as Peckinpah and actors such as Steve McQueen—not only because of their notorious "macho" qualities or image, but rather, and really chiefly, because of the softer core under their surface hardness—their emphasis on the virtues stressed, repeatedly and insistently, by John Woo's films: loyalty, friendship, personal integrity, courage in the face of reversal. To this list Woo adds a Christian (but almost traditionally Japanese) emphasis on victory through sacrifice. In films such as *The Killer* (1989), the defeated hero "wins" because his integrity is restored.

Such ethical *gravitas* anchors Woo's work. Not just "buddy" films, his action movies explore the limits of friendship and the need for self-sacrifice precisely to maintain such friendships. Fortunately, however, Woo is neither a superficial director of gunfights and car chases nor a tiresome moralizer, a heavy-handed message scenarist. One of the major aims of this book will be to show just how Woo avoids these two alternatives and instead succeeds in fashioning a surprisingly complex and articulated filming style, repeated but varied and enriched in each successive film.

My contention is that Woo is more than an "action director"; in fact, he dislikes this tag. He became quite expert at making comedies in Hong Kong and Taiwan, and he would very much like to make a musical as well as to work in the epic genre of *Lawrence of Arabia*.[11]

Woo's success is not an isolated phenomenon. Hong Kong (or Cantonese) cinema has a long history,[12] and several talented and innovative directors are now working within that tradition. Many directors and actors from Hong Kong—Chow Yun-fat, Danny Lee, Che Kirk Wong, Ringo Lam—merit closer attention and more widespread popularity. Undoubtedly more than a few of them will receive such attention since, like Woo, many began to emigrate from Hong Kong around the time of its transfer to mainland China.[13] Jackie Chan's recent visibility in the United States, on movie screens and television shows, is representative of the growing attention accorded Hong Kong movie people. As for John Woo, his newfound United States popularity, greatly accelerated by the success of his recent *Broken Arrow* and *Face/Off*, will contribute to a closer examination of other Hong Kong film personalities.

A Brief Biography

John Woo (Wu Yu Shen or Ng Yu Sum)[14] was born in 1946 in Canton (Guangdong), in what is now Guangzhou province, in the south of China.[15] When he was four, his family moved to Hong Kong (Wolcott 63). He became interested in cinema at school: "I started to make films—existential love stories—when I was in school. I was part of a small group of people who were stimulated by European art films, the French New Wave and contemporary Japanese cinema and were experimenting with film" ("Woo in Interview," 25). The family could not afford to send him to film school, but he was able to join the Cathay Production Company in 1969. His work as a "continuity person" there allowed him to earn just enough to create some experimental films; he also wrote film criticism.[16]

After working for Shaw Brothers studio,[17] where he was assistant director for martial arts specialist Chang Cheh, he co-directed an independent film, *Young Dragons* (1973/75). Its banning due to violence led to its being purchased by Golden Harvest Films,[18] who put Woo on a three-year contract. He directed some low-budget kung fu films and was able to help Jackie Chan get started in acting (in *Hand of Death*, 1976). Woo's next film, well-received by audiences, was *Princess Chang Ping* (1976), a Cantonese opera film.

Woo began to work in comedy, "as a production consultant to help the great comedian Michael Hui on his first two films." When Woo directed *Money Crazy* (1977), a "smash hit" comedy, he became a well-recognized name.

In 1981, he left Golden Harvest and began to work for the newly formed Cinema City.[19] His experience with this company was far from positive; sent to Taiwan to direct, he was, in his own words, "stuck there for two years." Upon his return to Hong Kong, director and producer Tsui Hark (*Peking Opera Blues*, *Once Upon a Time in China*) gave him a job at his company, the Film Workshop. Thus they came to collaborate on *A Better Tomorrow*.

With this film, Woo's career became of real importance, both for critics and for moviegoers. The film was an enormous hit in Hong Kong and established Woo as a high-energy action director (Wolcott 63). Often compared to Sam Peckinpah's style, Woo's frenetic action mode is in fact distinctive. He has set his own mark in shooting such sequences as the protracted destruction of a hospital, during multiple gunfights, in *Hard Boiled*.

In 1992, Woo moved to the United States to direct *Hard Target*, starring Jean-Claude Van Damme. The film cannot be regarded as a "total"

Woo work, since he took over the production with an existing script, and Van Damme and the producers exercised unfortunate control over the filming and the publicity (Wolcott 64). Still, it has very accomplished action sequences and some challenging performances (especially from the villains played by Lance Henriksen and Arnold Vosloo), and it served to expose American viewers to Woo's work.

Woo now lives in Los Angeles and pursues his directing career. His *Broken Arrow* (1996) was a major hit, as was his most recent release, *Face/Off* (1997); his TV pilot for Fox Television/Alliance Productions, *Once a Thief*, was aired in fall 1996. *Black Jack*, another TV pilot for USA-TV and starring Dolph Lundgren, came out in 1998.

Woo works in a tradition interesting because it is hybrid. He is a Western-influenced Asian director, a member of the Hong Kong "New Wave" which came to prominence in 1979 (see Li Cheuk-to 160–1). Woo subsumes influence and inspiration from traditional genre films (Raoul Walsh, John Ford), from contra-generic or revisionist films (by directors including Sergio Leone and Arthur Penn), and from American New Wave mavericks such as Sam Peckinpah.[20] To this mix Woo adds European filmmaking technique and allusions to now-iconic directors such as Truffaut, Fellini and Melville. Not to be forgotten is, of course, the great contribution of Asian film to his vision and style. He himself points especially to martial arts film master Chang Cheh,[21] but one would certainly add Japanese giant Akira Kurosawa, and, perhaps, Masaki Kobayashi and the late Cantonese director King Hu.[22]

Clearly Woo is "more than Mark Lester's Asian brother" (McDonagh 48)[23]; nor is he merely a Chinese Sam Peckinpah.[24] His range is greater than or at least different from Peckinpah's—one could hardly imagine *Once a Thief* (1991), a caper film with slapstick and sight gag comedy, from Peckinpah. Woo's work draws syncretically upon cinema, plastic arts, and music, as we shall see in studying his films.

His signature films are stories about male friendship and loyalty, usually featuring a *doppelgänger* relationship between a "good" brother and a "bad" one, a cop and a killer, a cop and a gangster, a "good" thief and a "bad" thief. This kind of relationship is not new to Hollywood or to literature; what is new, perhaps, is the currently fashionable disparagement or dismissal of such relationships as "macho male bonding." From the Sumerian *Gilgamesh* through Homer to the medieval German *Nibelungenlied*, epic has emphasized the role of male friendship, both in moral terms (loyalty, integrity, courage) and as a vessel of cultural transmission. With the rise of the novel, writers as varied as Cervantes and Conrad (two men who would not be thought of as *machista* apologists), Twain, Dickens,

Fitzgerald, Raymond Chandler and Yukio Mishima—to name a very few—have celebrated, parodied, investigated or critiqued male friendship and its tendency toward exclusiveness, defensiveness or misunderstanding of women. Filmmakers from Ford to Scorsese have been fascinated with the topic, each providing a distinct approach to it. John Woo, then, should be seen in this respect against a long tradition of thematic and structural focus upon the theme of male friendship. One is reminded here of films like those of Peckinpah or of Howard Hawks. Like Hawks, for example, Woo's films avow the importance of loyalty and integrity and also display stylistic formulae such as triangular relationships.[25]

Besides his employment of bravura stylistic effects and hyperkinetic action, other salient features of Woo's work are his interest in personal (especially family) relationships and the sentiment and comedy (whether intentional or not) so often a part of any interpersonal communication, male or female. Commentators on his films rarely notice, or at any rate fail to stress, his background in comedy. Like Howard Hawks, Woo approaches action filming with a leavening of wit and, to a greater degree than Hawks, he has worked in more purely slapstick or *opéra bouffe* modes, as in the Hong Kong *Once a Thief*. Critics attuned to the "strong" virtues of male loyalty and heroism so prominent in much of Woo's work or enamored of his technical displays have tended to point to his "lapses" into comedy as embarrassing defects. (So too with his sentimental interludes.) To see them as mistakes, however, is to misunderstand Woo. The keys to a more precise evaluation of Woo may lie in his interest in comic expression (a mode that rarely lies far from the extremes of pathos or farce) and in the samurai film and *bushido* tradition as well as the *wuxia pian* (Chinese swordplay) genre. One can easily find such sentimentality in Chaplin or Keaton comedies and such comic moments (often very broad) in Kurosawa films like *Yojimbo* (1961) or, even more noticeably, *Sanjuro* (1962).[26] (The parodic Japanese Zatoichi [blind swordsman] series, many with actor-producer Shintaro Katsu, would be an even more obvious example.) Woo's tone and pacing may annoy or perplex Western audiences (or at least critics), but one must understand that he is not inherently a Western director despite his Western film homages.

This book is not intended as an uncritically auteurist study, nor does its author wish to make inflated claims for John Woo's importance. Rather, it is hoped that the reader will come to understand the fascinating aspects of a director who crosses cultural, generic and artistic boundaries with a very engaging, bold and unpretentious manner and who displays a consistent aesthetic vision. Woo is the most visible representative of a generation of filmmakers from Hong Kong which includes

Tsui Hark, Johnny Mak (*Long Arm of the Law*) and Ann Hui (*Song of the Exile*). His career, now in its middle stages, can illuminate for Westerners probably unfamiliar with Hong Kong cinema its interesting approach to genre, to social and political challenges, and to the cross-cultural influence so familiar to societies (such as the Asian and Latin-American) "on the margin" of Western culture.

John Woo, Auteur?

One would not wish to defend a straightforwardly simple auteurist view of any director at this late date. Certainly too simplistic is the 1950s *Cahiers du cinéma* view, propagated in the United States chiefly by Andrew Sarris,[27] of the auteur as a kind of rugged individualist who progressively imposes his will and style on a recalcitrant studio system product. For one thing, it ignores or downplays the collaborative nature of motion picture making, and it fails to distinguish between the true role of the director and his image as director. Still, auteurism has left a definite imprint both on film criticism and on popular reaction—audiences are made aware, to some extent anyway, of the importance of directors.

Since a clearly auteurist emphasis is still apparent in U.S. film circles, it is not difficult to see why Woo has been hailed as an auteur by numerous critics and artists. Dave Kehr, for example, states, "There's very little doubt that John Woo is a director you'd call an auteur, a director who expresses himself very immediately, very directly through his films" (*Hard Boiled* 26).[28] And, as one might argue that the recent explosion of auteur talent in Hollywood (the Scorsese-Coppola generation) is fading somewhat, and that Quentin Tarantino is one of the few young directors to be positively embraced as an auteur (a debatable contention), one can understand even more readily the near-hunger for overseas auteurs to fill the void.

So, Woo has been touted in the United States, much more than in Hong Kong, as a new auteur. Despite the circumstantial reasons for such claims, they appear to be very justified, and in some very emphatic ways.[29] Woo is almost a better argument for pure auteur theory than was Hitchcock (who, after all, actively manufactured his persona)[30] or Welles (who was generally unable to exercise full creative control due to economic constraints). Woo has at times benefitted from a great degree of control over his scripts and shooting. While such control by the director is more common in Hong Kong than in the United States, it is by no means the rule. He is also a director who works, as Terence Chang puts it, in an "intuitive"

Woo on the set of *Bullet in the Head* (1990). Top: Woo setting up a shot. Bottom: Woo at the viewfinder with crew members and actor Jacky Cheung (to the left of viewfinder, with upraised right arm). (Both photographs courtesy John Woo.)

manner. This can result in more control for him, even if such a conse-
quence is unintended:

> I think John is by no means an easy director to work with. Because in
> Hong Kong he did not plan out all his shots. Nobody knew exactly what
> he was going to do the next day or the following week. Every single shot
> is planned in his head, you know, so it's really very difficult [for the stu-
> dio] to have some kind of control. I didn't think John did that on pur-
> pose, because he's a very intuitive filmmaker. Often new things popped in
> his head and he would change things accordingly. So it's very, very
> difficult to find out in advance what exactly he is going to do [Chang,
> "Commentary," *The Killer* 13].[31]

But if the auteur "theory" means anything, it means that an auteur
is a director with an artistic vision, with a consistent "something to say,"
in the words of cinematographer Bill Butler:

> There are a lot of things a good director has to be.... [M]ost of all, he has
> to have something to say. It doesn't have to be what's on the surface of
> the story. He has to have something to say that's in his gut. He has to be
> mentally disturbed about something, enough so that he will go out there
> and slip it into the story and the characters.... And you'll find that a
> director that does have something to say is successful and you will find
> that message in picture after picture that he makes; it doesn't matter what
> the title of the film is [Schaefer and Salvato 97].

This consistency from film to film would differentiate an accomplished craftsman, say Henry Hathaway or Richard Donner, from an artist
or an "author." The auteur may not be the sole creative force on the film,
but he must at least guide and shape the collaborative effort of filmmaking so that something bearing his stamp will emerge. And Woo does precisely that. Even in a film like *Hard Target*, without his accustomed Hong
Kong crew, and with as many as *nine* producers pressuring him (Woo,
interview with John Martin), one can see that the film is a John Woo product; that moving, intelligent, romantically charged camera is enough to
convince us. Here we can see evidence of auteur status for Woo. And this
is auteur status in the classic sense of a director who leaves his stamp on
a film in spite of the studio, the actors or any other distraction. Despite
their hyperbole, Bazin, Truffaut and their colleagues were decidedly on
the right track. Directors *do* make a great difference, and their work can
be approached as the work of an individual artist—who, however, has collaborators and whose work is informed by the contributions of a group.

If, with our reservations about the theory in mind, we are to take Woo
as an auteur, what is his vision? As it turns out, his vision is a very simple

but strong one, a highly romantic, almost "primitive" perspective. Woo is thoroughly convinced of the central necessity for self-discipline, integrity and loyalty for human life to have any ethical value. He expresses this belief—in some ways a very Chinese one[32]—through his great fascination with, as he says, "the true hero": the man (or woman) who embodies the chivalric ideal, who will die for a friend or a cause. Added to this conviction and this symbol is Woo's avowed Christianity, seemingly an odd attribute for one who has directed such violent films. But Woo feels and believes intensely, and so one should hardly be surprised that his depiction of violence is intense, or at least florid.

Floridity and intensity are qualities normally associated with the romantic. Woo in fact describes himself as a romantic and mentions the French Romantics as influences. His top ten film list certainly contains many characteristically romantic films and motifs. *West Side Story* is assuredly a romance in the pristine sense. *Raging Bull* and *Mean Streets* are romantic from the Shelleyan or Byronic mold, with frustrated and Promethean antiheroes. *2001* is also arguably romantic, but with a modern cautionary subtext. T. E. Lawrence of *Lawrence of Arabia* is, of course, a thoroughly romantic or romanticized figure.[33] *The Godfather Part II* and *Citizen Kane* are actually the least romantic or perhaps the most ironic of the list, but they do contain the all-important tragic hero motif. Although one might not wish to call *Seven Samurai* "romantic," it is certainly intense, and it does feature seven self-sacrificing heroes. So Woo is consistent in his self-characterization, even though he may be using "romantic" in a less restrictive sense than a specialist might.[34]

Woo is decidedly romantic in one precise respect: his disregard for formalism. If, with Walter Jackson Bate, we take the literary Romantics to have been "open" with regard to form, disdainful of literary rules—in other words, opposed to the neoclassical canon (while of course building upon it)—then Woo is a cinematic romantic. It is notable that his "models" are largely iconoclasts, rebels or just romantically inclined filmmakers: Peckinpah, Kubrick, Welles, Melville, Coppola, Scorsese. David Lean is perhaps an exception, if only in his very cleanly disciplined style of perception, but he still deals in romanticism—a Brahms to Welles' Berlioz.

A significant part of Woo's interest for us as a filmmaker is his unapologetic, even simple romanticism. This is a quality not often seen nowadays in cinema, at least in commercial cinema. Earlier analogues might be John Ford, in terms of sentiment, or Howard Hawks, in terms of boyish enthusiasm. But throughout Hollywood history, most directors have been concerned with schedules, contracts and so forth—not very romantic material. Or they have been, more recently, ironically self-conscious film school products. Woo's large appeal is that he seems to brush away studio politics and that he has no truck with directorial posing or intellectual posturing. As screenwriter Roger Avary says, Woo just loves to make movies and wants to tell stories (*Hard Boiled* 22)—to be, as he says, a painter with film.

In this book, we will consider Woo as a cross-cultural film artist who draws upon Asian and Western influences in film, literature, history, philosophy and religion. Along with specific chapters on his important films, the book will examine his inheritance from Asian tradition; his sources in Asian, American and European filmmakers; the question of his status as an "action director"; his influence on other filmmakers; and his use of symbolic material. In addition, his working methods will be highlighted with material drawn from extensive and numerous interviews conducted by the author. It is hoped that the reader will come to understand the special appeal of a unique director who appears to have begun a successful transition from cult status to wider viewership, but without destroying or losing the artistic force that first drew attention to him.

Chapter 1

Woo and the Asian and Western Traditions

> *Behind the complicated details of the world stand the simplicities: God is good, the grown-up man or woman knows the answer to every question, there is such a thing as truth, and justice is as measured and faultless as a clock. Our heroes are simple: they are brave, they tell the truth, they are good swordsmen and they are never in the long run really defeated. That is why no later books satisfy us like those which were read to us in childhood—for those promised a world of great simplicity of which we knew the rules, but the later books are complicated and contradictory with experience; they are formed out of our own disappointing memories.*
>
> —Graham Greene,
> *The Ministry of Fear* (1943),
> book 1, chapter 7, section 1

The Chinese Chivalric Hero

A central aspect of John Woo's romantic perspective is his long-standing interest in the chivalric legend or myth in Chinese history and literature. Like many neo–Romantics, Woo is fascinated by chivalric legends. In the West, such harking back to pop chivalry is evident on one level in the *Star Wars* trilogy and on another in a writer like Raymond Chandler.[1] Despite Woo's often Western turn of mind, in this case he appeals quite directly to his Chinese heritage, a fact that some critics have either overlooked or have treated as unimportant, preferring to see, and to misunderstand, Woo as merely a Western epigone. It is more accurate to say that Woo brings a Western-hued sensibility to his deep interest in, and romanticization of, his own heritage. Thus, as David Chute has noted, those who do not understand the influence of sources such as Chinese martial arts films on works such as *The Killer* are missing much of the key to Woo's films.

This generally overlooked dimension of Woo is indeed a rich one.

For, underpinning his gloss on martial arts films, such as those of Chang Cheh, is Woo's lifelong exposure to classical Chinese literature. His father was a scholar of that literature, and Woo mentions repeatedly his own affection for two classic novels: *Water Margin (Shui hu chuan)* and *Romance of the Three Kingdoms (San kuo chih yen-i)*.[2]

Why do these two novels, and other such sources, especially interest John Woo? In order to understand this, we must first examine not only the two works, but also the Chinese concept of "novel."

C. T. Hsia's useful discussion of the classical Chinese novel draws important distinctions between the Western concept of fiction, as genre and praxis, and the classical Chinese approach to fictional endeavor. He notes that little attempt at Western perspectivism, as for example in Cervantes, is usually made in "colloquial Chinese fiction":

> The modern reader of fiction is brought up on the practice and theory of Flaubert and James: he expects a consistent point of view, a unified impression of life as conceived and planned by a master intelligence, an individual style fully consonant with the author's emotional attitude toward his subject-matter. He abhors explicit didacticism, authorial digression, episodic construction that reveals no cohesion of design, and clumsiness of every other kind that distracts his attention. But, of course, even in Europe the conscious practice of fiction as an art was a late development, and we cannot expect colloquial Chinese fiction, with its humble oral beginnings, to have been designed for the cultivated modern taste [6].

In his introduction to the fourteenth century *Romance of the Three Kingdoms*, Roy Andrew Miller notes that classical Chinese novels were "guilty pleasures"[3] and that those genres normally considered "literature" in the West might not be placed in that category at all by the Chinese of that period:

> The traditional Chinese scholar has until recently [1959] hardly even been willing to consider worthy of study as "Literature" most works that the Occidental scholar would wish to include under the term; at the same time the major part of what the Mandarin would regard as important literature has been official prose and documents of a variety that most persons in the West could hardly be induced even to take seriously [v].

As in the Western literary tradition, we might expect that features of the classical Chinese novel have carried over into the present, of course with modifications and frequent deviations, and that fiction and film would display analogies in technique. If "classical Hollywood" films in the West have preserved many aspects of the fiction and theater of the nineteenth century (that is, more traditional literature), then we might reasonably expect films in Hong Kong or China to feature aspects associated traditionally with Chinese fiction and theater.

To summarize, then, the classical Chinese novel and Western fiction differ in at least three ways: (1) Genres not perceived as literature by Westerners (chronicles, official records and the like) were seen as serious literature by Chinese scholars, while fiction would have been thought frivolous; (2) Little attempt is usually made in Chinese fiction at overall, Jamesian perspective, lending a stubbornly episodic and fragmented quality to the work; (3) Character development is sketchy, with stock or stereotyped figures as the rule.

Woo in fact appeals to the latter of these points in discussing director Chang Cheh, associated particularly with swordplay and martial arts films. He cites not so much Chang's violent sequences as his expressiveness and exaggerated emotional content, features often associated with the use of stereotypes or with melodrama. He also notes his contribution of male bonding in swordplay films, an innovation at the time in Hong Kong film because female bonding had been the rule (Woo, personal interview, 7 November 1995).[4] Tony Rayns notes that Woo has been strongly influenced by films, like Chang's, from the *wuxia pian* genre with their stylish swordplay and costume drama feel (Rayns, "Chivalry's," qtd. in Supplements Text, *The Killer*). This would tie in with the background of Woo's *Princess Cheung Ping*, a Cantonese opera film. All anachronistic pieces, these films cultivate a style redolent of the dramas from the Yüan Dynasty (1264–1368) and of epic novels from the Ming Dynasty (1368–1644) such as *Water Margin* and *Romance of the Three Kingdoms.*[5]

The historical romance displays the elements to which Woo refers: male bonding, the relegation of the female role to a secondary position, and stress on emotionalism and florid gesture. It is also, as Hsia says, episodic, relying on vivid incident and linear plot development, with any density attained occurring within scenes rather than between them. Not to be missed by those familiar with Woo films is the fact that many of these statements could be applied to his movies. He even appears to have obtained some of the tone in his film dialogues from the idiom of these novels and from martial arts films: exaggerated politeness, over-the-top villainy expressed through hissing speeches, and so forth. The "courtesy" mode is integral to romance, and Woo has learned much from the romance form, whether cultivated by Lo Kuan-chung or Chang Cheh.

The historical romances, although not purely tales of chivalry,[6] tend to reflect the virtues ascribed to historical chivalric figures or "knights-errant." Liu lists these ideals as altruism, justice, individual freedom, personal loyalty, courage, truthfulness and mutual faith, honor and fame, and generosity and contempt for wealth (4–7). He points out that "the knight-errant forms a strong contrast to the Confucian scholar" in several respects; in general, he says, "as Professor Yang Lien-sheng has pointed out, the Confucians modified universalism with particularism, while the knights-errant acted on a universalistic principle" (7). That is, their morality was not parochial. The knights-errant "went beyond the call of duty" for a Confucian and showed a "tendency towards extremism"; their "generosity, even their self-sacrifice, would have been condemned as excessive by the Confucians" (8). Also, the knights were often vengeful and certainly used force repeatedly; the Confucians opposed both approaches; and the knights "valued personal freedom above family solidarity" (8). But, he concludes,

> ... the Confucians and the knights-errant did have certain similarities. As Feng Yu-lan [a scholar of Chinese philosophy] pointed out, both were faithful to the tasks entrusted them, even to death, and both showed personal loyalty based on a principle of reciprocity. To these may be added that both cherished honour and belittled wealth.... Indeed, Mencius's definition of a great man as one "whom wealth and rank cannot corrupt, poverty and humble position cannot change, and authority and power cannot bend" would apply to the ideal Confucian scholar as well as the ideal knight-errant [9].

Of course, not all, or even any, of the novels were serious expositions of such virtues. But they did represent a popular or "vulgar" presentation of some generally accepted knightly and/or Confucian values, much as the Horatio Alger stories or Western dime novels might present certain characters as virtuous and others as villainous, depending upon their respective accord with accepted societal norms. Similarly, the thesis that the Chinese–language kung fu films of the 1950s and 1960s presented Confucian values[7] must be qualified, as a strict Confucian would most likely disapprove of violent martial arts confrontations.[8] Still, their transmission of values such as loyalty, filial devotion and honesty probably had some effect on younger viewers and most certainly struck a chord in John Woo.

If one examines Woo's films, or at least those after *A Better Tomorrow*, one can easily find a Confucian cast to their value system. The values of loyalty, courage and integrity are repeatedly celebrated, as on another level is service to society. Woo's self-avowed Christianity has Lutheran roots, and the Lutherans are known for social and familial cohesiveness and for ethical seriousness. Thus, Confucianism and Lutheranism are easily combined in Woo's world-view and form two bases of his films' "messages."

The influence of Asian literary and cinematic conventions is evident in Woo's style, particularly as seen here in one of his early martial arts films, *The Hand of Death* (1976). In this scene, Dorian Tan unhorses an adversary. (Courtesy John Woo.)

Woo's frequent claims that he has tried to convey this message or that may surprise those who see him as an "action director." He in fact disavows such a label[9] and is not apologetic about his didacticism—another feature of neo–Confucianism. His films are filled with examples of filial loyalty, integrity, service, moral men resisting corruption or complacency and other virtues associated with Confucianism.

Among such examples we may list a few. Their mere presence, of course, does not argue for a director's Confucian background; but it is notable that they appear so importantly in Woo's films. He also seems to dwell on them, or emphasize them, more strongly than some other Hong Kong directors such as Ringo Lam or Kirk Wong. These directors usually tend to emphasize loyalty between friends or colleagues but do not normally stress the loyalty of son to father[10]; nor does Lam, at least, necessarily highlight the hero resisting complacency or corruption.[11] Woo is often considered one of the most Western of Hong Kong directors, and so he is in many senses; but in other ways he is very Asian in his sensibility—and his emphasis on family loyalty and cohesion is very noticeably Confucian.

A Better Tomorrow provides some of the best examples in Woo's work of such filial and fraternal loyalty and sense of duty.[12] Its message is that the traditional Confucian relationships of duty as between son and father, brother and elder brother, and husband to wife must be maintained, or society will be out of joint, as Julian Stringer comments regarding Woo. Much of the conflict in the film centers on Kit's lack of respect for Ho, his elder brother, whom he blames for their father's death. Kit cannot bring himself to fill his traditional place as younger brother because he feels that Ho has himself broken the chain by not respecting his father's wishes and leaving the Triad. Only after he witnesses Mark's "fraternal" self-sacrifice for Ho does he feel that Ho is now worthy of his loyalty; additionally, he understands that Shing was the real transgressor. Shing, in fact, violates the entire Confucian code in the sense that he rebels against his "father" Yiu and his *dailo* ("big brother") Ho; neither does he respect his other *dailo*, Mark. So he pays the ultimate penalty, while Ho and Kit are reunited, at least spiritually, since Ho must go to prison for killing Shing.

This kind of pattern is seen repeatedly in Woo's films. Those characters who follow the code are rewarded and valued; even those who rebel against their "elders," like Tequila, may be rewarded if they do so not from bad intentions but from an excess of emotion and moral outrage: thus, by the end of *Hard Boiled*, Tequila has, as Dave Kehr points out, been redeemed by his willingness to join the team once again, and by his unselfish support of Tony, who is in a sense his younger brother. The emphasis on the team, as opposed to the individual, is a common enough feature in Asian literature and cinema, probably more so in Japan than in China; but once again, we only have to compare Ringo Lam's work with Woo's to notice how much more "Asian" Woo seems. Lam's *Full Contact* (1992) would be unthinkable from Woo, with its privileging of the lone, vengeful hero who leaves his life behind to pay his blood debt; its parody of the Confucian family, with the vicious father or *dailo* figure, the aptly named Judge (Simon Yam Tat-wah), and the younger members—the not-so-virginal Virgin (Bonnie Fu Yuk-jing) and Deano (Frankie Chin)—would again seem anathema to Woo. He might admire the courage shown here by Jeff (Chow Yun-fat) and his loyalty to the innocent (he takes money at the end of the film to a girl who was seriously injured during one of his battles), but one suspects that Woo would not leave the essentially cowardly and disloyal Sam (Anthony Wong Chau-sang) in such an ambiguous position at story's end.

Nevertheless, Woo does admire and privilege the "knightly" type of hero who acts out of principle, regardless of consequences. Basically, this figure comes from the Chinese chivalric tradition and from Japan's *bushido* code[13] (and not necessarily from historical fact); and Woo is explicit about his admiration for certain aspects of this tradition.

One of his most important models in respect of chivalry is the figure of Ching K'o, perhaps historical, though certainly also somewhat anecdotal, from the *Shih chi* of the great historian Ssu-ma Ch'ien.[14] We have referred previously to this anecdote, in the Introduction, and to Woo's probable conflation of its details with some material from another important model, Chang Cheh's *The One-Armed Swordsman* (1969). In any case, one critical feature of both stories for Woo may escape us if we think only of the hero's courage or self-sacrifice. This element is the crucial one of loyalty: Ching K'o acts out of loyalty to his superior, just as Kang in the film (Wang Yu) risks death at the hands of the cruel and vengeful One-Armed Devil solely in order to protect his *sifu* (master, played by Tien Feng). His obligation discharged, he leaves for a life of farming.

Woo's most important characters are so because of their loyalty; their courage is actually secondary to this virtue. Thus, Li and John in *The Killer* are above all loyal to each other and to Jenny, as John is to Sidney. John, in fact, though very saddened and angered by Sidney's betrayal of him, seems most shocked and frightened by Sidney's revelation to him that the man behind the contracts is the younger Weng, who had hired him to kill his uncle: John had not until this point known the identity of the man paying the bill. This fact apparently horrifies him, perhaps because of its violation of Confucian norms: his facial reaction to Sidney's revelation seems peculiar and exaggerated unless interpreted in this light. John is in this way one of the most traditional of Woo's heroes; he is a direct throwback to the Assassin Retainers of the *Shih chi*.[15] Perhaps it is for this reason that, as Terence Chang says, many American viewers prefer *Hard Boiled*: it is "more accessible"—less Asian in its roots, perhaps (Chang and Wu, personal interview, 1 March 1996).

The quite traditional nature of the John character in *The Killer* becomes yet more evident if his actions and traits are compared to the list prepared by James Liu of the "ideals" of the historical "knights-errant" in China. Despite some differences—the most important being the nonprofessional position of "at least some of" these knights—the similarities are instructive.

Liu lists eight ideals for the knights (see above). The first, "altruism," is explained thus:

> They habitually helped the poor and the distressed, and often risked their own lives to save others. Their unselfishness extended not only to their friends but even to total strangers, so much so that the word *hsia* ("knightly" or "chivalrous") has become associated in usage with the word *yi*, which is usually translated as "righteousness" but, when applied to knights-errant, has quite a different meaning and comes close to "altruism." ... [*Y*]*i*, in the sense understood by the knights-errant, means doing more than what is required by common standards of morality, or in other words behaving in a "supermoral" way [4].

Can such a claim be made for John in *The Killer*? Clearly, yes; even at the beginning of the film, he risks his own life to save Jenny, although he does not yet know her. Even if one ascribed this motive to a sudden infatuation, it would be difficult to explain his actions toward the little girl who is injured during the "beach battle" later in the film; he is certainly unselfish towards her, taking her to the hospital at considerable personal risk to himself. He is also consistently unselfish with his friends, like Sidney and, later, Li.

Liu ties the altruism of the knights-errant to "a sense of justice, which they placed above family loyalty." He comments, "This respect for justice and insistence on 'fair play,' together with their altruism, are well illustrated by the common description of a knight-errant as someone who, 'seeing an injustice on the road, pulls out his sword to help.' Such action was often necessitated by the failure of the government to administer justice" (4-5). Again, John qualifies here, saving Jenny from some street toughs who are trying to rape her.

The knights-errant also valued individual freedom,

> ... living in what would nowadays be called a Bohemian manner and paying little attention to social conventions.... They had little respect for the law of the state or the conventions of behavior of the society in which they lived. The only rules they recognized were those of their own moral code [5].

While John is certainly not a "Bohemian"—he lives in a nice flat and dresses sharply—he clearly lives by his "own moral code." Unlike Sidney, he is not particularly respectful of "the rules" for killers (not betraying one's anonymity, for instance); and of course he sees little wrong, until later in the film, with killing those who, as he tells Jenny (ch. 26), "deserved to die."

"Personal loyalty" is central to the knight-errant code. This virtue is

particularly important to characters in Woo films and is seen with especial clarity in *The Killer*. Liu elaborates on the virtue:

> To a knight-errant, personal loyalty was more important than loyalty to
> one's sovereign or parents. Even when a knight died for a prince, it was
> not out of a sense of loyalty such as a subject owed his sovereign, but such
> as one man owed another who "appreciated him" (*chih-chi*). This is clearly
> illustrated by the lives of such men as Hou Ying and Ching K'o [the last
> of whom is the hero cited by Woo] [5].

Loyalty of this kind forms the center of *The Killer*. John is loyal not
in an abstract sense, but rather in a personal one. He is willing to die from
loyalty to those who "appreciate him" such as Li and Sidney, and, in
another sense, Jenny. He will sacrifice himself so that his money, and his
corneas if necessary, can be used to help the nearly blind Jenny: he is frustrated in this effort, as Johnny shoots him in the eyes, and Jenny apparently dies. Sidney and Li display similar loyalty towards John. Johnny
Weng is a villain precisely because he does not show or value such loyalty.

Courage is the fifth virtue discussed by Liu. Once again, the description could have been written about John (or Li, or Tequila or Tony from
Hard Boiled):

> It required physical and moral courage of the highest order to be a
> knight-errant. The question of danger seems never to have entered the
> minds of knights-errant, who faced death with a cavalier attitude that
> almost suggests they did not much care for life [5].

Like the knights-errant, John values "truthfulness and mutual faith";
he is thoroughly disgusted with both Sidney and their employer when he
learns of their duplicity. Liu ties this virtue to "honour and fame" and
calls the "desire for fame" of the knights-errant "their only selfish motive."
In this case, one would have to conclude that John does not totally fit the
category, at least in his lack of interest in fame. This is a question not
even raised in the film, nor generally in most Woo films, except in some
of his comedies, where such interests are perhaps lampooned (as in the
Ricky Hui character's comic obsession in *From Riches to Rags* with a female
movie star whose life is not as glamorous as he supposes).

Finally, Liu mentions "generosity and contempt for wealth" as typical of the knights (6). At first glance, "contempt for wealth" might not
seem to fit John, and we really have little evidence one way or the other;
but he does not appear to be a greedy sort. When John asks a very high
price for a hit and Sidney expresses surprise, John explains that this is
his last hit; what he does not explain to Sidney, but we see in interior

flashback, is that he wants the money to pay for an operation abroad for Jenny. So Liu's words seem appropriate in this context:

> A knight-errant might receive handsome sums from friends without any embarrassment ... or refuse an offer of household effects worth several million cash.... It was not that they had no use for money; they simply did not have a strong sense of proprietorship, and either lived lavishly while sharing their luxury with friends, or lived modestly themselves while giving money to the poor [6].

Liu stresses the evident fact that "not all those who claimed to be knights-errant actually lived up to these ideals" and further notes, "Even those who did live up to these ideals had serious shortcomings." The following comments could certainly be applied with justice to John, though not completely to Li or Tequila:

> ... they were too eager to fight and too quick to take offence.... Moreover, the knights-errant had a rather limited conception of justice. Therefore, in spite of their altruism, their action could only benefit a few, but not the whole community. Finally, they had no respect for the law, so that they further disrupted social order, though at the same time they brought redress to personal wrongs [6–7].

Bushido

A cousin to the Chinese chivalric code, Japanese *bushido*[16] has influenced Woo's films, chiefly through the samurai film (especially Kurosawa's *Seven Samurai*) and the Ishii Teruo film *Narazumono*.[17] Like the Western chivalric code, both the Japanese and the Chinese codes are idealized and not always effected practically. But it is precisely in the realm of popular culture, not in history, that such codes have great importance.

Woo appeals to the chivalric code as a model for his heroes, and his films are quite harsh and unforgiving toward those characters who violate it. Evidence of such codes in Woo films includes the comic courting of Tequila's girlfriend and colleague with roses and mock obeisance; Mark's unselfish willingness to suffer and die to avenge an injustice to his friend Ho; John's principles which do not permit him to see innocents harmed; Mad Dog's refusal (in *Hard Boiled*) to harm patients. Chow Yunfat commented to me, concerning Woo's films, that:

> [John] want[s] to show the audience, that right now the whole world is in need of discipline—even [if] you're a thief, a killer, you have your

discipline. He wants to say that men must have loyalty, purity, responsibility, must be loyal to family and to friends. They must have dignity [personal interview, 6 November 1995].

Woo's value system is indeed reminiscent of the samurai ethic (or rather of what we like to believe that ethic was), so that his killers and cops are men from the wrong century[18]: one is reminded of characters such as the young student Isao in Yukio Mishima's *Runaway Horses*, who would like to revive the *bushido* code by a demonstration of self-sacrifice and who feels that the sacred Shintoist ethic of military virtues has been profaned by Westernizing corruption. The curious interface with the sacred world is also seen in the films of Akira Kurosawa, one of Woo's acknowledged masters, as in *Seven Samurai* (1954), when the leader of the samurai band (subtly played by Takashi Shimura) shaves his head and poses as a Buddhist priest in order to trap and kill a kidnapper, or in the clear parody of Zen masters and their disciples in *Sanjuro* (1962), or in the macabre jokes on burial rituals in *Yojimbo* (1961). Such treatment of the samurai, or military and chivalric, tradition, fits neatly with Woo's films. Here, we often see a close juxtaposition not only of the sacred and the profane, but more precisely of the sacred and the violent, as for example in the final scene of *The Killer*, when a church is destroyed in a ferocious gun battle, and in the ironically elliptical reprise of this scene in *Face/Off*.

Symbolism in Woo's Work

Many of Woo's later films, such as *A Better Tomorrow*, *The Killer*, and *Hard Boiled*, might be considered in some critical quarters as not much more than restatements of generic action motifs, of the "buddy" film and so forth. Woo has noted, however, that he quite consciously pursues a Protestant ideology of redemption, expressed through overt Christian symbolism. These symbols include doves, Pietà figures, churches and allusions to Biblical scenes such as Pilate's hand-washing. And Woo's use of symbolism is not Western–specific; he derives more than a little inspiration from Chinese and Japanese sources.

Woo's work, as we have seen, has often followed a preset structure: Two men on opposite sides of the law find a kinship in their principled opposition to evil. Both undergo moral development or redemption by the end of the film, usually through self-sacrifice or displaced sacrifice (for instance, a close friend of one of the men may die). In the films with this structure, the men invariably discover, or cement, their friendship in the midst of battle—incomparably choreographed battles which recall the swordfights from Kurosawa films or from other examples of *jidai-geki*, or period pieces (see Richie 97), such as samurai films, with social significance; or of martial arts or swordfight films in Chinese.

The addition of the samurai film to the Woo mix is significant, as the *bushido* ethic, often expressed in such films, draws upon Shinto and, to some degree, Confucian and Buddhist elements. Thus, Woo, who refers to his interest in the samurai tradition and specifically to the implicit idealization of it in Jean-Pierre Melville's *Le Samouraï* (1967), also employs Eastern symbolism, as in *Hard Boiled*, where paper cranes are used to symbolize the fleeting nature of life.

The sacred clashes with the violently profane in Woo films in a very starkly drawn manner. For example, a church is profaned and destroyed (and, along with it, a statue of the Virgin Mary) in *The Killer*. A suspenseful scene in *Hard Target* is set in a cemetery; the tombstones are sullied and physically scarred by the murderous pursuit shown there.

I would not want to overstate the seriousness of Woo's religious message-sending. Or, perhaps, its pervasiveness. Though an unconventional and highly accomplished director, he is not Robert Bresson; his sensibility is not that delicate. Nevertheless, it is interesting that a director usually thought of as an "action master" should see himself as a moralist who employs a given form, action or comedy or melodrama, in a didactic manner. One should not go so far as to call his works sermons or extended homilies, but they are certainly well-melded amalgams of escapism, film buff fare, emotional tours de force and—sermons.

So, how do the sacred and the profane function in Woo's films? Despite my caveat about overemphasizing this aspect of his work, it is true that Woo has stated on several occasions that he consciously tries to instill Christian imagery into his work with the intention of communicating a message about morality or religion. One must conclude, therefore, that the numinous or the sacred does indeed play a significant role in his films. We also should eschew the temptation to classify the sacred elements in his work as merely another example of camp or postmodernist game-playing. Woo is quite serious, almost naïvely so, about his insertion of such signals into his movies.

Sacred signs often appear in unexpected contexts in Woo's later films. The viewer is probably rather shocked when the opening shot of *The Killer*, a dolly into a church that tracks towards its altar, reveals John and Sidney seated in a rear pew and agreeing to the final details of a contract hit. The scene is not used merely for decoration. Woo does not cheat the viewer by using the church as an "interesting" or "naughty" backdrop. He uses it to reveal an important trait in John. When Sidney asks him why he meets in churches, he denies any religious leaning, averring that he likes the "tranquility" in churches. But the viewer does not, and should not, totally accept this demur. We sense both that the killer John is suffering a *crise de conscience* about his work and that his very presence in the church, not to mention what he is doing there, is a profanation—and he knows it. We might even be reminded of Coppola's use of church scenes in the *Godfather* films to make a point about the corruption of the Italian immigrant promise.

The church building is established from the opening shot of *The Killer* as important in its imagery. It will recur during the film as a fixed backdrop against which John's moral journey is played out. We see the locale again after John's first hit of the film is completed. Having taken several slugs in his back, he has them removed by Sidney and the priest in a scene of intense pain with the altar and crucifix shown in the background. Not only does one make the obvious connection of John as a Christ figure, but also we draw the point that this is the beginning of John's atonement for his career. He begins to pay a high price for his profanation of human life.

The church is finally the setting for the climax of the film. This is a most unusual scene as the church becomes an active battleground, suffering irreparable and shocking desecration.

Again the temptation may be, as critics, for us to see the church setting for one of the most violently kinetic gun battles ever conceived for the screen as little more than an exercise in camp and the *outré*. But it is different from that: Woo very pointedly sets convention on its head, showing the nefarious effect of violence, hatred and betrayal on the sacred sanctuary of the church.

The first canonical violation is that churches historically have been places of refuge or asylum. Criminals or political refugees were free from state pursuit once they left the temporal realm and entered church premises. Here, though, the church that John has called "quiet" becomes a dangerous battleground. The heroes' pursuers—criminals, not the authorities—certainly respect nothing about the church and its spiritual significance.

Another violation of the sacred is the wanton murder of the priest by Paul Yau, Weng's hired killer. This act clearly separates the two sides in their profanation; although neither side is innocent of sacrilege, the "invaders" are acting on a moral plane much worse than are the defenders. (A similar incident is seen in *A Better Tomorrow II*, where one of the hit men pursuing Mr. Lung callously kills a priest who had been sheltering him.)

The most visually effective profaning of the sacred is the destruction of the Madonna and Christ figures, and indeed of the entire altar. Other sacred images and objects are also destroyed in the battle, such as cherubs and vestments. Again, Woo both shocks our sensibilities and alerts us to the price of a life led in opposition to society's and God's dictates.

In an ironic reversal of Saul's holy blinding in Acts 9, John suffers the horror of being blinded by gunshots at the end of the film. He had, like Saul of Tarsus, begun to see the value of self-sacrifice and moral redemption through love. But he dies blinded and unable even to touch his beloved, who had previously suffered damage to her own vision by the muzzle flash from John's gun.[19]

Profanation of the sacred, though recurrent in Woo films, is not always found in contexts as formal as those mentioned from *The Killer*. Woo sometimes scatters Christian or religious imagery in his films as seemingly incidental elements. One of the more striking examples of this, noted by Woo himself, occurs in *Bullet in the Head*. The scene is an arrest in Saigon following the satchel bombing of an official car during a protest demonstration.[20] The army and police, trying to find the bomber, rough up several people, including the three friends from Hong Kong, and finally find the real suspect. Intentionally echoing the famous photo of a South Vietnamese official shooting a suspected Cong member in the head in Saigon, Woo shows the young man executed by a pistol shot to the head.[21] In a masterful image, his falling body reveals a previously obscured *Pietà* group that now dominates the frame. The image is not really a political one (taking the side of the government opponent) but rather a humanistic one, deploring the suffering of wartime and opposing the mercy and kindness of Mary to the cruelty of the soldiers.[22]

In similar fashion, Woo injects a biblical reference into *A Better Tomorrow*. Because Mark has remained loyal to Ho, he is savagely beaten by Shing's men. Shing strikes him and reaches for a handkerchief to clean his hands. Woo says that this is a deliberate reference to Pilate's handwashing disclaimer of responsibility for Jesus' fate.[23]

Hard Target occupies a middle ground between the insistent use of sacred environs in *The Killer* and the sporadic employment of sacred images in *A Better Tomorrow* and *Bullet in the Head*. One of the most exciting but also saddening chases in *Hard Target*, when Chance's friend Roper is hunted down and killed, takes place partly in one of New Orleans' above-ground cemeteries. Amid religious figures such as a winged angel, Roper battles for his life, using his rusty Vietnam skills. Even he profanes the sacred precincts, popping out from a mausoleum like a grotesque zombie.[24]

These images of profanation, or of the sacred as a criticism of moral error, are not the only evidence of the numinous in Woo films. Woo very characteristically uses bird imagery, usually to represent the soul. Thus, in the last scene of *The Killer*, doves or pigeons escape flapping their wings from the church, ominously symbolizing the many deaths to come. The same imagery is used in *Hard Target* in the final scene. In *Face/Off*, the imagery is less foreboding. It signals the freeing of Archer from his earthly prison in Castor's body.

An unusual example of bird imagery appears in *Hard Boiled*. At the beginning of the film, a gunfight breaks out in a bar between gunrunners and the police. Guns have been hidden away by the criminals inside bird cages (hardly uncommon in such Hong Kong locales, but not thereby devoid of symbolic content). The image of the bird as the soul, as Cirlot says, is a long-standing one; the following vignette cited by him contains the image of the bird cage as a prison:

> There is a Hindu tale retold by Frazer in which an ogre explains to his daughter where he keeps his soul: "Sixteen miles away from this place," he says, "is a tree. Round the tree are tigers, and bears, and scorpions, and snakes; on the top of the tree is a very great fat snake; on his head is a little cage; and my soul is in that bird" [Cirlot 24–25].

In the *Hard Boiled* teahouse scene, such an image is surrealistically combined with the secreting of guns as if the souls of gunrunners (and cops) were underpinned by and tied to guns and violence. It is worth noting, in passing, that birds and guns have been regarded as phallic symbols (Cirlot 25). (The unusual juxtaposition of certain images with guns appears as a feature of this film. So, the gunrunner Johnny Wong has used the morgue underneath a major hospital to hide his huge arsenal: a provocative metonymy and one not calculated to express respect for the dead.)

Another example of bird imagery in *Hard Boiled*, the cranes made by Alan, alludes to *Le Samouraï*, the New Wave classic by Jean-Pierre Melville that admittedly was the model for *The Killer*. In this film, the hit man Jef Costello lives in a bare room with only one companion, a songbird in a cage. The symbolism of the imprisoned soul, or perhaps of the masculine principle hedged and restrained, is very clear. The bird is very nearly a spirit-brother to Jef; its chirping tells him that the police have planted a bug in his room. And Woo has stated that the shot on Alan's boat (when the crane appears to transition into his face) expresses his conflict about his work:

> It was the guilt shadowing him and he was just fed up with killing. He didn't want to kill anymore. And in that scene, with the crane, the wide

shot, and the closeup, it's a little bit like the opening of *Le Samouraï*, with Alain Delon on the bed, and the birdcage in front of the camera. Melville is using the bird to [show that Delon] doesn't have his freedom, just loneliness, nobody understands him or cares about him, he's in another world [Woo, personal interview, 2 March 1996].

Much of the imagery discussed here has been primarily Western or at least generalized cross-culturally. Woo does use iconography normally associated with Asian culture. A very affecting example of this is the use of cranes in *Hard Boiled*. According to Beryl Rowland in *Birds with Human Souls*, cranes have often symbolized old age, death or the soul's passage to another plane:

> Next to the phoenix, the crane was the most celebrated in Chinese legend.... The crane was one of the commonest emblems of longevity and was usually shown under a pine tree—also a symbol of age. The soul of the dead was represented as riding on the crane's back to the "Western Heavens" [Rowland 32].

Although known to Western culture, crane imagery, then, is very frequent in Asian art and culture. In *Hard Boiled*, Alan customarily makes a paper crane to commemorate every person he has to kill. He sometimes hangs the cranes inside his boat like little mobiles; Woo shows them wreathed in (presumably) cigarette smoke, as if to emphasize their ethereal quality. Alan sometimes drops them in the water; Woo's camera shows them being borne off like little funeral barges. This rather peculiar revision of an old image associated with the sacred (that is, matters of the spirit and of death) gives an unusual beauty to this very violent and kinetic film.[25]

The paper cranes are not the only example of Eastern imagery in Woo's films, and all the instances of Eastern symbolism in Woo's work are not sacred in nature. So, an important figure from Chinese history plays a central visual role in two scenes from *The Killer* and *Hard Boiled*. This figure is that of Kwan Yi, who, as Woo notes, was an important general from "2,000 years ago."[26] His statue appears in the police stations in *The Killer* and in *Hard Boiled*. A Chinese viewer would understand the imagery, much as a Western spectator might react to a statue of Abraham Lincoln. For Western viewers, of course, the good general needs some clarification, so Woo explains that he symbolizes loyalty and that all policemen in Hong Kong must show respect to his statue (Woo, *The Killer* 8). Additionally, we should mention a point not brought out by Woo, which is that Gen. Kwan's statue is painted red. Red is a symbol of loyalty or steadfast nature in the Chinese Opera (see Chang, *Chinese*

Opera 52), so the statue's identity as well as its coded visuals are significant to the Chinese viewer.

While it is true that Woo is a very Western-influenced director, the fact remains that he is not Western, and must not be interpreted along solely Western lines, or, worse, as some sort of "wannabe Westerner" who hides his Asian heritage. His Western influences are there for all to see, but he patently has strong Asian roots.[27] Certainly he is not a heavily symbolic director, like, say, Bergman or Ozu, but he does employ symbols consciously, and symbols also appear in his work in a manner that may be unconscious or unwitting. A general statement about symbolism in his work would be that he deliberately uses Christian and Western symbolism and naturally employs Asian traditional symbols.

We have seen how Woo uses Christian symbolism. But how do we see Asian symbols in his work, besides the examples already mentioned? One example of a Chinese symbol appearing in his films can be found in *The Killer*. Its use seems so off-handed that it rather calls one's attention. The scene in question is in Jenny's apartment, when John first goes there after defending her in the street (*The Killer* ch. 6).

When John and Jenny are about to enter her apartment, they hear a noise. John tells her to stay back while he investigates. The noise is "only a cat," as John soon says; Jenny replies, "It often gets in and scratches my furniture." Introducing the cat into the narrative may be little more than a device to add suspense, or to humanize John, who seems taken with the animal (rather like Alan Ladd's hit man character in *This Gun for Hire* [1942]); but to the present writer, at least, the use of such a symbolic creature seemed quite noticeable. And, in fact, the traditional symbolic cluster around cats in China is fitting with regard to John and Jenny. According to Doolittle's *Social Life of the Chinese*,

> The coming of a cat to a household is an omen of approaching poverty. The coming of a strange cat, and its staying in a house, are believed to foreshadow an unfavorable change in the pecuniary condition of the family. It is supposed that a cat can foresee where it will find plenty of rats and mice in consequence of approaching dilapidation of a house, following the ruin or poverty of its inhabitants [Doolittle 571, qtd. in Williams, *Encyclopedia* 58].

While one might not think of Jenny's approaching predicament as necessarily one of poverty, she certainly will have a future of bad omen—and so will John.

Also, later in the film, when Li and John confront each other as "Spy vs. Spy," the cat appears suddenly, startling Li's partner Chang. And, in one of his verbal thrusts at John, Li tells Jenny that there is a "rat" in the apartment, thus associating the cat with its prey and perhaps reminding us of Doolittle's words about rats' association with impending bad fortune.

Besides the cat, an animal prominent in *The Killer* is the dragon. One of the finest scenes in *The Killer* is the assassination of Tony Weng during the Dragon Boat Festival. Normally, one might think the choice of the Festival is for decorative purposes, or for the opportunity of a big crowd setting, perhaps. But what about the meaning of the Festival itself, and that of its featured animal?

Dragons are a cynosure of Chinese civilization. Emblematic animals, they are, however, almost free of the negative opprobrium contributed by Christian symbolism to the Western dragon, a metonymy for the serpent: "The Eastern dragon is not the gruesome monster of mediaeval imagination, but the genius of strength and goodness" (Okakura, *The Awakening of Japan*, 77–78, qtd. in Williams, 131). As a Lar-like, protective animal for the Chinese, the dragon lends itself to festivals commemorating positive events. Thus, the Dragon Boat Festival appears to have originated in a memorial to a famous culture hero:

> The Dragon Boat Festival ... is held on the fifth day of the fifth moon....
> The festival is popularly believed to have been instituted in memory of a
> statesman named Ch'ü Yüan ... who drowned himself in the River *Mi-lo*
> ... in 295 B.C., after having been falsely accused by one of the petty
> princes of the State, and as a protest against the corrupt condition of the
> government. The people, who loved the unfortunate courtier for his
> virtue and fidelity, sent out boats in search of the body, but to no pur-
> pose. They then prepared a peculiar kind of rice-cake called *tsung* ... and,
> setting out across the river in boats with flags and gongs, each strove to
> be the first on the spot of the tragedy, and to sacrifice to the spirit of the
> loyal statesman. This mode of commemorating the event has been carried
> down to posterity as an annual holiday [Williams, *Encyclopedia* 138].

The importance of the dragon symbol lies here not only in its associations with traditional symbolism, but also, as so often with Woo, in its relationship to the characters. The image is ironic in several respects. The association of the dragon with the function of safeguard or protection contrasts with its total failure to guard Tony, who is shot immediately after "dotting the dragon's eye" (a part of the ceremony); even close contact with the talisman does not save him.[28] His character, as well, which is corrupt and hypocritical, flies in the face of the dragon symbol's thrust of anti-corruption. Finally, in a twist of dramatic irony, the dragon's association with the virtue of loyalty (and its related quality, friendship) might seem odd in view of the betrayal of John by his friend Sidney, a fact made clear soon after the Dragon Boat scene.

The use of symbolism and of traditional content in Woo's films is further evidence of his sophistication as a film artist. As his films demonstrate, Woo draws on Western and Eastern film techniques and symbolic content to present a mixture which enriches the action genre. We will see that his employment of such techniques and such motifs is both indebted to and parallels their use by other directors.

Chapter 2

Woo and the Cinema: Influences, Parallels, Inspirations

Originality is nothing but judicious imitation.
—Voltaire

*The merit of originality is not novelty, it is sincerity. The
believing man is the original man; he believes for himself,
not for another.*
—Thomas Carlyle[1]

Hollywood

PROLOGUE

A critical truism on Woo is his indebtedness to the work of Hollywood directors such as Peckinpah, Scorsese and Coppola, as well as to other directors such as Leone. But when questioned about "modeling" a scene or a shot on one film or another, only in rare instances does Woo note deliberate allusion, even in his direction or casting. One could call this a mere reluctance to acknowledge artistic indebtedness from fear of being accused of lack of originality, but Woo is not shy about acknowledgment when he believes that he has in fact alluded to a director, or quoted a film. It is more accurate to say that Woo's quotation of directors and films is relatively limited or at most not particularly conscious. Instead, he may parallel the work of a director or actor, or he may independently achieve a result that *looks* like another director's work. This fact explains why Woo is not like some of his imitators, or why he is not like directors who self-consciously quote others' work: this is what saves him, too, from being campy. As Kehr says, those who see Woo as "tongue-in-cheek" simply misunderstand him (Commentary, *Hard Boiled* 23).

A very good example of what we might call Woo's "parallelism" is the case of Samuel Fuller. When I asked Woo about Fuller's possible influence on him, he told me:

> Martin Scorsese says the same thing. To be honest, I wasn't influenced that much by him. I didn't see his films much. Maybe we have something in common, maybe we have a similar sense of the film and the same kind of emotion, [similar] character [treatment] and camera movement as well [personal interview, 7 November 1995].

He did cite one Fuller film as a favorite (but one which he only saw after making his own famous films): *Shock Corridor*. As he says, he and Fuller may *share* close-ups, concentration on character and an impatience with theory. Another element of Fuller that probably caught Woo's attention is his focus on what Woo would call "the true hero" (often played by Gene Evans in Fuller's films) whose principles frequently lead him into difficulties. Fuller's films repeatedly feature a lone male lead who "fights the system" in one fashion or another: Skip McCoy (Richard Widmark) in *Pickup on South Street*, Johnny Barrett (Peter Breck) in *Shock Corridor*, Sgt. Zack (Gene Evans) in *Steel Helmet*, Merrill (Jeff Chandler) in *Merrill's Marauders*.[2] Fuller's handling of action scenes would surely have interested Woo as well: as he notes, Fuller focuses on the character and his reaction to the moment, forcing us into a human connection with the film:

> The way he emphasized true human values and his camera movement. [This was] very emotional—always focused on the characters' expression and emotion. When his camera is focused on the character he never cuts away to something else; he never cares about the background or the landscape. Always, the camera is *on* the character [personal interview, 7 November 1995].

Also notably present in both directors' films is an unabashed emotionalism. Neither Woo nor Fuller is afraid or embarrassed to show characters openly mourning their loss or sentimentally rejoicing in their friendship. Thus, for example, Fuller shows the tough, callous Zack weeping over the death of his little friend Short Round; and Woo has Inspector Li sobbing at the loss of his partner Chang.

Like Fuller, Woo has an essentially romantic sensibility; and like Fuller, Woo makes very personal films that do not apologize for their "lapses" in style. Neither director is especially interested in the "accepted" way of doing things, except in a very basic sense (Woo notes that continuity should not be violated); both use whatever means may be at hand to bring across their desired effect. Woo is the flashier of the two, using more visible "tricks"—freeze frames, slow motion, extreme close-ups, flash cuts, editing surprises—but both are quite idiosyncratic directors who view style as a means to an end, that end being the expression of a personal vision without academic preoccupations.

Woo and Scorsese

A longtime admirer of Martin Scorsese, Woo dedicated his Criterion laserdisc edition of *The Killer* to him. They have met and corresponded, even to the point of exchanging parts of their video collection:

> About four years ago Scorsese wrote me a letter after he saw *The Killer* and then we met in New York. Scorsese said he saw my movie the same way as Sam Fuller's and then I told him I got so much influence from Jean-Pierre Melville. And then I went back to Hong Kong and he sent me all of Sam Fuller's films on tape or laser disc. Then I sent all my Melville collection to him [Woo, personal interview, 7 November 1995].

It is not hard to see why Woo feels an artistic kinship to Scorsese. Both deal extensively with Christian themes (in Scorsese's case, specifically Catholic); both prefer urban settings; both are fascinated with male friendship and *topoi* such as loyalty, honesty and integrity. Both find these qualities in unlikely places: a Mafia family or a Triad group.

Artistically, the two are similar in some ways. Both directors delight in moving the camera, preferring dollies over static shots. In fact, the similarities between the two directors extend to their rapport with their crews. Russell Carpenter, the director of photography for *Hard Target*, said that the crew did not object in any way to Woo's changes in setups:

> [T]here was no resistance from us because—I think by that time, everybody had seen his films and they knew who they were dealing with and I think the crew loved him so much they would just do anything for him. And often we were laying out several long dollies, and something about the timing wouldn't work—and he'd say oh, I'm sorry we have to move the dolly track. And these are *long* dolly tracks, it didn't faze the crew at all—they knew he was going for something that was in his head [personal interview].

Chapman reports similar experiences with Scorsese on *Taxi Driver*:

> Marty loves dollies, Marty loves to move the camera around and around and around, all the time.... And Marty is a real charmer when he wants to be, like anybody who has real charisma.... And after a while they loved him.... And so they really went out of their way to make all these elaborate moves, well and fast. So Marty just dollied and dollied and dollied and the guys did it [Schaefer and Salvato 107].

And, at least in *Raging Bull* and *Bullet in the Head*, both appear to glamorize the lead character's beloved object: the centering of the camera's attention on Jake's future wife Vicki (Cathy Moriarty) and Ben's girlfriend Jane (Fennie Yuen) in *Bullet in the Head* is quite similar in effect.

Both directors deal in nostalgia, although it is far from being a facile treatment. Like Scorsese, Woo is fascinated with the tone of his own past, so that *Bullet in the Head* becomes autobiographical in a historically inexact but emotionally precise sense. It dramatizes, as does *Raging Bull*, the loss of center by the lead characters. The need to belong to an ethnically united neighborhood, a cohesive, longed-for hearth, is prominent in both filmmakers' work.

Woo has expressed particular interest in three of Scorsese's films: *Raging Bull* (1981), *Taxi Driver* (1976) and *Mean Streets* (1973). We will begin with *Mean Streets*, as the earliest of the three and therefore presumably the one with the influence of longest standing on Woo.

Mean Streets deals with the issues of loyalty and obligation. Charlie (Harvey Keitel) feels morally obligated to help his friend and "younger brother" Johnny Boy (Robert De Niro) out of his problems with loan sharks. Although Johnny constantly betrays everyone's trust by not paying back the loan, not working and not keeping appointments, he manages through force of personality—a kind of winning devil-may-care insouciance—to override such concerns in Charlie's mind. And then, too, Charlie, like Pike in *The Wild Bunch*, or Steven in *Ride the High Country*, believes in standing by one's friends, even if those friends show themselves to be unworthy of such loyalty. Charlie obeys an almost Christian moral code in continuing to forgive Johnny's transgressions. The result is tragic. The loan sharks apparently kill Johnny and seriously wound Charlie; furthermore, Charlie's dreams of advancement in his own street business are destroyed.

This drama is a rather small-scale one, and is told almost like the story of a family quarrel. It has little of the operatic sweep of Coppola's treatment of Mafia material. Scorsese uses a small cast and limited locations and emphasizes the character conflicts and dilemmas inherent in such a situation. The viewer does experience quite an intimate connection to the New York Italian community; Scorsese's attention to rich detail makes this film a microcosmic vision of a certain aspect of Italian immigrant life.

Woo differs here from Scorsese, because he does not generally concentrate so heavily (in his mature films) on the "ethnicity" of his Hong Kong characters. While it is true, as Beatrice Reynaud points out ("John Woo's Art Action Movie" 23), that the Hong Kong of John Woo is almost totally Chinese—there is a curious absence of British faces—still, he does not focus on local color and evocative detail as does Scorsese. *Bullet in the Head* is a possible exception to this, with its wedding scene and the material that Woo originally wanted to include as back story on the three protagonists.

Despite this distinction between their styles, the two directors have much in common, and this is apparent in Woo's preoccupation with loyalty, a central theme of *Mean Streets*. As with Charlie's loyalty to Johnny, so too in *A Better Tomorrow* Ho remains loyal to Mark, refusing to leave him at the mercy of Shing; Ben tries to avenge Frank in *Bullet in the Head*; Sidney, in *The Killer*, sacrifices himself from obligation to John; Ken is fiercely loyal to Mr. Lung in *A Better Tomorrow II*. Also as in Scorsese's films, the "punishment" scenes in Woo's films—the depictions of up-close, physical retributive violence—are very hot and physical, a particularly intimate and powerful form of emotional contact between very driven men. The characters seem almost ready to explode out of the frame in scenes such as Mark's beating by Shing's men in *A Better Tomorrow*, or Sidney's by Weng's; or, similarly, from *Mean Streets*, in the (comic) fight between Johnny, Charlie and a fat bar owner or in the deadly confrontation between Johnny and the loan shark in the bar near the end of the film. And, of course, the famous boxing scenes in *Raging Bull* appear to have contributed not a little to Woo's staging of beatings in *A Better Tomorrow*, *The Killer*, *Hard Boiled* and *Broken Arrow*.

If the general tone and ambience (as well as the character relationships) in *Mean Streets* and Woo's films are akin, so too are there specific instances or tributes by Woo to this film. One of these is seen in *The Killer* and in *Bullet in the Head*, when Chang is shot by Weng's killers through the window of his car; and, in a very different scene emotionally, when Ben shoots Paul through his car window during the climactic duel of *Bullet in the Head*. Woo explicitly links these two scenes (Commentary, *The Killer* ch. 27), and we may see influence here from Johnny's fate in *Mean Streets*. Perhaps, too, the bar fight in *Mean Streets* inspired the rumble at the beginning of *Bullet in the Head*: both transpire, as if choreographed, against a background of raucous music, although there is nothing comic about the rumble in *Bullet in the Head*, as distinguished from Scorsese's bar fight.

Mean Streets has clearly been important for Woo as a source of imagery and as a film expressing emotions and ethics closely attuned to the Woo worldview. But it is not the only Scorsese film to inspire Woo: *Taxi Driver* has also been very important to him. Woo has said, for example, that the final gunfight in *Taxi Driver* is a scene that he "will never forget" (Woo, Commentary, *The Killer* ch. 17). We can perceive clear echoes of this dramatically violent scene in *A Better Tomorrow*, when Mark guns down the men who had set up Ho: the same quick eruption into violence, the same arrangement of motifs are in evidence (the lone avenger entering the villains' lair and dispatching them with great skill but not without cost; both Mark and Travis Bickle suffer serious injury). And the scene in *The Killer*, in John's apartment, when John eliminates Weng's hit team (ch. 17), is, Woo says, directly modeled on the *Taxi Driver* scene (Woo, Commentary, *The Killer* ch. 17).

Woo does imbue the scene with a different feel than the one in *Taxi Driver*, since our sympathies are totally with Mark as they are not with Travis, whom we know to be psychotic. But Woo seems to favor the inclusion of such revenge scenes in his films, and of course they are not all chips off the *Taxi Driver* block. Equally important to Woo in such instances is the samurai film tradition: Mark could just as well be the nameless "Yojimbo," or the father in *Hara-kiri*. Still, *Taxi Driver*, in its violence and in its depiction of justice done (however equivocally we may feel about the agent and the methods of that justice), is clearly in line with Woo's own perspective.

Taxi Driver contains another motif often found in Woo's films: the relationship between a protective man and a vulnerable woman, younger than he. From his comedies to his action films, the motif is repeated: *Follow the Star* (1977) has Roy Chiao protecting Rowena Cortes; *Plain Jane to the Rescue* reverses the motif, thus confirming its presence; *The Killer* has John (and Li) protecting Jenny; *Hard Target* centers on Chance and Nat. *Taxi Driver*, of course, dwells at length on the peculiar relationship between Travis and the Jodie Foster character.[3] Woo is interested in this kind of motif chiefly because of his concern with the chivalric. So, we should scarcely be surprised that his attention is drawn to *Taxi Driver*, since the relationship here is quite unusual and striking.

If *Taxi Driver* contains the elements of revenge, poetic violence and the "protective knight-errant," *Raging Bull* concentrates, certainly, on violence, but even more so on failed potential and self-destructive hostility. Jake La Motta (Robert De Niro) is not an attractive figure, any more than Bennie (Warren Oates) in Peckinpah's *Bring Me the Head of Alfredo Garcia*, but both are "John Woo characters" in one important respect: they are tragic losers. La Motta's story is one of sad irony, with the fighter becoming a publicly self-parodying figure, reciting Brando's "contender" speech without, perhaps, noticing how neatly it applies to him.

Woo has shown interest elsewhere in tragic figures like this, although he usually prefers to show them, or remember them, in their "comeback" moment. Thus, Lung (Dean Shek) in *A Better Tomorrow II* is wrenched out of his insanity by the sight of his friend Ken being threatened with death; Sidney regains his former prowess long enough to redeem himself; comically, Jules (Chow Yun-fat) in *Once a Thief* turns out not to be crippled and enjoys a physical "comeback." Woo has mentioned characters such as Borrachón (Dean Martin's drunken deputy) in *Rio Bravo* and Jansen (Yves Montand) in *Le Cercle rouge* as further examples of this type. The "comeback moment," a form of peripeteia and often an element of revenge narrative, is at least as old as Samson and is seen in many works from *The Odyssey* (with Odysseus' revelation of himself as the avenging husband) to innumerable popular novels and Hollywood films, where the revenge subgenre (*Death Wish, Rolling Thunder*) is almost a paradigm.

But *Raging Bull* would appear to fall into line with another of Woo's concerns, family loyalty. Scorsese spends a large proportion of screen time on the relationship between Jake and his brother (played by Joe Pesci). His brother is the only character with whom Jake really has any emotional connection, and even that is frozen by the end of the film. In Woo's filmography, one thinks immediately of *A Better Tomorrow*, in which Ho and Kit have a very stormy fraternal relationship. Woo is more positive here than is Scorsese in *Raging Bull*, since the brothers are reconciled at the end of the film—rather, in a sense, like the two friends Gil and Steven (Randolph Scott and Joel McCrea) in Peckinpah's *Ride the High Country*, who begin the film distanced and distrustful of each other, and end it close friends again.

This contrast between *A Better Tomorrow* and *Raging Bull* is instructive, since it shows that Woo consistently focuses on the hero—Kit and Ho are both heroic; they simply fail to reach an understanding until the end of the film. Kit cannot forgive Ho for their father's death; he refuses to accept the truth about Ho's loyalty. This situation is quite different from the barrier between Jake and his brother: Jake blames his brother for betraying him (setting him up to throw a fight), but Jake's rage and self-centeredness are such that he finds it nearly impossible to grow past his resentment of his brother, and so he must suffer greatly. In any case, the familial relationship is central here, as so often in Woo's films.

Francis Coppola

If a critic might not think immediately of the importance of, say, John Frankenheimer for John Woo, the same would not be true of Francis Coppola. Like Scorsese's, much of Coppola's work has entered the language of film and popular discourse. We are all familiar, of course, with scenes and lines from the *Godfather* trilogy and from *Apocalypse Now*. Woo does allude to specific instances from Coppola's masterpieces, but not usually, or only rarely, in the manner one might expect at first: no superficial references to "offers one cannot refuse" or to horses' heads. Woo, as one would expect, both pays homage to and parallels Coppola's use of film language.

Like Coppola, Woo has a taste for bravura and baroque. Although Woo doesn't share Coppola's frequent fascination with chiaroscuro, he does display a similar tendency towards Guignolesque and operatic effect. Many comparisons could be drawn between the two directors' respective Gothic displays of bloodletting.

But this is really a surface comparison; the similarities go deeper. A less apparent parallel lies in the two filmmakers' scene setups, their specific employment of *mise-en-scène*. At least in the *Godfather* films, Coppola often follows a reductivist strategy of stripping away other characters until he is left with two characters confronting each other. This is done either by stage technique (artful exits) or by framing, so that the other characters in the scene become background or periphery. One good example of the latter would be the meeting between Senator Geary and Michael at the beginning of *The Godfather Part II*; another would be Connie's subsequent meeting with her brother Michael.

Woo also exhibits a preference for two-shot confrontations, but he usually approaches this in a simpler fashion: the two characters may meet in an apartment (Sidney and John) or, as in *Hard Boiled*, on a boat (Tequila and Tony), by a pier or in an office. But even in "social" settings, Woo's focus is frequently on the confrontation between two characters: thus, the bar scenes in *A Better Tomorrow* or *Hard Boiled* (between Alan and Johnny Wong).

Woo clearly refers to the *Godfather* movies in several instances. Of course, in a macro-structural sense, anyone making a gangster film in the 1980s or 1990s is hard-pressed not to refer to the Coppola films, or at least not to be influenced by them. But Woo appears to have assimilated certain aspects of these films and to have put them to good use in his own work.

Some of these examples are in the form of general motifs, like Mr. Lung's escape to the States after his betrayal by his "friends" in the Hong Kong triad. Like Michael (Al Pacino) in the first *Godfather* film, he must go into hiding. The reasons are different, but the manner is similar, most especially in that the criminal "world" is in Woo's film divided into two geographical parts: "here" (Hong Kong) and "there" (New York). For Coppola's characters, Sicily (Michael's place of refuge after his murder-execution of Sollozzo and McCluskey) represents a dream of security and a nostalgia for the vanished past, as opposed to America, the land of the future, of opportunity, but also of great risk. Significantly, Michael soon asserts himself and fits very well into the Sicilian setting, but the same cannot be said of Mr. Lung; for him, New York is an alien, frightening place, especially after he must confront the loss of his daughter back in Hong Kong. While Michael knows that his life is not meant to be spent in Sicily but rather back in the States, Lung and Ken (Chow Yun-fat) want only to return to Hong Kong: the reference to 1997 seems inescapable, with its uncertainties and its dislocation of families and homes, since many are leaving Hong Kong for the United States or Canada.

An example of a very direct reference to one of the *Godfather* films is also found in *A Better Tomorrow II*, a film unusually rich in such allusions. When Ken "rescues" Lung from the sanitarium in New York, he takes him to his own apartment. One night, as they are attacked by men firing through the windows, the scene is set up very much like the frightening attack on the Corleone compound in *The Godfather Part II*. Woo confirmed the source of the allusion; he has said, in fact, that *A Better Tomorrow II* was intended as a sequel in the spirit of *The Godfather Part II*. And, in fact, the second film does compare easily with *The Godfather Part II* in one important way: the perspective of the director on his characters. Coppola stated that he wanted, in the sequel, to correct the positive view of Michael Corleone left with some viewers in the first film—to demonstrate the character's core amorality and the cost of that amorality for him and his family (Chown 103). Allowing for the clear difference in quality (not even Woo defends the finished *A Better Tomorrow II*) and tone, both films attempt to portray the destructiveness of violence and illegality for family and friends. And, if Woo does not reveal a contempt for his protagonists akin to Coppola's, he does treat them from a less than serious perspective. He claims that this was his vision for the film: "I intended to do [the sequel] like a comic book" (personal interview, 8 November 1995).

We might also note that both Coppola and Woo emphasize the importance of the family. Although this emphasis may seem opportunistic in the *Godfather* films, nevertheless Coppola sincerely tries to defend "family values" in his work: *Tucker*, *Peggy Sue Got Married* and *Rumble Fish* are examples; and we should remember that the Corleones' downfall is precisely that of a family with distorted values. So, too, Woo shows how the familial relationships in Chinese society are crucial, and, as Julian Stringer notes, how in *A Better Tomorrow* their violation leads to "disaster" (Stringer 31).

The *Godfather* films and Woo's gangster stories share another element, one we might term "morality askew." Producer and screenwriter Bill Laurin, discussing the "Godfather" character (Robert Ito) in Woo's TV-movie *Once a Thief*, compares him to Vito Corleone in the first *Godfather* film, observing correctly that Vito's code of ethics is not inconsistent with itself but is instead "screwed": "[I]t's not that Corleone's uniformly evil, he loves his family. It's just that his sense of priorities is somewhat screwed. His ethical order is confused rather than absent" (Laurin and Davis, personal interview). Vito's code is not the morality of the rest of America, including those to whom Vito enviously but disparagingly refers as "pezzonovanti" (big shots). Vito sees nothing wrong in killing to defend one's honor or family. In the former respect at least, he is remarkably like the ancient Chinese knight as described by James Liu; certainly, Vito would find much in common with men who could be characterized thus:

> ... these men were individualists who objected to any rigid regimentation. They had little respect for the law of the state or the conventions of behaviour of the society in which they lived. The only rules they recognized were those of their own moral code [Liu 5].

He also compares closely to John in *The Killer* (after all, a descendant of those very knights),[4] for whom killing is a way of life insofar as it only involves those who, as John tells Jenny, "deserve to die." And certainly for John, as for Vito or Michael, killing is necessary when one's friends are threatened. But, like Vito or Michael, John draws the line at "innocents" being harmed: and it is precisely because of his remorse for and concern over innocents (Jenny, the girl at the beach) that he is weakened and finally destroyed.[5]

So Woo's characters, like Coppola's, normally pursue a moral star which differs from society's but which is remarkably consistent internally. Michael's downfall begins when he strays from his father's consistency (or perhaps allows it to become his hobgoblin) and starts to destroy or mistrust those who are actually loyal to him (Pentangeli, Hagen) or to condemn members of his family who have betrayed him from weakness (Fredo). Unlike John, who forgives Sidney for his betrayal, even becoming closer to him than before, Michael is too limited and egotistical to forgive Fredo his transgression. And Pentangeli must die as well, not so much, it seems, simply because he betrays Michael out of fear, but, more ominously, because he reminds Michael of the past and indirectly of his father, of the old style of "doing things" with that peculiar integrity.[6] Neither Woo nor Coppola, in his *Godfather* films, seems particularly optimistic about the survival of true morality in the modern context: either such morality will be "askew," taking on grotesque or combative trappings, or it will become totally outmoded and fatal to its practitioners.

STANLEY KUBRICK

John Woo very much admires Stanley Kubrick's work. He listed *2001* as one of his ten favorite films and he speaks of Kubrick in terms he reserves for only a few other directors, contrasting his attitude towards them with his respect for Ingmar Bergman:

> Ingmar Bergman, I saw several of his movies, he's a great master, but maybe I didn't get that much of a strong feeling [from him]—although his movies are always a pleasure to watch. I feel in pretty high spirits when I'm watching his movies. [His work is] so elegant—so much like a poet's. But not like Sam Peckinpah or Chang Cheh, Scorsese or Stanley Kubrick—*wow!* They touch my heart [Woo, personal interview, 7 November 1995].

Woo's admiration for Kubrick can be seen in *Hard Boiled*, although the particular reference may not seem obvious. This is the scene in the corridor, when Tequila and Tony fight off numerous gunmen who jump out at them as in a penny arcade. Masterfully choreographed and apparently seamlessly shot, this part of *Hard Boiled* is a set piece which looks, and is, quite original. Nevertheless, it is based on, or inspired by, the chase at the end of *The Shining* (Stanley Kubrick, 1980), when Jack (Jack Nicholson) tries to catch and kill his son Danny in the gazebo maze, covered with snow. The fact of Kubrick's influence on Woo would be obscured in this instance, were it not for Woo's pointing to this scene and acknowledging the source. This process exemplifies how Woo works as a director: an inspiration is often so hidden as to be nearly unrecognizable, since Woo has assimilated the influence and recycled it so that he does not seem merely imitative.

Woo appears to have taken two elements from the Kubrick scene and expanded on them. His interest was not in making a tribute so much as in learning from the way Kubrick used his camera:

> In *Hard Boiled*, in the hospital fight, there was that over three-minute-long shot with Chow Yun-fat and Tony Leung, where they start from the corridor and run and kill the bad guys. When I made the shot, it came from *The Shining*—the ending scene with the kid running scared in the maze, and [Kubrick] used the handheld camera to follow the kid. That camera technique I was very impressed with, so I used it in *Hard Boiled* [Woo, personal interview, 7 November 1995].

In the Kubrick scene, the Steadicam runs down the maze like an out-of-control worm from *Tremors* (1990), in a bravura point-of-view setup that takes off from the John Carpenter–inspired "killer point of view" shot. Woo takes the Steadicam run and applies it in *Hard Boiled* to gain a different effect: Tequila and Tony are not horror-film killers, with a psychotic point-of-view camera lending tension to their visual field. Instead, the subjective point-of-view track unifies them as partners, with a double, yet unified vision. Furthermore, their deft switching of positions is justified not only from an intradiegetic "tactical" perspective—to exchange fields of fire—but also from an extradiegetic one: the alternating chiasmic rhythm actually serves to triangulate or focus the viewer's perspective into the vanishing point of the hospital corridor. Tequila and Tony's options, and their goal, are visibly and geometrically narrowed and focused. And, of course, the point-of-view shot adds to the suspense of the scene, identifying the viewer's perceptions with the characters'.

Still more is to be revealed in this striking scene. Kubrick used the image of a Jack-in-the-box Nicholson to shocking effect, as when he leaps out of the darkness in the hotel corridor and kills the Scatman Crothers character with an ax blow. Woo reverses this image, causing the gunmen through whose gauntlet Tequila and Tony must pass to pop out as in an arcade.[7] And we can easily see that, while Kubrick's scene in the maze may have inspired Woo to do the corridor scene, the inspiration is of a specific and limited order. Woo derives from Kubrick the extended point-of-view shot and the spatial imagery of the long corridor with many entrances and exits, but not the thematic complex of the demented father trying to kill his son, nor the supernatural penumbra of the Overlook Hotel, nor the setting itself. Here is more evidence, were it needed, that Woo's derivations are functional, not imitative, winking or shallowly parodic.

DON SIEGEL AND ROBERT ALDRICH

Two underrated directors who reached their peak in the 1950s and 1960s, Don Siegel (1912–91) and Robert Aldrich (1918–83) have been cited by Woo as important to his own formation as a director. Both Siegel and Aldrich are associated with the action film, and specifically with the depiction of strong and sometimes ruthless male protagonists, often antiheroic ones. Aldrich's perspective is darker and more complex than Siegel's, but both directors explore, in their best work, the nature of individual responsibility and the consequences of personal and leadership decisions.

Siegel first became known as a competent and notable B–movie director with his 1956 *Invasion of the Body Snatchers*. As Stuart M. Kaminsky has noted,[8] the film contained the kernel of his vision: the concern with individuality in a world where society suppresses individualism—thus, the Kevin McCarthy hero struggles valiantly to retain his separateness from the alien "pods" taking over his small town. Siegel went on to become a very recognized director with films like *Hell Is for Heroes* (1962), *Madigan* (1968) and especially *Dirty Harry* (1971), which launched the tough, anti-corporate cop vogue and arguably contributed to the later series of anti-bureaucratic heroes like Rambo.

Aldrich, a bluff, blustery, large man whose exterior belied his considerable intelligence, education and sensitivity, became known as a "man's man" in directing principally because of *The Dirty Dozen* (1967). But he was always a director restless with conventional films and brimming over with ideas about expanding cinematic form; thus, one of his enduring masterpieces is the seminal *Kiss Me Deadly* (1955), with its subversive appropriation of Mickey Spillane's Mike Hammer character (played by Ralph Meeker). He also made interesting political films such as *Twilight's Last Gleaming* (1977), allegories like *Flight of the Phoenix* (1966) and, especially intriguing to Woo, the badly received and flawed but powerful *Emperor of the North* (1973).

Both Aldrich and Siegel have made films dealing with strong male figures, usually in an antiheroic mode—thus, from Aldrich, most particularly *The Dirty Dozen* and *Emperor of the North*; and from Siegel, especially *Hell Is for Heroes* and *Dirty Harry*. Although this kind of emphasis does not exhaust their production, nevertheless for Woo much of their interest as directors inheres in such films.

Siegel was usually linked particularly to *Invasion of the Body Snatchers* and *Dirty Harry*, and the latter film has influenced Woo, especially in the construction of the Tequila character; but Siegel received less attention for one of his minor masterworks, *Hell Is for Heroes*. This platoon film, focusing on a small squad of U. S. Army soldiers, worn out and hoping for orders home, who are sent back "on the line" during the Battle of the Bulge in 1944, features a remarkably non-clichéd script "cowritten" by Robert Pirosh (*TV Movies 1998*) and notable work from Steve McQueen (in a career-making role), Nick Adams, Harry Guardino and Fess Parker. (The film was also Bob Newhart's debut.)

Hell Is for Heroes is typical of its period, with flat lighting, oddly two-dimensional depth of field, and "stark" groupings of men in stress. But it is also a grimmer portrait than most war films preceeding *Apocalypse Now* or *The Deer Hunter*, with its depiction of men left to die in a seemingly impossible job—to hold a position against overwhelming numbers—with little apparent support, until the end of the film, from the rear.

Individual initiative is not prized by higher command; the organization man Larkin (Guardino) seems a good fit here. Reese (McQueen) does not, and it is his character that draws Woo's attention.

Reese is introduced to us as an unkempt, surly, hostile and tight-mouthed soldier who arrives by transfer on the day when the squad will go "on the line." He had been busted down to private for insubordination and has a fondness for drinking alone. But these negatives conceal, or rather explain, his positive attributes: He comes alive "on the line," much like Ulysses S. Grant, who was aimless as a civilian and as a peace-time soldier, but who found his prime calling as an obsessively tenacious and ruthless commander. Reese is a man who relishes the hard life of combat—perhaps, we suspect, in the secret hope that he will be killed, or perhaps just because he likes living "on the edge." He proves himself capable nonetheless of generosity and self-sacrifice but will not bend to authority easily nor soft-pedal the truth about battle predicaments.

In short, he is very much like a John Woo hero. McQueen's characters often feed into Woo's; the 1960s icon struck a chord not only with Woo but with other Hong Kong film figures like Chow Yun-fat, Danny Lee, David Wu[9] and Terence Chang. The Don Siegel version of McQueen is much more hard-bitten, or in Kaminsky's terms, much more "mad" (see Kaminsky 175–76) than the Peter Yates "cool" McQueen in *Bullitt* (1968), or the John Sturges–directed professional gunman in *The Magnificent Seven* (1960), or the rather flippant and devil-may-care prisoner Hilts in *The Great Escape* (1963). Only under Peckinpah's direction in *The Getaway* (1972) does McQueen, as Doc McCoy, come close to the tight-lipped and misanthropic Reese of *Hell Is for Heroes*. What all these McQueen characters share, though, is an aversion to taking orders and a tendency to live by their own lights. Like Tequila, who seems in fact more like Bullitt than like Dirty Harry (he is more humanized than Harry), McQueen's characters buck the system, refusing to "join" if joining means selling out.

Thus Hilts in *The Great Escape* is nicknamed "The Cooler King" because he keeps making escape attempts and being sent to the "cooler" (solitary). But his true development as a character, particularly in moral terms, takes place when he is asked by Ramsey (James Donald) and Bartlett (Richard Attenborough) to escape for vital reconnaissance and to allow himself to be recaptured. His initial reaction of incredulity at this request yields to a sudden turnabout, a willingness to sacrifice his own goals for those of the community. Like Tony in *Hard Boiled* or Ho in the two *A Better Tomorrow* films, Hilts learns to join the group; and though he eventually fails to escape, his early heroism contributes to the escape of some of his fellows and to the disruption of the German war machine. Also like Tequila, and to some extent Inspector Li, Hilts is sometimes rather rude, eliciting the comment from the camp commandant, the well-mannered Col. Von Luger (Hannes Messemer), "Are all American officers so ill-mannered?"

Parallels between Siegel's *Dirty Harry* and *Hard Boiled* are clear enough and have usually been mentioned in connection with Tequila's similarity (not an exact one) to Harry. But we might also note that Woo's original storyline called for a villain even more like Siegel's Scorpio (Andy Robinson) than is Johnny Wong. Johnny, though psychotic, is not a lone serial killer but the leader of a gang who operates from understandable if reprehensible motives, in the mold of "mad" gangsters like Dutch Schultz. Even after the change in storyline, though, the opposition between Tequila and his "evil double" Wong mirrors that between Harry and Scorpio. Like Harry, too, Tequila is alone, though in a more comic fashion— Harry's wife is dead; Tequila and Teresa have merely split up. And Harry and Tequila have similar trouble with the higher-ups, although Harry is certainly meaner as a personality than is Tequila. Chow Yun-fat even appears to do a take on Harry's famous nonchalance in the midst of violent action: Harry stops an armed robbery while still munching a hot dog; Tequila munches on a sandwich while inspecting a dead body, the result of a hit by Alan, at the crime scene.

Siegel appears to have contributed mainly to Woo's vision in his character types and in his fondness for oppositional structures like the one between Harry and Scorpio. Aldrich's influence is less pronounced but generally turns on the same axis: around character—in this case, male groups led by a strong figure (like Lee Marvin in *The Dirty Dozen* and *Emperor of the North*, or like James Stewart in *Flight of the Phoenix*). Woo has also commented on his respect for Aldrich's staging of violent scenes, especially in the wrenching fight atop a rail car that closes *Emperor of the North* (Woo, personal interview, 8 November 1995).

John Frankenheimer

If Scorsese and Peckinpah are often mentioned as influences on John Woo, John Frankenheimer (1930–) has never, to my knowledge, been noted as important to him. Yet a close examination of Woo's films leads one to perceive similarities in their style and their content—specifically, their moral tone—to some of Frankenheimer's work. Woo's positioning of his characters in obliquely related two-shots seems very "Franken-heimer." So do his use of sometimes strange long shots and his placing of characters in isolated, alien environments which do not seem alien at first glance—for example, Ken and Lung's conversation outside New York City before returning to Hong Kong, when they seem strangely alienated from the American city, like Asian Popeye Doyles stuck in the United States instead of in France.

Woo in fact confirmed this intuition about Frankenheimer in conversation with me. While he did not specifically admit to "influence," he did point to Frankenheimer's importance for young filmmakers of his generation in 1960s Hong Kong: "Frankenheimer was a big name in Hong Kong in the '60s and '70s, [with a big] following. We loved his movies" (Woo, personal interview, 2 March 1996).

In the same interview, Woo mentioned two films by Frankenheimer that have particularly impressed him, *Birdman of Alcatraz* (1962) and *Black Sunday* (1977). These are two of the director's most interesting films, if perhaps less cited than *The Manchurian Candidate* (1962) or *Seven Days in May* (1964). As far as *Birdman* is concerned, Woo would most likely have been impressed with the dignity of "birdman" Stroud (Burt Lancaster) in the face of adversity, with his romantically heroic refusal to give up his bird studies, and with the friendship that grows between this prisoner and a sympathetic prison guard (played by Neville Brand). Woo has also commented on his own firmly held belief that even the worst of people have some good qualities (Woo, Commentary, *The Killer* 20). Stroud is certainly no angel; he is a convicted (and guilty) killer; he is arrogant and brusque; he is capable of extreme coldheartedness. But he develops, through his rapport with the birds, into a person of rare wisdom and compassion. He also reveals an unusual gift of native intelligence.

Frankenheimer filmed the story of Stroud with consistent reliance on facial close-ups of the pensive inmate. For Woo, perhaps this film language has contributed to his own featuring of close-ups and of long-held shots of meditative characters, such as we see repeatedly in *The Killer*.

Finally, one might observe that Stroud's resistance against an unjust or unfeeling "system" is right in line with one of Woo's favorite themes. Woo says that he detests totalitarianism and dictatorship (and has little truck with politics in general) (Woo, Commentary, *Hard Boiled* ch. 31). Frankenheimer has dealt with such themes on other occasions—in *The Manchurian Candidate*, *Seconds* (1966), *The Train* (1964), implicitly in *Dead-Bang* (1989), synecdochically in *52 Pick-Up* (1986), allegorically in *The Island of Dr. Moreau* (1996) and in conjunction with terrorism in *Black Sunday*.

Turning to *Black Sunday*, we might at first wonder why Woo chose this film as one of his favorites by Frankenheimer. This is because Woo normally eschews political themes and *Black Sunday* is openly concerned with Arab-Israeli politics and terrorism, with the 1972 Munich Olympics attack as a subtext. Nevertheless, the film has certain features which would definitely appeal to Woo.

One of these is Frankenheimer's totally assured sense of scene management. He works with a very big palette, the Superbowl stadium, and achieves some dazzling and suspenseful effects in the story of an attempt by Arab terrorists to bomb the Superbowl game by misappropriating the Goodyear blimp. In the process of creating his effects, Frankenheimer uses documentary footage of his stars at the Superbowl so as to create a verisimilar montage. Woo brought off similar effects, on a smaller scale, in the Dragon Boat scene in *The Killer*. In another way, that is, in filtering history through a fictional structure, he parallels Frankenheimer's recasting in *Black Sunday* of the terrorist attack at the Olympics by recreating the famous murder of a Vietcong prisoner by an ARVN officer in *Bullet in the Head*.

Black Sunday also may have helped to form Woo's notion of the hero-villain pair who complement each other in their vices and virtues. Although certainly not comparable morally to Woo's pairs of self-sacrificing heroes, Israeli Major David Kabakov (Robert Shaw) and Palestinian terrorist Dahlia (Marthe Keller) are an intriguing opposed pair. While it is true that they remain enemies until the end, when Kabakov kills Dahlia, still they are siblings under the skin. Both are ruthless in their cause, both have lost family members and friends to the other side. A Palestinian official, Col. Riaf (Walter Gotell), even reproves Kabakov for Dahlia's nature, reminding him, "After all, in a way, she's your creation." In short, the heroes and villains in this film are not one-dimensional. Each has some good or admirable qualities as well as some less attractive ones. And, significantly from Woo's perspective, each is thoroughly prepared to die from a sense of duty and integrity—even though this integrity might not be the morality commonly held by others.

Woo and Frankenheimer also share a fascination with the visual and plastic potential of the human face. Frequently cited in the literature on Woo is his recourse to the extreme close-up, sometimes in association with freeze-frame (as, for example, in *The Killer*). One purpose of this device is to place the subject *sub specie aeternitatis*: not only the freeze-frame but the close-up assist in this. The subject, becoming much larger than life, is suggestively placed above and beyond it (see Fuchs for this idea regarding buddy films). Frankenheimer may not have the same intention as does Woo in such cases (that is, heroicizing or eternalizing the character), but both share an interest in the moral psychology of their characters. Thus,

John in *The Killer* is shown in sweating emotional agony in a progressively nearing tracking shot following Johnny Weng's attempted hit on him and Sidney's concomitant betrayal. His moral anguish, self-doubt and loneliness are patent (as well as strikingly Chinese; a Western character would be more outraged than anguished at such a breach of friendship). Jiggs Casey's moment of decision, to betray his superior officer Gen. Scott (but for a higher moral reason than in Sidney's case), in *Seven Days in May*, also features a "growing close-up." Though never as exaggeratedly tortured as the shot of John, this Frankenheimer setup does convey the deep guilt and self-doubt experienced by Casey. Frankenheimer also uses the close-up in a more peculiar and disturbing fashion when the camera focuses obliquely on Mudd (Andrew Duggan), who has just begun to realize while talking to Senator Clark (Edmond O'Brien) that treason may be afoot. This close-up shows Mudd both as if sickened and as if distanced from his environment (because of the angularity of the shot). Although Woo usually does not attempt such grotesqueness, still he uses the camera for psychological inspection, as in numerous close-ups in *The Killer* and *Bullet in the Head*.

Although Woo has not specifically mentioned *The Train* as an important film for him, it is a Frankenheimer work that features both character types and concepts similarly elaborated by Woo. The theme of art as national expression is certainly not alien to Woo, and the poignant depiction by Frankenheimer of the French resisting Nazi theft of their art at great personal risk is a fine example of struggle against dictatorship. But even more striking is the nature of the decision by railroad man Labiche (Burt Lancaster) to involve himself in this struggle. He is a member of the Resistance, but he feels no particular loyalty to high art; for him, people are much more important. Labiche demurs at first when asked to stop the train; he suggests that it be blown up. The story of *The Train* is in large part the record of Labiche's growing involvement in a struggle for an ideal—but, it must be remembered, he acts for personal more than for idealistic reasons. He sees too many friends killed, and his attempt (ultimately successful) to stop the train becomes the settling of a score with the German colonel (Paul Scofield) who has ordered the artworks transported.

Labiche is a good example both of an existential protagonist, who becomes a "hero" by personal choice, and, even more, of a "reluctant hero," who acts in no small part to avenge the death of his comrades. In this sense, he is a spiritual brother to Inspector Li, to Ho and to other such Woo heroes; he also mirrors them in his distaste for authority and in his general stubbornness and quirky integrity. Finally, we should take note again of Labiche's fierce loyalty to his comrades and of his meting out of lethal justice to the colonel, whose soldiers have just massacred hostages carried on the train as human shields. Woo's villains often suffer such personal retribution at the hands of the hero: Johnny Weng in *The Killer*, Ko in *A Better Tomorrow II*, Johnny Wong in *Hard Boiled*, Shing in *A Better Tomorrow*, Deakins in *Broken Arrow*, Castor in *Face/Off*—that is, Woo does not permit the machinery of movie convention, the *deus ex machina*, to destroy his villains. This function is vouchsafed to the avenging hero.

Alfred Hitchcock and David Lean

Although the influence of these two directors on Woo is not extensive, it is significant. Hitchcock's films in particular inspired Woo to learn technically. *Strangers on a Train* is cited by Woo as a model for developing and sustaining suspense while not losing narrative and visual fluidity.[10] (He might also have mentioned its opposed pair of good/evil doubles.) This film lent more than a little to *Face/Off*, both in its sane/psycho doubling and in its related mechanism of parallel editing or narrative. Like Bruno (Robert Walker) in *Strangers*, Castor Troy (disguised as Sean Archer) is shown in a series of scenes preparing to take over Archer's life and then to take it, as Archer (disguised as Castor) tries to rescue his family. And Woo appears to be paying direct tribute to Hitchcock in the film's opening scene, with its juxtaposition of innocence (Archer's son) and evil (Castor) with a merry-go-round as the setting.[11]

Hitchcock's work seems to have helped Woo in the elaboration of suspense and character conflicts, particularly those expressed through doubling. The importance of David Lean for Woo is more in the nature of his handling of heroism and of epic *mise-en-scène*. *Lawrence of Arabia* (1962), one of Woo's personal favorites, is a fine model for his longtime aspiration to direct a grand epic, as he wishes to do with *The Devil Soldier*. And Lawrence himself, or the picture of Lawrence given us by Lean and Peter O'Toole, is a rebel against the "system," an unlikely hero who rises to prominence by his disregard of personal risk and his reliance on intuition. His loyalty to friends is also beyond question. All these are qualities to be found in the Chinese chivalry tradition and in Woo's modern-day revisiting of that tradition. And Lean's *The Bridge on the River Kwai* (1957) focuses on the role of the moral man confronted with tyranny, as well as on the effects of moral rigidity and pride on one's life. British Col. Nicholson (Alec Guinness) pays dearly for his inflexibility about the Geneva Convention, but not as he had anticipated: he wins over camp commandant Col. Saito (Sessue Hayakawa), but then joins, or rather takes over, his bridge-building enterprise, to prove the worth of the British soldier. But his pride and his uprightness blind him to the fact of his co-opting by an immoral enterprise (his more detached colleague, Major Clipton [James Donald], is not so blinded) in aiding a tyranny. *Kwai* also contains powerful examples of self-sacrifice, notably by the commandos who sabotage the bridge. Regardless of possible overt influence on Woo, these Lean films certainly express moral concepts akin to his own.

Sam Peckinpah, a Seminal Influence

Sam Peckinpah, the director of American screen masterpieces such as *Ride the High Country*, *The Wild Bunch* and *Straw Dogs*, has importantly influenced John Woo. But his influence is not necessarily of the kind usually mentioned in reference to Peckinpah, who has (like Woo) been often misunderstood as a purveyor of macho action bloodfests in gory slow motion. Much more complex than this caricature, Peckinpah was a combination of vulnerable romantic and tough-guy stoic. And he celebrated the stoic virtues in films like *Ride the High Country* and *The Wild Bunch*, whose heroes, far from being nihilists (an accusation often leveled, particularly at *The Wild Bunch*),[12] are frustrated idealists who long for a simpler time when technology had not overshadowed human relations and when big corporate enterprise had not intruded irrevocably into the garden of the American dream.

Woo's characters can in many cases be better understood when placed against Peckinpah's. Tequila, John and Li are all spiritual kin to Pike, Steven Judd, and Dutch Engstrom, both in their secretive idealism and in their generally tragic denouements. At least as important as these aspects is their masculine or, if one prefers, their macho stance toward the world around them. One reason that many of these characters fail is that they do not fit into an increasingly feminized, civilized world (so that the Wild Bunch, for instance, symbolically destroy such a world in their early gunfight in Starbuck when the Temperance marchers and local citizens are caught in the crossfire between the Bunch and the railroad gunmen led by Deke Thornton [Robert Ryan]). So, Pike and Dutch discuss the passing of their kind, and John and Sidney lament the ending of a way of life (obliquely referring to 1997 but also to the passing of a "nobler" age). Both Peckinpah and Woo mine the *ubi sunt* trope in their narratives.

Furthermore, both directors express alienation from political systems and from the corporate world. Woo and Peckinpah express individualism and self-reliance—both tempered, however, by loyalty to the friendship group and by a sense of duty—over and against the demands of politics and governments.

Thus, when the German "military advisor" to Gen. Mapache asks Pike where he got the weapon he is carrying (a 1911 issue .45 pistol, available only to the military), and whether he is affiliated with the military or the U. S. government, Dutch Engstrom (Ernest Borgnine) replies in quiet detachment, "No, no. We're not associated with anybody." And Pike offers some reassurance about their willingness to help Mapache: "Well, we share very few sentiments with our government." *Ride the High Country*, an early Peckinpah film, shows the company that hires Judd and his men to carry a payroll for them as duplicitous and penny-pinching. By the time of *The Wild Bunch*, Peckinpah has arrived at a much more thoroughly corrosive view of corporate America. He portrays Harrigan (Albert Dekker), the head of the railroad who hires Thornton and his bounty hunters to capture or kill the Bunch, as not only a callous man indifferent to civilian casualties in the Starbuck gunfight but as a totally uncompromising capitalist who sees Thornton as a tool and threatens him with going "back to Yuma" (the territorial prison). (An insert shot shows us the sadistic mistreatment endured there by Thornton, nicely tying together the cruelty of political and business authority.)

Woo is not as blackly cynical as Peckinpah, but he does display negative attitudes toward big organizations, which he views as potential dictatorships. The corporation in *Plain Jane to the Rescue* is an Orwellian enterprise run by a vicious man who mistreats his father ("Uncle" Sha, rescued by Jane and Fang) in a very non–Confucian way. *From Riches to Rags* shows the Ricky Hui hero as victimized by his unfeeling and pompous boss. Woo has also said that he uses uniformed gunmen as characters (that is, as in *The Killer*, all dressed in the same white clothing) to show that the big gangster organization is like a dictatorship which demands conformity (Woo, personal interview, 2 March 1996). Woo's films have displayed this perspective since his earliest work. In *The Young Dragons*, the criminal organization run by Mr. Lung demands absolute obedience and employs anonymous killers. Woo has expanded upon such one-dimensional treatment. In *Hard Boiled*, three big organizations are implicitly contrasted. The outfit run by Wong is cut from the same cloth as Mr. Lung's, with the added twist that Wong is unbalanced psychologically. Mr. Hui's organization is actually parallel to the police force run by Chief Pang. The strong authority at the top is not faceless, nor is it capricious; both organizations feature leaders concerned about their subordinates. So, Wong's mob here, like the outfits in *The Killer* and the *A Better Tomorrow* films, represents the dictatorial kind of organization criticized by Woo. Such parallels between Woo and Peckinpah show us that the Peckinpah influence on Woo, or perhaps Woo's kinship of spirit to Peckinpah, is hardly limited to the "macho bonding" or "tough guy" motif, nor to the slow-motion filming style usually seen as Peckinpah's major contribution to Woo. The directors share moral and social concerns as well, although Woo adds his own perspectives to his commonality with the American director.

Europe and Asia

JEAN-PIERRE MELVILLE AND SERGIO LEONE

Few other directors receive as much praise from John Woo as does Jean-Pierre Melville (1917–73). A true cult figure, in the sense of a director with esoteric appeal, Melville never attained the fame of his contemporaries Truffaut, Godard and Resnais. He seems a little too off-center and "disreputable" in his choice of subject matter and in his frequently downbeat, minor-key films. His gangster movies are difficult because they spare no one, neither the gangsters nor the police, from the sense of moral slipperiness, and because they are spare, minimalist and typically pessimistic (though not always without humor and limited warmth).

Those viewers and critics thinking of John Woo only as a "shoot-em-up" action helmer would be hard-pressed to explain his interest in a director like Melville (or for that matter, in a film like Peckinpah's strange *Bring Me the Head of Alfredo Garcia* [1974]). Woo, though, responds strongly to films about losers or failed heroes who nevertheless win, in a sense, by preserving or rediscovering their integrity, both in moral and in emotional terms.

Notably, Alain Delon's signature lead roles in Melville's *Le Samouraï* and *Le Cercle rouge* portray men who have no real inner life; they live in and for their work, their métier as criminals, their next hit or score. Their Sartrean existence, alienated and rootless, leads them to act in reckless and self-destructive ways—but they both are men with defined principles, including a strong sense of loyalty and a contempt for moral weakness.

The above sketch might apply to Woo characters like John or Tequila, but Woo has added a significant element to the Melville type: Woo's heroes come to experience real and effective human warmth, even love, and may sacrifice themselves or risk their lives from motives other than the often murky impulses that drive Melville's characters. Woo characters are impelled by varying motives: protectiveness (John, Tequila, Ben), love (John, Li), loyalty (many characters, including John, Tequila,

Alan and Sidney), and more rarely, negative forces like greed (Paul). But the heroes, or protagonists, in Woo films like *A Better Tomorrow, The Killer* and *Bullet in the Head* decidedly do not act because they know little else to do (as in *Le Cercle rouge*) or chiefly because they feel trapped (as in *Le Samouraï*). So, the analogy between Woo's work and Melville's is qualified despite the admitted influence.

But the analogy is certainly valid in some important ways, one of which is the redemption theme. Woo commented at some length for a program note at the 1995 Toronto International Film Festival on his admiration for Melville and *Le Samouraï*:

> Jean-Pierre Melville's *Le Samourai* is the closest thing to a perfect movie that I have ever seen. It is an amazingly pure and elegant film about a criminal who is facing death and coming to terms with a life devoted to violence.... The picture has been a major influence on my own work, *not because of the story or even the way it is shot, but because it is a gangster film that is as much about the way a gangster thinks and feels as about the way he behaves.* Melville understands that when Jeff ... chose this life he was embracing his own death.... [Jeff] achieves a kind of redemption at the end by accepting his fate gracefully. To me, this is the most romantic attitude imaginable [Woo, Program note, qtd. in Chute, Publicity for *Broken Arrow* 32; emphasis added].

Like John, Jef Costello (Delon) pays a kind of penance for his life and redeems himself to at least some extent. Jef does this by not killing the chanteuse who had actually betrayed him; he comes to meet her at the club with an empty gun and aims at her, knowing the police will kill him. Woo deepens the gallantry of John's death by conflating the Melville story with that of *Narazumono*, so that John dies trying to save Jenny. Additionally, it is John's newfound altruism and love for Jenny that has led to his demise. He stays in Hong Kong, inviting death, because he wants to be able to pay for her operation.

Another important parallel between the two directors is the "comeback" motif. We have referred to Woo's affinity to characters who bring their lives back from rock bottom to a semblance at least of their former level of expertise and competence. As we will see in Chapter 6, he stresses Jansen's comeback moment in *Le Cercle rouge*, when he shoots out the lock, as one of the central inspirations for his own film sensibility. This moment is quoted by Woo in two of his canonical films, *The Killer* and *Hard Boiled*, although as so often with Woo, the allusion or quotation is only partial. Or, if one prefers, Woo integrates the reference into his own work so that it is not a mere reprise. When John shoots Tony Weng in a fantastically accurate series of unbraced shots from a motorboat, and Tequila shoots the primer cap on one of his .357 magnum shells with a from-the-hip shot from about 25 paces, the viewer should be reminded of Jansen's feat. But neither John nor Tequila is, at this moment, experiencing a moral or technical "comeback" similar to Jansen's. The emphasis is rather on the imagery of the shots and on their amazing competence: the quickly fired or drawn weapons, the eyeline between shooter and target, and, importantly for the effect on the viewer, the Eisensteinian editing used in both cases to expand the moment so that we experience it even more fully.[13]

As we have seen, Alain Delon, the actor whose character Corey hires Jansen (Yves Montand), reappears in several contexts in Woo's films. His trenchcoated laconicism fits well with Woo's image of the strong, silent hero, while his cold good looks lend force to analogous spiritual coldness. Not by accident is his the face of a killer in films like *Le Samouraï* and *Le Cercle rouge*. So Chow Yun-fat pays homage to him in the *A Better Tomorrow* films and in *The Killer*, and we can even see his presence in some of Woo's villains: the dark glasses worn by Paul Yau (Weng's hit man in *The Killer*) and by Mr. Chong (Ko's hit man in *A Better Tomorrow II*) might have been worn by Jef Costello or by Corey. Woo in fact adopts a certain "French style" in his costuming of gangsters (whether villain or hero): the formal black suit-on-white-shirt style favored by the heroes in *A Better Tomorrow II* recalls the austerity of Melville's costuming, most especially in Delon's case.

And Delon carried his trademark dress into the films of other directors. We see his black trenchcoat in, for example, Jean Herman's *The Honorable Thief* (*Adieu L'ami*, 1968), where he costars with Charles Bronson.

Terence Chang says that this is one of Woo's favorite films (personal interview, 2 March 1996). The film seems a made-to-order Woo story. Its two male leads, ex-Legionnaires and mercenaries Deano Barron (Delon) and Frank Propp (Bronson), do not particularly like each other. Deano is recruited by Isabel Moreau (Olga Georges-Picot) to do a strange black-bag job. He is supposed to *put back* 50,000 francs in bearer bonds into a time-lock safe in the basement of an office building where he hires on as a doctor. Propp follows him and ends up trapped with him in the basement; they soon understand that the job was a set-up.

The fact that Deano's nurse-lover Waterloo (Brigitte Fossey) and Isabel have set him up is not what interests us here; rather, it is the extraordinary degree of (nonsentimental) loyalty that both men evince towards each other. We discover that Deano did the job solely to pay his moral debt to his friend Mozart, whom he had accidentally killed, mistaking him for an enemy. This revelation elicits a very Woo-like remark from

Propp: "Well, you can't always tell your friends from your enemies. Come right down to it, maybe they're the same thing." And Propp, who is captured by the police, refuses to tell the no-nonsense but not unsympathetic police inspector that he knows Deano; he stands up under many hours of interrogation by sleep deprivation without admitting any knowledge of Deano. Clearly, each man's professional code overrides other considerations. (Deano returns the gesture at the end of the film by not admitting to a knowledge of Propp.)

Woo appears to have integrated some elements of this film into his own work. Besides the clear parallels between the character relationships here and in his own movies, Woo's films contain scenes that clearly echo *The Honorable Thief.*

In *Hard Boiled*, Tequila and Tony are trapped in the basement, actually the morgue, of the hospital, and must escape in order to stop Wong and his men. Perhaps the germ for this idea was the two men's predicament in *The Honorable Thief.* Weight is added to this notion by a small detail: Propp tries to free the two by cross-wiring the elevator (he actually shorts the air-conditioning, compounding their problems) and is shocked insensible. Tony, attempting to open the sealed door in the morgue, joins two cables together and is nearly killed. In both cases, the man's partner revives him. Woo's treatment of a similar event as in Herman's film is much more elaborate and hi-tech, but this is also the case with his treatment of scenes such as the first hit in *The Killer*, a scene reprised from *Le Samouraï* with much more florid style and a great deal more lead and cordite.

The other scenes from *The Honorable Thief* that may have directly influenced Woo concern Propp's capture and interrogation. As in *The Killer*, one of the partners is captured at an airport. Like Sidney, Propp creates a diversion, allowing his partner to escape while he is captured. After being arrested, Propp, like Sidney, makes light of the episode to the police. But neither reveals any connection to the partner or friend.

Woo's airport scene, whether based on this one or not, differs in some important ways from the scene in *The Honorable Thief.* The emphasis in *The Honorable Thief* scene is on the two "partners," one of whom (Deano) did not expect the other even to be at the airport. In *The Killer*, Jenny has betrayed John's plans to Li and Chang, believing that she must do so to save him. At the last minute, she changes her mind and tries to warn him, so the scene really has shifting foci: Woo cuts back and forth from Jenny's face to Li's, connecting the two in their concern for John (and in Li's for Jenny). He also pans slowly around the airport, the camera (Li's POV) resting tantalizingly on a figure whom we suspect to be

John, but whose face is not fully visible, and then tracking past crowds of people.[14] Finally the track begins to follow a running figure whom we discover to be Sidney; now photographed in full-face, he kicks out at the police and is arrested while John and Jenny escape by lying on the baggage belt. The French film scene is much simpler, since the camera is not identified with the pursuers, there is no Jenny present at all, and the question of identity is moot—the faces of the two are not obscured. The similarities between the two scenes are nevertheless clear, and perhaps this scene gave Woo the inspiration for his much more elaborate conception. In any case, Alain Delon provides a connection between this film and two of Woo's other important inspirations, Melville's *Le Samouraï* and *Le Cercle rouge*.

Woo repeatedly mentions *Le Cercle rouge* as an important film for him. Both *The Killer* and *Hard Boiled* refer explicitly to its sharpshooting scene. Besides the "big scene," though, the film contains elements which would certainly appeal to Woo.

One of these characteristics is the "brotherhood of bandits" theme, central to *Water Margin* and reprised in *A Better Tomorrow* and *The Killer*. The motif is understated, in fact, unmentioned in Melville's film, and not, as with Woo, made an overt part of the script. But it appears clearly at the plot level when Vogel (Gian-Maria Volonte, familiar to Leone and Eastwood fans), on the lam after escaping from custody, hides in the trunk of Corey's car. Though aware that he is in the trunk, Corey (Delon) does not betray him at the police roadblock. When he stops the car and tells him he can get out, Vogel trains a gun on him, and he offers Vogel no explanation of his motive for protecting him. But he patently did so for two reasons. He needed an accomplice for a job, and (a point he certainly would not admit) he sensed a kinship under the skin, or perhaps felt some vague loyalty to the "brotherhood" of criminals. In any case, the two become partners, and even closer ones after Vogel saves Corey from being hit by the man he had just robbed (but who had taken his lover).

In critical and review articles about Woo's films, the name Sergio Leone is recurrent, at times concerning Woo's acknowledged influences, and at others with regard to their seemingly comparable perspective on filmmaking: epic, revisionist, generically innovative and quirkily idiosyncratic. Sometimes the import of such comparisons is not so favorable to Woo, or to Leone, since the implication seems to be that both are "enfants terribles," not too reputable and not to be taken too seriously.

Like Woo, Leone had trouble with the critics. He was often accused of excess, of distorting the Western myth, of cultivating sleaziness (especially in his early films with Eastwood), and so forth. He was not always a very subtle director, but he was a very intelligent, forceful and visual scenarist, as well as a keen observer of humanity. And he made at least two masterpieces, *Once Upon a Time in the West* (1968) and *A Fistful of Dynamite* (1972), as well as another film which came close: *Once Upon a Time in America* (1984).

Woo has been a close student of Leone's work. One of his personal favorites among Leone's films is *Once Upon a Time in the West*, but he has also mentioned *A Fistful of Dynamite* as influential on him (personal interview, 8 November 1995). Leone's influence on Woo is often considered in terms of their mutual use of long, suspenseful stand-offs between duellists and in the degree of violence found in the work of both filmmakers. Woo, however, does not acknowledge this type of influence from the Italian; he sees his own use of the stand-off as a parallel rather than a borrowing, and in fact such moments can be found quite readily in another Woo influence, Kurosawa, who certainly predates Leone's work. More correctly, Leone's influence is one of tone: Stephen Teo is certainly right to point to Leone's operatic quality as inspirational for *The Killer*, although he relatively underplays the considerable importance of Scorsese, Melville and Coppola (Teo 177–78).

CHANG CHEH

As we have already seen, Woo is quite indebted to Chang Cheh's films for showing him the possibilities of martial arts choreography and the use of male friendship in chivalric terms. While he freely admits this influence now, for some reason, according to Terence Chang, "It was only after John came [to Hollywood] that he began to acknowledge the influence of Chang Cheh. In Hong Kong he always denied that. I don't know why" (Chang, personal interview, 4 November 1995). In any case, it is clear that Woo learned a great deal from Chang Cheh about staging action sequences, but also, and probably more importantly, about the necessity of "staying on" the characters. One of the reasons that Chang films like *Invincible Fist* or *Vengeance* are so memorable is that Chang, unlike many less talented martial arts directors, focuses almost obsessively on his heroes and villains, showing them in big close-ups before, during and after battles. Even though he shows his heroes in trademark battles against multiple adversaries, a factor that has been noted as contributing to Woo's films, Chang never lets his important characters become part of an undistinguished mass. The viewer remains interested at all times, in Chang's best work, in the heroes and in the villains, perceiving them as personal adversaries.

Like Chang, Woo never loses sight of his characters as human beings and as the "center of attention" for the camera. Even in the most furiously staged gunfights, Woo does not let his camera wander; the major characters are always clearly at "center stage." In the hands of a less sophisticated director, John's dispatching of his putative assassins in his flat would be a routine bloodbath, perhaps filmed with set piece shots of men being mowed down, intercut with shots of John blasting away. But Woo follows John around the room, now in the middle of the room, now against a door. The camera changes angles to accommodate John's movements and to focus on his point of view or on his weapons. We thus are made to feel vicarious participants in the action, but we also are made to identify somehow with John's perspective and with his tense effort. This feature Woo has very much in common with Chang Cheh. But he surpasses his master in his innovativeness and flexibility as far as the camera is concerned: Chang would not have dreamed of such mobility and complexity as Woo's in the use of the camera.

One elemental image that Woo owes to Chang is that of evisceration. Often noted as a feature of Chang's swordplay films is the death of many characters by cuts to the stomach, as in *Vengeance* or *The One-Armed Swordsman*. Woo has borrowed this imagery and adapted it generally to the gunplay film. The first gunfight in *The Killer* shows John dispatching a door guard with multiple shots to the stomach; Alan kills Mr. Hui in *Hard Boiled* with a shot to the stomach; and John repeatedly eliminates adversaries in *The Killer* by holding them by the arm and shooting them in the midriff. Evisceration is a displaced symbol of castration, and it is no accident that many of the characters killed in such fashion (albeit by bullets) in Woo films are authority figures about to be displaced, or protectors of such figures: Mr. Hui is a father-figure killed by his "son" Alan; the many bodyguards and gunmen killed by John are surrogates or protectors of gangster higher-ups. Woo has even used the evisceration imagery in more traditional form in at least two notable examples. At the end of *A Better Tomorrow II*, Ho uses a sword to disembowel one of Ko's henchmen (played by Shing Fui-on). And, memorably, in *Face/Off*, Castor Troy slashes Archer in the belly with a boat tool and is in turn dispatched with a spear graphically shot through his own stomach; he dies impaled to a wall.[15]

Woo borrows and extends imagery and themes from Chang Cheh's greatest films, but he is not a Chang Cheh epigone, dressing up Chang Cheh swordfests in modern dress. Chang Cheh's work, like Melville's, Leone's or Peckinpah's, became a part of the mix that is a John Woo film. But Woo added his own special touches and interpretations to each of these sources of inspiration, enhancing and enriching them by recombination and commentary.

Japanese Influences: Kurosawa and Kobayashi

Like many filmmakers, Woo owes much to the magisterial work of Akira Kurosawa. Woo has never been reluctant to note his interest in Kurosawa, naming *Seven Samurai* (1954) as one of his "ten best" films in a director's poll (Supplements text, *The Killer*).

It is not hard to see why Woo would admire Kurosawa, and in particular *Seven Samurai*, as opposed to, say, *Rashomon* (1950) or *Ikiru* (1952). Some directors would highlight Kurosawa's investigation of truth-claims and his melding of Western and Eastern philosophy and ethics in *Rashomon*, or his great probing of the humanity in a "little man" in *Ikiru*. Woo would certainly admire these qualities in both films, but significantly he lists *Seven Samurai* as one of the great accomplishments of world cinema. This film, not usually seen in the West in its complete version until rather recently, is, at its full length of nearly four hours, an astounding exercise in kineticism and a moving exploration of the humanity residing in even the toughest warrior.

The story of *Seven Samurai* has been retold several times, most famously in John Sturges' excellent, and often unfairly maligned, remake, *The Magnificent Seven* (1960). A small group of unemployed samurai, or ronin, is recruited to defend a village from 40 bandits who return every year after the harvest. The twist to the story is that the ronin agree to defend the village without pay, and we see that the men rediscover their humanity and begin to understand the value in the lives of the simple villagers by helping them without strings attached. One of the samurai is in fact a farmer's son, played by Toshiro Mifune, who always hated both farmers and samurai but who dies heroically, at last finding a place for himself in society. At film's end, the bandits are all dead, and only three of the samurai survive. They leave the village, aware that the farmers are the real survivors and that their own lives will consist of wandering.

Here we can see themes dear to Woo: self-sacrifice, loyalty and camaraderie. Additionally, a strand of the film that may not be so noticeable is its emphasis on the gulf between villager and samurai, and the effect that this has on the normalcy of the samurais' lives. Two of the samurai are farmers' sons: Kikuchiyo (Mifune), and the youngest of the warriors, Katsushiro (Ko Kimura), who wishes to become a samurai but finds that the "way of the warrior" will ostracize him from farm society (he must leave behind his beloved). In characters such as these two, we might see the germ of some Woo heroes, particularly the two leads in *Last Hurrah for Chivalry*, one of whom, Magic Sword, presumably becomes alienated from his relatively normal life, and girlfriend, by taking up with his friend Green and becoming fatefully involved with the treacherous Fan. The other, Green, sacrifices himself to save his friend Magic Sword. It is not much of an effort to see the similarity between these two figures and the Mifune and Kimura characters from the Kurosawa film. Of course, Woo may not have consciously derived the characters from this source, but still the ethos and the conflicts are much the same.

Another important feature of Kurosawa's work generally, but especially of *Seven Samurai*, is its constant impression of great energy. No doubt this impressed Woo, who has himself become synonymous with high-energy filmmaking and rapid-fire editing. The techniques used by Woo are different from Kurosawa's, especially as far as superimposition is concerned. Where Kurosawa creates a tableau of intense activity from which he abstracts certain sections (as for instance with the wonderful shot of Takashi Shimura, the samurais' leader, drawing his bow during the climactic battle), Woo fashions a seemingly chaotic setting of unpredictable violence, both by rapid editing and by superimposing shots taken from different angles and at different speeds. His filmmaking is in this sense less realistic than the Japanese master's. But we may see some of the origins of Woo's fantastically controlled yet intense action sequences in scenes such as the final battle in *Seven Samurai*. The sudden explosions of violence in Kurosawa's *Yojimbo* (1961), as for instance in its opening scene, when the anonymous ronin (Mifune) kills or maims several assailants, also find their analogue in Woo films like *Hard Boiled*, with its often shocking injections of intense violence, for example when Tequila suddenly attacks Johnny Wong and is coldcocked by Alan. Like the Kurosawa heroes in films such as 1962's *Sanjuro* (the sequel to *Yojimbo*), Woo heroes, particularly those played by Chow Yun-fat, consistently communicate a sense of barely hidden aggression and of extreme competence in carrying out violent acts.

Woo responds especially to the strong emphasis on ethical heroism in the work of Kobayashi, an important Japanese director who is not as famous in the West as Kurosawa. Woo lists Kobayashi's *Hara-kiri* (1962) as one of his ten favorite films. Certainly it is not difficult to see, in this harrowing story of a young samurai forced by an inflexible clan to commit *seppuku* (hara-kiri) in a particularly cruel manner, and the futile but magnificent vengeance wrought by his skilled and courageous father (Tatsuya Nakadai), plenty of material to interest Woo, whose own treatment of loyalty and heroism is so integral to his work.

Woo told me briefly of his reasons for being interested in *Hara-kiri*, emphasizing the look of the film as well as its theme of heroic self-immolation and rebellion:

> The visuals and the self-sacrifice—the special thing of those movies is the true hero who really beats the system. I mean spiritually. It's a true man who can struggle against the system and against fate. That's how I got a strong feeling for the movie [Woo, personal interview, 7 November 1995].

Seen from Woo's perspective, the Nakadai hero is a spiritual cousin of Inspector Li, of Ricky Hui's character in *From Riches to Rags*, or of Lam Ah Chun (Plain Jane in *Plain Jane to the Rescue*). All are heroic, even the comic ones, in the sense of opposing "the system" and fighting for morality and individuality.[16] The doomed hero of Kobayashi's film is particularly admirable in that his rebellion expresses a yearning for a "moral" guideline in a society governed by fixed ritual: "Fighting the weight of a tradition that has left a code and ritual void of all meaning as its legacy, Kobayashi demands a return to the authenticity of a moral law" (Billard, qtd. in Mellen 134).

Nakadai's hero is also very much like a character from Woo's films who is not as often studied as are the flashier figures like John or Tequila. This character is Sidney Fung (Paul Chu Kong), John's friend and colleague killer in *The Killer*. Sidney melds together elements of several fictional types: the samurai, the professional hit man, the gunman who has hung up his guns, the punched-out fighter. And, especially, the crippled or disabled combatant. Like Fang Kang (Wang Yu) in *The One-Armed Swordsman*, Sidney has lost the use of one hand. He has no confidence in his ability under such conditions, averring that "a one-handed killer's out of the action" (*The Killer* ch. 9). Reminiscent of favorite characters for Woo like Dean Martin in *Rio Bravo* or Yves Montand in *Le Cercle rouge*, Sidney has a brief comeback to his former stature, taking on Weng and his men and almost defeating them before being beaten nearly to death and escaping. Unlike Kang, he does not really avenge any wrongs, nor does he triumph; he is killed by his friend John (an incident reprised in *Bullet in the Head*) to end his suffering, recalling perhaps the end of Kubrick's *Spartacus*, when Spartacus (Kirk Douglas) kills his friend to save him from crucifixion. But Sidney does redeem himself morally, a very important point for Woo, because he is killed when trying to get John's hit money back for him; Sidney feels that this is an obligation he must discharge to balance accounts with John for having betrayed him.

Woo also mentioned the "visual elements" of *Hara-kiri* as impressive to him. This film is indeed strikingly beautiful; shot in black-and-white, it achieves its effects by working within ranges of grays and rich blacks and whites. Kobayashi implicitly contrasts the understated beauty of some of its scenes (like the centerpiece scene in the graveyard) with the agonized turmoil experienced by the two protagonists, and especially by the Nakadai hero. In another interview with the author, Woo noted the importance of the black-and-white photography in this Kobayashi film, relating it to the impact of the story: "I like that movie—so tragic. And the way he uses black and white is so strong. It's a big contrast and also it's the tragedy of human life" (personal interview, 2 March 1996).

The tragic ending of the film also struck Woo, who spoke of it in the following terms: "Especially I love the final scene [the father's attack on the clan]—it's all done in one shot. Like an opera. So strong" (personal interview, 2 March 1996). If we can judge from *Hara-kiri* and *Rebellion*, Kobayashi is comfortable with a structure which, as John Gillett says about his later *Inn of Evil* (1971), "reserves his main action until the end" (qtd. in Mellen 137). Like Chang Cheh in *Vengeance*, and like Woo in *The Killer*, Kobayashi allows the inevitability of the tragedy to accrue until the viewer begins to accept the fatality of the hero's death. As is typical with Chang and Woo, the hero undergoes an apotheosis by combating multiple adversaries, braving overwhelming odds for a principle. Woo tends to admire stories which feature this kind of resolution: thus, *Butch Cassidy*, *The Wild Bunch*, the tale of Ching K'o in the *Shih chi*, *Hell Is for Heroes* with Steve McQueen. One might almost be tempted to see a little auto-heroicizing in Woo's privileging of such narratives, and the fact is that he does identify with the "little guy" who wins out, or at least tries to win, against the system, the big organization, overwhelming odds and so forth.

These varied directorial influences have contributed to Woo's unique blend of styles and techniques. He can hardly be considered a "straight" action director, as we will see presently. His background, and his sensibilities, are just too complex for such a simplistic labeling.

Chapter 3

Woo as a Unique "Action Director"

Editing Style

John Woo is very much a product of the Hong Kong cinema. This statement does not deny his originality; it merely situates him within a general style of directing. Commentators on Hong Kong cinema usually note its preference for rapidity and flashiness over contemplative, thoughtful *mise-en-scène*. An implicit analogy is sometimes made between the fast pace of Hong Kong life, or at least business, and the style of many Hong Kong films. Whether or not the analogy is valid, the classification certainly fits Woo, at least insofar as his "signature style" is concerned. What gives his work its peculiar poignancy is its marriage of flashy, supercharged kinesis in *mise-en-scène* to a core of well-contemplated moral lessons and meditations on human failings.

Woo's style is nonetheless often described as if in passing. Critics note his employment of various techniques but do not really delve into the synergy of their multiple juxtaposition. One of Woo's most effective, indeed gripping tactics is a combined forward dolly, done rapidly, and a cut to extreme close-up for a reaction shot. In action scenes, like gun battles, he may, in the next frame, switch to slow motion. The cumulative impact is not only wrenching, or arresting, but also peculiarly distorting, skewing the viewer's perception of time on film and adding to an uneasy (or thrilled) feeling that the gunfight is happening in a Borgesian eternal moment.[1] Time appears literally to stop, and then to extend, and the camera executes this metaphor. This element of time distortion is important in determining the fascination felt by many viewers in watching the gun battles in Woo movies: they are poetic set pieces in the sense that they live in an eternal present.

Woo shares this quality with some interesting company. Like Sergio Leone, he is a partisan of the extreme close-up, freezing time in an eternalized psychic moment;[2] and like Howard Hawks in *Rio Bravo* (1959), Woo presents a geometrically precise tableau of violence.[3] Woo's action style is probably best compared to Kurosawa's in its fluidity and use of rapid cutting, but Woo generally lacks Kurosawa's delicately poetic grace. Woo's art is one of barely controlled explosiveness and unexpected juxtaposition; he often sacrifices delicacy for effect, and his additive style, like Peckinpah's but more manic, derives especially from his use of super-impositions and difficult and complicated camera placements.[4]

Also like Peckinpah, Woo employs slow-motion filming for effect. But his touch is different from Peckinpah's. That is almost a tautology, as everyone's use of slow motion is apart from Peckinpah's. Nothing else feels or looks quite like a Peckinpah slow-motion scene—the time seems to have been disjointed and jerkily reassembled, yet it flows into a new whole. Despite Peckinpah's occasional use of slow motion for emotional effect (that is, individual emotional expression, as in the final death scene in *The Wild Bunch*), he seems chiefly interested in the technical and pictorial aspects of time expansion. Woo is more direct. His slow-motion shots are almost always used to express personal suffering or to illustrate a point in the plot. A good example of the former would be the shot of Mark's knee being devastated as he unwisely turns his back on one of his adversaries at the end of his revenge hit in *A Better Tomorrow*. His physical pain is intensely presented, and the slow motion serves also as a synecdoche for the slowing of his life after his crippling injury. Woo also uses the technique to romanticize or to mythify his heroes, as in the ending shot of the same film, when Kit and Ho are shown walking off-camera in slow motion. Often, too, Woo uses slowed action as inserts into his gun battles, in clear homage to Peckinpah.

Woo's slow motion, though, is technically more akin to that used by Scorsese and director of photography Michael Chapman on *Raging Bull*, since the speed changes are done in the camera.[5] Added to this is the fact that Woo uses dolly movements within and associated to speed changes, so that the effect is complicated considerably.[6]

Woo employs slow action, then, in several ways, including mythification of his hero figures. He has specified, and differentiated, his debt to Peckinpah and Scorsese with respect to slow motion:

> I admire Martin Scorsese so much.... [E]specially *Mean Streets*, I really love that movie. I learned from his powerful technique, and ... from his dramatic slow motion. Now the way he uses the slow motion, especially, it wasn't on the action, it's on the emotion. Sometimes he likes to use slow motion to capture some beautiful movement from the acting ... or to capture some expression from the actors, and it looks so beautiful and so dramatic, so I use it in my films.... [I]n some of the acting, I also use slow motion on the actors, not only on the action. The action is from Sam Peckinpah's films. My camera movement [is] also influence[d] by him [Woo, supplements text, *The Killer*, 2: 5245–6750].

And he uses extreme close-ups, often in freeze-frame, to such an extent that they have been noted as part of his signature. This combination of stylistic effects, both so noticeable as to be baroque in their showiness, is one of the features of Woo's style that sets him apart from many other directors who may use one device or another, but not so floridly and so consistently as a logical part of their lexicon. Woo uses the freeze-frame rather more liberally than did his models, Truffaut and the French New Wave. His positioning of the freeze-frame within his narrative is sometimes surprising, as when he shows a still shot of Inspector Li (Danny Lee) in *The Killer*, near the middle of the film (18:29853). Normally, the viewer, conditioned by Truffaut and others (for American viewers, perhaps by George Roy Hill's ending to *Butch Cassidy and the Sundance Kid*) to perceive this effect as signaling the end of the narrative, is at first deceived into thinking the film finished and is then startled to see that the freeze-frame was in fact a transitional punctuation mark. It signals the dividing point between Li's role as the pursuer of John who perceives him from the outside and Li's gradual entrance into John's world, with his consequent alienation from his life as a cop. When Li draws on his partner Chang, visualizing him as one of the assassins who had tried not long before to kill John, and Chang asks him "Are you nuts?" Li's smile intimates and underlines his release from the conventions by which he has lived and communicates a secret alliance with John—his Mona Lisa smile seems to hide an awareness of a truth to which Chang is not privy. This smile of Li's is the one preserved on the transitional freeze-frame: not a flashy, empty tactic, but rather a critical suture in the narrative of *The Killer*.

Just "Buddy" Films?

John Woo might fairly be characterized as shooting nothing but "buddy films." Many, perhaps all, of his movies contain the "buddy" kernel: *Last Hurrah for Chivalry, Young Dragons, Money Crazy, From Riches to Rags* and, of course, the *A Better Tomorrow* films, *The Killer, Hard Boiled, Just Heroes* and *Bullet in the Head*.

Why is Woo so fascinated with "buddies," pairs or groups of heroes? He has stated repeatedly that one of his major themes is friendship. Often, his focus on male friendship has been misconstrued as "homoerotic." Critics pursuing feminist or "queer" readings of films have naturally seen in Woo's work aspects that resemble those in Hollywood buddy pictures such as *Lethal Weapon* and *Tango and Cash*. As Tony Williams so aptly cautions, though, such critics have misunderstood the role of male physical contact and emotional display in Asian culture ("To Live and Die" 48). Extending his point, we should take care in any case when drawing parallels—or neat contrasts—between Western and Asian films without recognizing that we may not be dealing with cultural universals.

The sources for these John Woo "brother" pictures are to be found not, as one may argue regarding *Lethal Weapon* or *Tango and Cash*, in the conservatism and anti-feminism of the Reagan and Bush years (see Fuchs 196), but instead in specially Asian influences (as one might logically expect). These backgrounds are a melding of Shaw Brothers studio films, in particular those directed by Chang Cheh, and the literary sources which contribute to such films, like the Chinese romance novel. The counterparts to Ho and Mark in *A Better Tomorrow* are to be seen in films such as Chang's *Vengeance* and in literary works such as *Water Margin* and *Romance of the Three Kingdoms*.

We may see an analogy to the frequency of paired heroes in Chang Cheh's, and then in Woo's films in the Chinese romance genre. C. T. Hsia, discussing the typical characteristics of Chinese "military romance" heroes from the T'ang and Sung epochs, notes that "...all principal heroes are attended by companion-heroes" ("Military" 359–60). Whether or not the romances directly influenced filmmakers like Chang and then Woo, it certainly seems more than coincidental that such a similar structure in the character relationships exists in the case of the films and the novels.[7]

Woo and the Double

Commentators on Woo's films have frequently noted his recourse to the double as a central motif. Doubling is a common enough device or motif in literature and film, but it does not always have the same significance in a given text as in another.

A double may be, as in Dostoevsky's *The Double* or Gogol's *The Overcoat*, an unconscious projection, a sinister shadow which represents the darker side of one's own nature. These are the double types of Hoffmann's *The Student Prince*, Gogol's *The Nose*, and of *film noir* generally.[8] In *film noir*, as in *The Student Prince*, the double is presented as a literal mirror-image, a reflection in a mirror or on a window, thus recalling the old Gnostic doctrine of the reflected duality of the soul. The double may also be a concrete entity, that is, another person in the narrative who exhibits similarities to the original figure. This is the case in many works, such as Conrad's *Heart of Darkness*, Argentine writer Julio Cortázar's *Hopscotch* (*Rayuela*), and, again, much of *film noir*. Both of the types detailed here, the "apparitional" double and the ontologically existent double, may appear in a single text. A good example of this would be *Out of the Past* (1947; with Robert Mitchum, Jane Greer and Kirk Douglas), Tourneur's canonical *film noir*.

Woo prefers to use the actually existing double, although he may use reflecting mirror images, images in glasses and so forth. But his temperament and approach are not those of Dreyer or of E. T. A. Hoffmann. Woo is too grounded in reality and in human interaction to engage in fantasy, in its original sense of "imagination."

Woo uses doubles not as a game, as some directors might, nor as a compositional strategy, but rather as a kind of exemplum for his characters. John and Li, as the best case of this usage, discover their kinship, and the audience learns about it *along with them* by Woo's use of experimental editing and continuity violation. The two characters learn truths about themselves by being juxtaposed to one another. Woo seems to believe that we only learn about ourselves through others; his message is profoundly social, and his frequent recourse to extreme situations only underlines the point.

While *The Killer* is the most balanced example of doubling in Woo's work, his other films often contain instances of this signature characteristic. The cop and killer motif of *Hard Boiled* is a variation on *The Killer*, with Tequila finding his "opposite number" in Tony, the undercover cop who has been living as Triad killer Alan. Just as in *The Killer*, Woo underscores the double nature of his heroes by tying them to similar "accidents." Tequila kills a cop whom he does not know to be working undercover[9]; near the end of the film, Tony also kills a policeman by accident, in the confusion of a fierce gun battle. Woo is more intentional here even than in *The Killer*, for example actually posing Tequila and Tony on parallel or opposite sides of a hospital corridor near the end of the film, then causing them to exchange places repeatedly in a chiasmatic effect.

Woo also uses another image appearing in *The Killer* but he changes its significance here. In the final scene of *The Killer*, Li and John, side by side, face down Johnny Weng (Shing Fui-on), who is holding a gun to Jenny's head. Li, holding his own gun to the head of Weng's hired gun Paul Yau, tries to end the stalemate, but Weng kills his own man, breaking the parallel standoff in an unexpected manner.

This little set piece is repeated in *Hard Boiled*, but with some crucial differences that transform it into an imaging of the double. At the end of the film, Tequila, alone, faces Johnny Wong (Anthony Wong), who is holding a gun to Tony's head. Woo has split the two doubles from each other, placing one with their adversary. The space between the figures only serves to underline their essential closeness. Wong becomes the symbol of the past separation between the two characters. Standing behind Tony like his evil shadow, his sinister double, a wicked imp, this trickster figure threatens to destroy the hope of friendship and self-realization for these two men.

That the double is crucial for Woo should not be surprising. The double is a recurrent figure in European romanticism, an acknowledged source for Woo.[10] Several of his favorite films feature the double; in some instances they revolve around it: *Strangers on a Train*, *Lawrence of Arabia*, *West Side Story*, *Citizen Kane* and *The Shining* would be good examples. Woo's tendency is to recur to this figure, even in circumstances when it may degenerate into formula, as in *Hard Target*.

So, if Woo recurs time and again to the double figure, one may wonder if there is a deeper reason for such interest. Perhaps, for some psychological reason, the double theme fascinates Woo. Without engaging in facile psychologism, we might record that even in casual conversation about Woo and his films, people often remark that he "works out" his "aggression" in his violent films. I would not take this too literally—I don't think that Woo is a Paul Schrader or maybe an Oliver Stone—but it is true that his heroes are wish-fulfillment figures. He has noted that Chow Yun-fat, as the best example of the Woo hero, is "himself," and that his heroes do things he can't—right injustices, make statements about society by warlike means, and generally conduct themselves as present-day samurai (Woo, personal interview, 7 November 1995).

Thus, we can explain the strong personalism in Woo's work: like Samuel Fuller, he identifies and almost merges with his heroes in a way quite unlike "action" directors of the usual sort. This personal infusion of emotion helps to account for the hypnotic quality of films such as *The Killer*, where it is a strong element, and for the relative flatness of, say, *A Better Tomorrow II*, where Woo's heart doesn't seem really to have been in the work.

Cinematography

Woo has earned a reputation as a master of camera movement and setup. In the course of my research for this book, I have been told repeatedly in interviews with Hollywood people who have collaborated with Woo that they have never seen anyone work with the camera as Woo does. Much of the fascination of watching a mature Woo film is the ever-intriguing camerawork. His camera is as peripatetic as anyone's since Kurosawa and much more intelligent than that of most directors.

The background to the camera setups, that is, Woo's preparation for a day of shooting, is revelatory of his intuitive approach to filmmaking. As Russell Carpenter observed, "His sequences are well-thought out, but there's a feeling that he's definitely putting the final touches at least on his blocking the morning that he's there." This is a decision on Woo's part, or rather a studied but spontaneous approach (*pace* the oxymoron); as Carpenter also said, "With John, the intellect is there but you see the heart, the intuition is driving him" (telephone interview, 8 January 1996).

And so Woo sets up his shots with a preconceived notion of how they will fit together but without a rigid structure for how they will do so. This allows him, as Carpenter explained, to work without shooting a large, patterned master. In response to one of my technical questions involving master shots and using Richard Brooks as an example, Carpenter placed Woo into context:

> Richard Brooks is not going for that overall defining shot because he knows his cutting pattern. And John works very much that way. He did not go for the big master. He's not conservative in that way. Some people shoot very, very beautiful, wonderful masters—now, Kurosawa's shots would start and develop in the camera and the action would move and move. And that was a very well-thought-out master [telephone interview, 8 January 1996].

Some notable features of Woo's camera style include his use of alternately nearing tracking shots, rack focus, triangular setups and violation of continuity. These effects or signature techniques account for much of Woo's interest as a filmmaker. Of course, their mere presence is no guarantee of originality, since many directors employ an assortment of them without really understanding their effect; however, Woo uses them in such a conscious and aware manner that his directorial intelligence is always discernible behind the lens. And most importantly, he places technique with the lens at the service of his desire to express character relationships on the one hand and to design a pictorial tableau on film, on the other.

The first of these techniques, the tracking or dolly shot that "alternately approaches" its subjects, is one of the most immediately apparent features of a Woo film, at least since *A Better Tomorrow*. The effect of this kind of camera movement is twofold: one, to cause the viewer to concentrate more forcefully on the faces of the characters, and, two, to disorient the viewer as to his relative position as spectator. The origins of the technique appear to lie, as does so much else, with the work of Alfred Hitchcock, who used such movement in his films since *Murder* (1930).[11]

Many directors have since adopted it, though few have used it intelligently or have really adapted it to their style. The most notable examples of directors using the "alternating dolly" are John Frankenheimer, Sergio Leone, Martin Scorsese and Woo.

Woo readily confirmed to me his use of the technique, and was also aware of its employment by other directors. He explained his cultivation of it as:

> It's maybe inspired by painting. So the framing in my movies and the camera movement [are like a] painting frame. With me, Scorsese, Coppola, Hitchcock, the lens becomes like a pen or the brush. And the lens also represents our eyes—how we see things, how we feel things. And the other thing is that we are very much into the character and into the scene. While we are shooting the scene, and the people are talking, we know their feelings, and we put our feelings into the scene [Woo, personal interview, 2 March 1996].

The characters' "feelings" are so strongly brought forward by these camera moves that one must ask why this intensity is proper to Woo films: in a John McTiernan film like *The Hunt for Red October* (granted, the product, well-made and entertaining, of a lesser director), for example, the intensity is present, but it is all on the surface, chiefly at the service of suspense. What causes these moves in Woo films to differ so spectacularly from their counterparts in others' work?

We might note first that Woo uses his slowly moving camera to highlight character relationships and to emphasize mood. His tracking shots of this type often end in a full-face close-up of an actor with an emotive expression. A good example would be Sidney's horrified expression, shown us while John is dispatching Weng's gunmen in his flat; another would be John's anguished, retrospect countenance when he touches Jenny's bloodstained scarf in her apartment. Such shots have the effect of "training" the viewer to expect strong emotional reactions at the end of certain camera movements—that is, the slow dolly becomes a suspense-building reaction shot which translates point of view into character-viewer identification and which also charges the very fact of camera movement with emotion—often of a negative or certainly not a "sunny" type.

Music

One important aspect of Woo's films not often noticed is their scoring.[12] Although Woo is usually celebrated for his action sequences, his attention to musical elements is rarely mentioned. When it is noticed, in fact, the music in Woo films is often dismissed as "syrupy" or "corny." Once again, such reviewers miss the point—about the scripts of the films and about their musical texturing.

Woo has in fact created several films with very interesting and complex scores. Even when the score's quality is uneven, as in *A Better Tomorrow*, the audience will remember signature themes from the film and will, probably unknowingly, associate those themes with characters and situations.

This trend in Woo films began to appear, very noticeably, in *A Better Tomorrow*, with music by Joseph Koo. The plaintive, homey, almost rustic little harmonica melody that accompanies Ho (Ti Lung) at the beginning of the film gradually acquires added poignancy as it reappears in more intense situations. And the theme becomes associated not only with events and circumstances involving Ho and his friends, but, significantly, with his face: after seeing *A Better Tomorrow*, it is difficult to visualize Ho without "hearing" the melody, or to recall the melody without "seeing" Ho.

This linkage of the visual to the auditory is very important for Woo and is one of the keys to his romantic thrust. Woo has mentioned on several occasions his preference for editing his films while listening to symphonic music, in order to achieve the proper rhythm. As with some other comments by Woo about his work, this observation has passed unnoticed; not surprisingly, most critics and reviewers would be more interested in commentary on action staging, heroics and so forth. But this method of editing reveals that Woo is thinking along paths followed by the Romantics and the Symbolists. One of the principal underpinnings of Symbolism, an outgrowth of Romantic theory, was the practice of synaesthesia: the mixing of senses in a work of art. And, like the Symbolists after them, the Romantics had preached the essential correspondence between the arts (an exaggerated form of *ut pictura poesis*).[13]

One result of this Romantic theoretical argument was programmatic music, usually most associated with Hector Berlioz, and later, with Richard Wagner. The program music of Berlioz' *Symphonie fantastique*, in which the music is tied to a storyline, is theoretically extended into Wagner's supersized *Musikdrama*.

I think that in Woo's films we often see something of the same sort. This tendency is very pronounced in *The Killer*, and to a lesser degree is present in *Bullet in the Head, A Better Tomorrow, Hard Boiled, Hard Target* and *Broken Arrow*. As we have so many times in this book, we will turn again to *The Killer* to examine this technique.

The marriage of text to music in *The Killer* is not immediately obvious. As we have seen, many critics have dismissively evaluated the score or have not even seen fit to mention it. But if one closely examines the score, listening carefully to its repetitions and variations, its fine appropriateness to the script and to the characters' personae becomes very apparent. I believe that this score, and its intricate relationship to the film as edited, is a very underrated achievement for Woo, Lowell Lo and film editor David Wu. Its close connection to the storyline and the characters' personalities explains much about Woo's approach to this film and also a great deal about the success of *The Killer* as Romantic art.

The film opens with a haunting theme, with a vibraphone lead, which accompanies a *Citizen Kane*–like tracking shot that begins with the Hong Kong skyline and approaches a church. This is the first instance of the theme's being tied directly to Chow Yun-fat, the first actor we see in the film. The music continues as a second character enters the church; we discover the second man to be Sidney, the killer's contact and friend. The two have a conversation rather unusual for two hired gunmen, discussing briefly the fact that John likes to meet in this church. As the contracting proceeds, the music shifts to a vocal; the song that we will discover to be a signature theme for the film and for John and Jenny, the *chanteuse* who performs the song.[14] This song continues until John enters the inner sanctum of the club where Jenny is singing and attacks the object of his contract.

Almost unnoticed by the casual viewer, then, is the fact that Woo has introduced two major musical motifs for the film and has also tied them to three significant characters and to some very important plot themes and incidents. The vibraphone tune has been identified with John and Sidney, with the church, with nighttime, with the Hong Kong skyline, and with the impending autumn, signaled by the Coppola–like vision of leaves blowing across the churchyard.[15] The tune has also been tied directly to spirituality and to John's loneliness.

The second tune forms a transition to John's new life, or his attempt at one, and is here associated not with John and Sidney but with John and Jenny (one of its lyrics is "Who needs dreams when we have each other?") (ch. 3). The theme is played with the camera concentrating on John's face and his slow-motion walk towards his fulfillment of the film's first contract. The song's lyric is also uncannily and ironically fitting for its context; the song fades out on the lyric "Who needs tomorrow when we have today?" just as John knocks on the door where his target is playing cards.

The song is heard again as John has slugs extracted from his back, in the church; now the song's text has been thematically overlaid with the elements of murder, the accidental blinding of Jenny by John's gun; and, most importantly, it has become a kind of musical *petite madeleine*, bringing to the surface memories painful to John.

Once the song has been, so to speak, encrypted with these emotional and narrative features, it only gains in richness as a filmic motif when it is used in other contexts. The song grows in complexity of allusion as the film proceeds.

We next hear the song when John visits Jenny's apartment. The song is not extradiegetically performed, but is instead, significantly, played on cassette by Jenny (as if she were calling up a shadow or a double of herself and unknowingly forcing John to relive the occasion of her blinding). John instantly enters a reverie, experiencing again the contract hit and their injuries.

The song serves here as a transitional device between John and Li, as Woo, in one of the most inspired shots in the film, tracks from John's face to Li's, shown sitting in a city park thinking, in a position complementary to John's. Li, Woo says, has not yet met John; still, he "senses" him (personal interview, 2 March 1996). So, the music serves as a bridge and as a sign of emotional communication between the two. The song's lyrics also join the two adversaries, indicating their common bond, since these lyrics play over images of the two (chs. 5-6).

Woo and Lowell Lo have thus extended the associative web concerning this song, since it now includes several characters and embraces several scenes and emotional responses. Soon, the theme will reappear, with an added dimension.

After Sidney comes to John's apartment and tries to kill him, completing his reluctant betrayal, and John successfully defends himself against both Sidney and Weng's assassins, we are offered a reprise of an earlier scene. Before Sidney had come to see John, Woo had shown John sitting in a chair, waiting for Sidney. The soundtrack plays a plaintive melody. Now, after the attempted hit on John, Li and the police come to the apartment. Li stays in the apartment for a while after his colleagues depart, sitting in the same chair as John had and listening to a melodically related song on the tape player (ch. 18). Woo shows him acting as a double of John, drawing his gun and apparently (but only apparently) firing as Chang enters the room.

The plaintive "reverie" song had already become associated for Li with both Jenny and John: she is singing it when Li comes to see her in the club (ch. 16).[16] He asks her to sing the song again, but she replies, "I only sing for one person" (John). Li tells her, "Your singing is so filled with emotion, I feel I already know him." At this point, Li has begun to merge into John's persona; they are becoming explicit doubles. So, Li says to Jenny, "Part of him will always be here"—whereupon John is shown standing in his doorway playing a tune on his harmonica. We are momentarily deceived into thinking that Li actually sees John, rather than a mental image of him. But, on the other hand, we have no reason to doubt that this is exactly what John is doing at the moment, since the psychic communication between the two men has already been established as fact. In any case, the harmonica motif is another musical element that reappears throughout the film.

This harmonica motif brings to mind especially the music of Ennio Morricone, both generally and specifically. In general terms, harmonica themes appear in many places in Morricone-scored films, particularly those directed by Sergio Leone, and are often combined with other rustic elements, like Jew's harps and whistling, to provide a unique effect. But more specifically, a very important hero of one of Leone's best films, *Once Upon a Time in the West*, is known as "Harmonica" because he announces his presence by playing a particularly mournful harmonica tune.[17] This character, played with great intensity by Charles Bronson, inherited the harmonica from his brother under terrible circumstances and has sworn revenge against his brother's murderer, Frank (Henry Fonda). Whether Woo intended a specific allusion or no,[18] the revenge theme and its association with the harmonica would have an especial relevance to *The Killer*, and probably Woo would not object too strongly if viewers made this particular connection. In any case, the harmonica motif also adds a homey, familiar, humanizing touch to John's character. Li says of John earlier in the film that "He doesn't look like a killer…. [He] acts like he has a dream" (ch. 13).

For all his love of classical music, Woo rarely uses it in his films (although he does use it to accompany his editing sessions). But it does appear in some instances, and usually quite notably. One important example of its presence is in the concluding scene of *The Killer*, when Weng's gunmen blow up a Madonna statue in the church. The soundtrack transitions from the previous "action" music to the "Hallelujah" chorus from *Messiah*. This abrupt insertion of the Handel music is, of course, quite clearly related to the sacred context, and was David Wu's idea, intended to break up the numbing effect of the violence and the kinetic music (Wu and Chang, personal interview, 1 March 1996). What is most interesting about the *Messiah* insertion is not its rather obvious aptness to the context, but instead the fact that the characters—even the gunmen—are frozen in horror when the statue explodes. They seem almost to be listening to the music, which is of course played extradiegetically and is presumably not accessible to them. It is a measure of the power of this moment in this film masterpiece that we are momentarily deceived into believing that the border between the fictional plane and the level of artifice has been breached.

Often the characters in Woo's films do listen to or even perform music. As we have noted, most commentators on Woo have overlooked or deprecated the musical dimension of his work. But Woo is a lover of musicals and has repeatedly expressed his interest in making a musical. Audiences or interviewers usually respond to this statement by laughing a little nervously (what is my action-director idol *talking* about?) or by changing the subject. The fact is, though, that to understand Woo and his characters one must see that music and rhythm are basic to them. Already in *The Killer*, the integration of music with character and situation was very important. In Woo's later Hong Kong films, this tendency is often more overt.

Bullet in the Head is the most notable example of the importance of music for Woo. This film continues the associative tendencies from *The Killer* and adds to them a more intentional and overt linking of certain characters to musical pieces. *Bullet in the Head* also generally eschews Asian pop music (like Jenny's songs in *The Killer*) in favor of Western standards. The film is in fact, at least for its first third, close in spirit to *West Side Story* (Robert Wise, 1961), one of Woo's admitted favorites.

The score for *Bullet in the Head* differs, too, from that of *The Killer* in its relative lack of romantic pathos. The music in *Bullet in the Head*, unlike that of *The Killer*, frequently works against the action, or sets up an ironic commentary upon it. Thus, the Monkees standard "I'm a Believer" recurs at various points in the narrative, but generally serves merely to underscore either the characters' *lack* of belief in themselves or in society (so highlighting Paul's cynicism) or the irony of Ben and Frank's misplaced belief in Paul. Similarly, we hear a variation on "Venus in Blue Jeans"[19] when we first see Ben's girlfriend.

Two other musical elements in this film are of interest. One of them concerns the rumble that opens the film. This intensely violent street fight is effected against a driving rhythm based on "I'm a Believer." The rumble seems choreographed or at least rhythmically accented, recalling the (highly) stylized fights in *West Side Story*. Woo's rumble segues into some back stories on the lead characters, including the second musical element which will interest us here: the dance class that Ben is shown attending.

Ben is just one of a set of musical performers in Woo's films. Musicians and singers have always been important in the Chinese chivalric tradition, and so they are in Woo[20]; of course, such an interest on his part is also explained by his own dance study. Still, he highlights musical performers in many of his movies; thus, Jenny and John are both musicians; Ben studies dance, and Luke plays jazz piano; Tequila plays jazz saxophone; Jackie in *A Better Tomorrow* plays cello; Jules in *Once a Thief* plays flute; and Fouchon in *Hard Target* is an accomplished pianist.

Music is central to *Hard Boiled*, but in a way rather different from *The Killer* or *Bullet in the Head*. As with these films, *Hard Boiled* features bar and jazz scenes, but it adds to them a prominent iconic treatment of jazzmen. Music is also tied directly to the heroic and the tragic. When a cop is killed, Tequila customarily writes and plays a song for him, in a personal twist on the well-known importance of music for policemen's funerals.

Additionally in *Hard Boiled*, music is a crucial element of the plot. The police captain Pang has worked out a code with his undercover agent Tony/Alan which is based on musical notes. This code provides an added dimension of witty suspense to the film and also serves to highlight Tequila's relationship with Teresa and to accentuate his musical training. This is accomplished in a very economical manner by placing Tequila in his ex-girlfriend's office when she is receiving one of Tony's flower messages. The code requires her to sound out the notes of a song title included in the bouquet. This provides some comedy, but it also furnishes a means for Tequila to intervene in Teresa's life again in a cooperative, if still sardonic, fashion, since he has to correct some of her notations. So, Woo has used a narrative device (the code) as a neat method of bringing two of his heroes together. Music is again a communal and a reconciling activity, even when it is used for less than innocent purposes.

Later, Pang is shown placing the transcribed message on his computer in order to decode it. He sings a little duet with Teresa to get the melody. On this and other occasions, the musical code serves as a link between Tony, Tequila, Teresa and Pang. Thus, all the heroic or positive characters are joined by means of music. So we see that, while the means of introducing musical material into the narrative is quite different from *The Killer*, the effect is similar. A community of heroes is created by the meaning and emotion of music.

In *The Killer*, *Hard Boiled* and *Bullet in the Head* (and to some extent in *A Better Tomorrow*), the music acts as an important complement to the narrative and to the characters' existential status. Sometimes, Woo's work is not so fortuitously harmonious. In *Once a Thief*, the music is not always totally effective, or perhaps its rationale is not as apparent as in the other films cited. This is not to say that the film is not interestingly scored, only that its music does not always mesh completely with its narrative. The problem is as much with the narrative itself as with the score, however.

As with *The Killer*, David Wu was the film editor for *Once a Thief.* He contributed much to the appropriateness of the music here (relative as that may be, given the problems of conception and execution with this movie). Woo also had a hand in the music selection, as the snippet from Handel's *Joseph in Egypt* demonstrates.[21] This bit appears during a high-speed robbery of a painting from a truck, carried out flawlessly by the three thieves. As with the *Messiah* piece in *The Killer*, the selection of *Joseph in Egypt* comments intelligently on the narrative. Like Joseph, the characters here live in a kind of exile from their homeland, plying their trade in the foreign environment of France. Other forays in the film into Western music are not as fortuitous, especially in the trendy use of Lambada music to accompany Jules and Jim's limbo dance under the laser beam during the robbery.

Chapter 4

Woo's Early Films:
A Selected Treatment

The Young Dragons

One of Woo's earliest films (credited to "Wu Yu Sen"), *The Young Dragons* was independently produced and then distributed by Golden Harvest. Set in the warlord era of the 1920s, its plot concerns the conflict between two factions of arms smugglers.

The Young Dragons bears the strong influence of Chang Cheh (especially his *Vengeance*), both in its staging (several scenes of corruptly sensual gangsters in lacquered surroundings) and in its choreography (extended *wing chun* sequences). This is hardly surprising given Woo's apprenticeship with Chang.

But even in this early film (and, in fact, rather more clearly than in some of the later pre–1986 films by Woo), one can discern marks of Woo's later style and themes. We can see the prototypes for Woo's familiar tracking shots, as he brings the camera sharply closer into the faces of the main characters. This aspect of Woo's technique has been ascribed to influence from Sergio Leone (Teo 177). This is partially true, but Chang Cheh was even more clearly influential, especially when we examine such early films as *The Young Dragons*. In this case, Woo is not very fluid with the camera, rushing the dolly track abruptly into the actor's face. The appearance of these shots, though, is very similar to that of Chang's work in films like *Invincible Fist*. No doubt Woo was influenced or intrigued by Leone's insistence on facial framing and slow dollying, but developed his own techniques slowly with such early experimentation, with sources like Chang Cheh as a point of departure, as in *The Young Dragons* and *Hand of Death*.

Woo was also beginning to develop his distinctive character groupings. A notable example of this in *The Young Dragons* occurs on the bridge, after the Kid has stolen Fan Ming's purse, and Brother Kin is attacked by a man and his friends (the man had lost to Kin at gambling). As if the whole fight scene were designed to bring Fan (Lau Kong) and Kin (Yu Yang) together, Woo pulls in on a shot of the two framed on the bridge, one in profile, one in full-face. Clearly he had begun to work with the imagery of doubling and was eschewing both the unique focus on one protagonist and the visual privileging of the group: *The Young Dragons*, from this point on, becomes a story about the friendship between these two men on opposite sides of the law (Fan is a detective, Kin a freelance thief) but on the same side against a ruthless enemy—not so different after all from *The Killer* or *Hard Boiled*.

In this prototypical Woo film, plot is built around the growing friendship and loyalty between policeman Fan Ming and entrepreneurial thief Kin. In Kin's character we can see an early forerunner of "Green" and Mark: the heroic and ultimately self-sacrificing Steve McQueen type whose sensuality and hotheadedness are belied by a cool surface. Kin lolls around with his prostitute friend, smoking and looking world-weary, but his words betray his true quality as a Woo hero: "A man can sacrifice for his ideal. It is the most beautiful experience." And Fan Ming, an early version of Inspector Li, though without Li's degree of rebelliousness, insists on going to arrest Lung and his men even when convalescing from a bad injury, because he knows that Kin may be in trouble. He arrives with his police friends only to find that Kin has died in the process of killing Lung's hatchet man Yun Fei, after having first dispatched Lung.

Lung himself is a villain from the Chang Cheh film mold—a middle-aged, corrupt, vicious man, a bad ruler according to Confucian theory. As such, he does not closely resemble later Woo villains like Johnny Weng in *Hard Boiled*. But his henchman Yun Fei is a little more intriguing. His cruelty and killing ability will later abide in men like Paul Yau (*The Killer*), Chong (*A Better Tomorrow II*) and most memorably in Mad Dog (*Hard Boiled*). Unlike Mad Dog, though, he has no redeeming qualities, no principles about whose death is within the rules of the game. He simply kills for killing's sake, as in the opening scene when he needlessly murders a sparring partner. His boss amusedly comments that he's just as ruthless as ever.

From Yun Fei to Mad Dog we can measure the distance in Woo's maturation as an artist: Mad Dog is one of the more interesting characters in *Hard Boiled*, precisely because he has that integrity shared by Tequila and Tony. This link is underlined by the scene at the end of the film when he and Tony lay down their guns to avoid harming the innocent patients. The inspired touch of adding such a dimension to Mad Dog's character also adds another dimension to the film. It allows Tequila's and Tony's darker side to be reflected in Mad Dog's, and conversely it forces Mad Dog's better angels to be understood in conjunction with the two heroes'. No such dimensionality is possible in *The Young*

Dragons, despite an important face-off between Kin and Yun Fei (they kill each other). Still, this is an important early Woo film because it adumbrates the directions his career was to take, and its very "creakiness" permits us to see how Woo's style operates at a level not always so easy to perceive in his mature, more sophisticated work.

Plain Jane to the Rescue

Plain Jane to the Rescue (1982) was the third film in a series which contained a character named Lam Ah Chun, created by star Josephine Siao Fong-fong. It was one of Woo's more artistically successful comedies during his time at Golden Harvest. The film provided a showcase for the extraordinary Josephine Siao.[1] Not just another "silly comedy," though, *Plain Jane to the Rescue* attempts to address concerns particular to Hong Kong people facing 1997. Jane[2] and her sidekick Fang, played by the talented Ricky Hui, and their cause to be championed, the about-to-be-robbed old millionaire Sha, played with considerable panache by a non-actor, represent for Woo Hong Kong individualism and quirky self-reliance as opposed to totalitarian, faceless corporate enterprise and distanced authority. Although uneven and not always pointed enough in its jabs, the film does manage to insinuate its message home while providing for the wackiness one would expect from Siao, Hui and Woo.

Woo always seemed comfortable with the "moony" Ricky Hui[3] (as David Chute so aptly called him [Publicity release, *Broken Arrow* 43]), using him in several of his Golden Harvest comedies, but he had not previously worked with Siao. Their collaboration produces some entertaining results, and Siao and Hui play well off each other. A real cynosure of the film is the bedeviled patriarch. Woo told me that the man who played this role "wasn't an actor, he was an artist" (Woo, personal interview, 8 November 1995). Woo showed here a fine touch in getting a very natural and unadorned but funny performance from him.

The film is somewhat unusual for Woo in that it features a strong female lead. One need not draw too many conclusions from this, since the character is, after all, Siao's, and Woo is to some extent providing her with a showcase. Still, we might take note of the fact that, despite critical commonplace, Woo has not always relegated women characters to backseat positions.

The Plain Jane character is a very peculiar mix of several comic strains. At times, she seems like Lucille Ball's Lucy Ricardo in her befuddlement and ineptitude, as in the opening scene, where she loses a job as a

"Plain Jane" (Josephine Siao) gets a facial from the makeup department for *Plain Jane to the Rescue* (1982). (Courtesy John Woo.)

street-line painter by continuing to paint a stripe in the wrong direction. At other times, she is reminiscent of sharp-tongued Jean Arthur or maybe even Jackie Gleason's irascible Ralph Kramden. And Siao clearly harks back to silent comedy, with her mastery of physical humor, at times Chaplinesque, at times like Keaton or Lloyd.

Particularly noticeable is the Bergsonian strain in her comedy, one which Woo seems to have relished, as the scenes with this effect are particularly humorous. Bergson had emphasized the mechanical aspect of comedy,[4] and Siao plays marvelously on this under Woo's direction, as in the scene where she tries to administer a numbing injection to a guard in the asylum where Sha is being held. The injection, as we ruefully expect, ends up in her own arm and leg, so that we have additive humor (and what next?), but the comic effect of the scene is really to be found in the rag-doll quality imparted by Siao's suddenly numbed arm and leg: she looks precisely like a store dummy. So, with our thoughts leading in this direction anyhow, Woo and Siao clinch the point, or make the sum, as it were, as she finally drives the needle straight into her head.

Siao is often "mechanical" in the film, an aspect of her character which adds to its comedy: she is often the passive butt of abuse (or flattery) and seems dumbly not to notice. On the level of characterization, then, her mechanistic appearance is central. But this also functions on the level of the script as a whole: Woo takes advantage of this element of her character by playing it off against situations in which regimentation is demanded—thus, the highway department, the film shoot, the big corporation. We are reminded of films like Chaplin's *Modern Times* (1936) and René Clair's *A nous la liberté* (1931) which deal from the same deck.

Like Dean Shek in Woo's *Laughing Times*, Siao alludes freely to Chaplin, not least in the running references to *Modern Times*. Jane is placed repeatedly in assembly line settings for which she provides a comic analogue in her mechanical reactions, but she ends up surpassing her environment in all cases. For instance, during the film shoot, when she plays a second team stand-in for an actress in a soapy story, she repeatedly takes real beatings from the lead actor. Again, the comedy is based on repetition; the viewer is asked to wonder when the worm will turn. Finally, her true spunk gets the better of her and she assaults the actor, nearly destroying the set.

Scenes such as this force the issue of individualism versus corporate sameness and restriction, but as the film progresses, Woo turns down the temperature somewhat, and Jane begins to act subversively rather than rebelliously. An example of this shift appears in her first encounter with "Uncle" Sha, whom she has been hired to teach good manners (that is, conformity). She comes to meet him at a playground where, implicitly analogized to the children, he is "protected" by a kids' bodyguard team who "assault" Jane. Previously, his other trainers had quit at this point, embarrassed and exasperated. But Jane appears to endure the "attack" meekly (actually ironically), and then "attacks" the kids herself. Not merely an indication of her determination to do her job, this little performance shows her disdain for appearances and social forms; she will not be embarrassed because keeping up the good side does not matter to her. She and Uncle are kindred spirits.

Like other Woo pairs (and she and Uncle are really more of a pair than she and Fang, at least in this sense), they team up against cold, even vicious enemies who seek to repress difference. Jane, Magic Sword (more, Green), Mark and John are siblings, Woo characters who fight for principle and freedom and who sometimes pay heavily for it—Green, Mark and John all die. An added note of irony is provided here by the contrast between Uncle's innocuous "bodyguards" and the impersonal, potentially ruthless myrmidons at his son's company. Again, though in the comic realm, the son's guards are really not far here from the companions or servants of Fan, Johnny Weng or Shing.

These aspects of *Plain Jane to the Rescue* fit well into that tradition of Cantonese comedy which privileges the "little guy," pitting him (or her) against faceless corporations, impersonal police forces or well-organized criminals. We see such oppositions in films like Michael Hui's *Chicken and Duck Talk* (1988) (the Chinese barbecue store battling against the new fast-food restaurant) and Sammo Hung's *My Lucky Stars* (1985) (the innovative crimebusters—criminals themselves—fighting the ruthless mob), and even in hybrid films like *Mr. Vampire* (1984), in which the resourceful but rather wacky ghostbusters, led by Lam Ching-ying, win against the undead when the organized police cannot. All these films, and many more, privilege traditional Chinese folk wisdom against Western-inspired macro-organization.[5] It is not too hard to see here a rehearsing of the ancient fears of foreign intervention or of, for example, extreme Legalist control over government.[6]

Certainly it is no accident that Woo's contributions to Cantonese comedy have fallen squarely into the populist tradition represented by figures like the Hui brothers (especially Michael Hui) and Siao Fong-fong. Woo's own proclivities would almost dictate his identification with such comedy. He does, though, bring his own spice to the mix; as he points out, "Before my movie [*Money Crazy*], all Michael Hui's comedies were pretty realistic, pretty real, but I tried something different, because I like Jerry Lewis so much. I must say I was the first one to use the visual comedy. I started that" (personal interview, 8 November 1995). One can also see his special contributions to comedy in Hong Kong by comparing his work with Siao with another of her previous efforts starring her Lam Ah Chun character.

This film, *Lam Ah Chun* (1978),[7] is competently but unimaginatively directed. The straight-on shooting style effaces the directorial personality and provides Siao with a series of opportunities to display her remarkable talents. But the film, while engaging, has little of the zaniness, or the underlying seriousness, of *Plain Jane to the Rescue*, and this is due chiefly to the flatness of its style. The camera frequently remains stationary while Siao and the other actors deliver their dialogue; basically the movie is an extended filmed skit, or series of skits. Still, it focuses more centrally on the Lam character than does *Plain Jane to the Rescue*; it is a series of predicaments or situations to showcase the character. Woo's film is more ambitious; he attempts to use the character to experiment with comedy effects and to advance a narrative with overtones of filial disloyalty, political and economic injustice, and populistic anarchism.

In fact, *Plain Jane to the Rescue* is a significant early text in the 1997 canon, since it features an overt treatment of the subject. According to Woo, it "was the first Hong Kong film to talk about 1997" (personal interview, 8 November 1995). Woo's treatment begins near the end of the film, with a wild rush through a traffic-choked tunnel with the object of beating the deadline for Uncle to revoke the fake will he had inadvertently signed. As in Woo's films generally, and his comedies in particular, the irrational intervenes in the person of a pyromaniac who threatens to immolate himself and explode the tunnel in the process. The fact that he uses gasoline to douse himself and to threaten the tunnel adds to the irony of the scene. The very material that made possible the traffic jam in which he escapes is the instrument he will use to blackmail the authorities.

But Jane does him one better. She claims that she'll die right along with him, becoming an unlikely "people's heroine" by her unexpected action. She takes the phone and demands that Uncle be brought to her. Following her lead, other people in the tunnel begin to communicate demands, the most telling of which is the request that all drivers in Hong Kong blow their horns to protest the traffic problems. In the meantime, a woman has a baby in the tunnel and other women begin to file up to deliver. The tunnel becomes a comic laboratory of freedom.

This scene extends the Lam character well beyond her status in *Lam Ah Chun* as essentially an ordinary person placed in a bizarre situation, as caretaker for an eccentric, rich young man. Again, Woo experiments, within the limits of his budget, with visual jokes, mobile cameras and odd settings, to create a film of which Lam Ah Chun is an anchor but not really a centerpiece.

The Lam character enters new territory here as well in the realm of purely physical comedy. Although *Lam Ah Chun* was not bereft of such comedy, much of its emphasis was placed on situational and verbal humor, and less, insofar as Lam herself was concerned, on mime and other forms of visual humor.[8] But in *Plain Jane to the Rescue*, Siao is put through the physical paces, particularly in the film shoot scene and in another important scene (the hypodermic fiasco) from later in the film.

The latter scene, referred to previously, is a clear nod to Chaplin and Keaton, with its aforementioned Bergsonian mechanism. Jane and Fang sport Chaplinesque disguises, and Jane acts in mime and eventually falls victim to her own stratagems with the hypodermic. This little homage to silent comedy appears less forced than the generally derivative *Laughing Times*, in which Dean Shek's admittedly accurate Chaplin impersonation begins to wear after a short time.

Perhaps one would not care to make exaggerated claims for Woo's earlier work, like *Plain Jane to the Rescue*, but these films are not always negligible, nor are they exclusively mere preludes to his later work. Tempted though we might be to hunt retrospectively here for Woo's later work in germ (and this is certainly a justified approach), the fact is that *Plain Jane to the Rescue* is a self-contained little comedy. Often Woo's earlier work suffers from low budgets; he was frequently forced to cut corners to a nearly impossible extent. Nevertheless, he sometimes did very original work in these films, and *Plain Jane to the Rescue* at least occasionally bears the mark of his talent for absurdity.

Last Hurrah for Chivalry

Woo has said that "most people didn't like *Last Hurrah for Chivalry*" (qtd. in Chute, *The Killer* 30). David Chute defends the film while admitting its faults:

> *Last Hurrah* looks like a typical cheap martial arts picture, from the bad wigs to the overlit studio exteriors. But it's recognizably a real movie; there's an effort to make the characters talk and behave naturally, and the emotions are authentic. It's a meditation on the decline of the old swordfighterly virtues, and upon that nagging fear that they may never have existed at all except as cherished illusions in the minds of a few weirdos: our (doomed) heroes [*The Killer* ch. 30].

Though hardly a masterpiece, the movie does show early signs of Woo's later preoccupations. It also looks backward to his earlier work in some respects.

Last Hurrah for Chivalry (1978) opens as if with a take on Chang Cheh's *Vengeance*: a treacherous attack by the villain Pai on Kao's family at his own birthday party. Kao (Lau Kong)[9] swears vengeance and is only with great difficulty calmed by his *sifu*.

The scene switches to introduce Magic Sword (Wei Pai), whom Kao mentions as the only one who can kill Pai. Soon, another important character appears: Green, a drunken swordsman (Damian Lau Chung-yun, seen more recently in the two *Heroic Trio* films as the husband of "Wonder Woman" [Anita Mui]) who comes to Magic Sword's aid in a fight. Woo is clearly trying to set up one of his paired hero situations. It is here

"Green" (Damian Lau, left) and "Magic Sword" (Wei Pai, right) try to entrap villian Pai in an intriguing setup from *Last Hurrah for Chivalry* (1978). (Courtesy John Woo.)

that the film becomes something other than, or in addition to, a Chang Cheh gloss.

The narrative begins to shift between scenes showing Magic Sword and Green's growing closeness and scenes of Kao's planned vengeance. Gradually, Kao drops out of the foreground as Woo concentrates on the two young swordsmen. They begin to have adventures together, not very serious ones. But later, enlisted by Kao, they enter into open combat with Pai.

Their battles are choreographed in Shaw Brothers style and might remind one of Chang Cheh or King Hu. But the growing friendship and banter between the two young men is pure John Woo.

Thus, Woo extends and develops the Chang Cheh motif of the moral, self-sacrificing male hero, which he has noted as the master's contribution to martial arts films:

> He was the pioneer. Before him, in all the Hong Kong movies, the major lead was a female. His films are always about chivalry, honor, loyalty, and

a true hero—and at that time, not many people would dare to do a thing like that, because usually only the female lead movie could work. But ... Chang Cheh changed the whole thing and gave the movies a new look. And the action and choreography also changed [Woo, personal interview, 7 November 1995].

Woo almost seems more interested in the interplay between the two men than in their sometimes perfunctory battles with adversaries. But in some of these battles, Woo shows hints of his later choreographic brilliance and depth.

In particular, we may note the prolonged battle between the two heroes and their apparent adversary ("apparent" because Kao has tricked them into fighting someone with whom they should have no quarrel). This extended fight is filled with spectacular stunts and frenetic attacks and recalls more than anything else the great slapstick battles in some of Woo's comedies like *From Riches to Rags* and *Money Crazy*. Woo had not yet settled on his tonal approach at the time of making *Last Hurrah for Chivalry* and seems unsure of the cast to give to his staged battles. Thus, the film wavers between frantic comedy-action and intensely dramatic struggles to the death.

The highlight of the film in dramatic terms is the amazing final battle between the two heroes and their real adversary, Kao. Besides the truly spectacular swordplay and martial arts stunts (especially considering the film's low budget), the real fascination of this battle is its undercurrent of betrayal and self-sacrifice.

The battle opens between Green and Pai and his henchmen. Green appears to be overwhelmed, perhaps to end, dying even if victorious, as did the David Chiang hero in Chang Cheh's classic *Vengeance*, or perhaps to fail entirely, as Chiang did not, when he is suddenly rejoined by Magic Sword. Green had supposedly killed him, betraying him to be paid by Kao. Woo shows the death scene to have been an optical trick. The blood splash on Magic Sword at the time is revealed through flashback to have come from an adversary behind him, killed by Green's thrust. While Woo does not yet have the sure touch of a Peckinpah, still Magic Sword's reappearance is reminiscent (with moral roles reversed) of Gil Westrum's galloping entrance into the fray to help Steve Judd at the conclusion of *Ride the High Country*. The "grand entrance" in *Last Hurrah for Chivalry* is also somewhat marred by the limited acting skills of the two leads, and if one keeps *Ride the High Country* in mind, by the relative lack of depth of the characters when contrasted to the cachet brought by actors like Scott and McCrea.

The final confrontation between the duplicitous Kao and Magic

Sword and Green allows Woo to emphasize some of his favorite themes. The solid friendship and loyalty between the two heroes are sharply drawn, contrasting to the amoral cynicism and evil opportunism of Kao. Woo drives home the point by having Green repeat his earlier, seemingly ironic line about friendship in the flashback which reveals that the line, far from being cynically ironic, is actually heartfelt and sincere. Woo's signature is just as noticeable here as in *The Killer*, even if the mature consistency of the later work is not yet evident.

A further Woo note is central to this film: the sacrifice of one friend for another. Like Mark or John, Green sacrifices himself to kill the villain and to save his friend. Even more than in *A Better Tomorrow* or *The Killer*, though, Green's sacrifice is deliberate and willing. He not only vindicates himself in Magic Sword's eyes for any possible waverings in loyalty, but also redeems himself from his earlier dissolution as a drunken ne'er-do-well.

The comparison with Mark is no coincidence. Woo says that the two are "the same character" (qtd. in Chute, *The Killer* 30). Both recall in their rather boyish sensitivity and willfulness heroes from Chinese tradition like Lu Ta from *Water Margin*.

Not only does *Last Hurrah for Chivalry* prefigure the themes of *A Better Tomorrow* and *The Killer*—loyalty to one's family or friends, courage in the face of death, self-sacrifice—but it also deals with these topics in ways different and less formulaic than does a film such as *The Killer*. Another way of expressing this point is to note that the swordplay film has more iconographic and visual conventionalism than the police or "lone gangster" film, that is, it is more stylized and restricted in its visual vocabulary. Paradoxically, though, the swordplay film is more varied insofar as narrative conventions. After all, the cop, even the plainclothesman or the undercover agent, must operate within a set of rules and work from a given "base" (the police station, the patrol car and so forth). Similarly to the Western, the cop film is highly stylized in the narrative sense. Its basic conflicts and oppositions are more limited than are the possible scenarios for the chivalry or swordplay film. Of course, in any generic narrative, certain elements recur and characterize that narrative. But it is still true that in *Last Hurrah for Chivalry* Woo was working in a form with less innate simplicity, or, if one prefers, more variability than the gangster-cop genre to which *The Killer* and *A Better Tomorrow* belong.

Last Hurrah for Chivalry is less intensely dramatic than *A Better Tomorrow* or *The Killer*, and this is due partially to the "wider" limits of the genre. Woo had learned much from Chang Cheh about action staging and about the importance of character in action films, but he was

"Magic Sword" (Wei Pai, right) battles one of his enemy's henchmen in *Last Hurrah for Chivalry* (1978). (Courtesy John Woo.)

clearly trying to reach beyond the limits of Chang's work. It is notable that while in films such as *The One-Armed Swordsman* (an important model for Woo, according to him) or *Vengeance* (a probable model), Chang is more interested in working out the hero's resolution of his inner conflict, whether by revenge or by defense of one's master, Woo is, by the time of *Last Hurrah for Chivalry*, trying to expand the parameters of such formulaic, didactic drama to include a strong focus on friendship between opposites or former enemies. Chang's heroes must often fight their battles alone, but in Woo the heroes are paired, as if one were incomplete without the other.

This new thematic territory explored in *Last Hurrah for Chivalry* causes the film to become curiously static in places. When Magic Sword and Green begin to become friends, Woo simply sets aside the storyline about Kao's attempted revenge on Pai by using Magic Sword and Green as his killers, for a nearly pastoral dialogue between the two heroes as they

discuss friendship and loyalty, and Green indulges in his favorite pas-
time, drinking. As can be discerned in this scene, Woo was already relying on the large close-up as a preferred method of revealing a character's
feelings.

Not only do we see the Woo signature close-up in this film but other
elements of his cinematography as well. He relies frequently on rack focus
to highlight the importance of a character. While this is by no means rare
in film, it is significant that Woo begins to employ it repeatedly in films
such as *Last Hurrah for Chivalry*. Rack focus lends a dreamy effect, as well
as a contrastive one, to scenes, since the primary object of the camera
comes into sharp focus, while the other characters and the background
recede into soft focus. This kind of technique is not associated with Welle-
sian "deep focus" practice, in which, according to Bazin, the viewer is not
directed to see but is instead forced, as it were, to choose from the scene
presented as a tableau. The director does not make choices for the viewer.
Woo is, by this criterion, not an "open" filmmaker; he is, like Hitchcock,
a director who wants his viewer to see certain things at the expense of
others. This tendency is very apparent in *Last Hurrah for Chivalry*, because
Woo's use of rack focus is rather crude or at least obvious; perhaps he was
simply not as proficient in his handling of such shots as he has since
become, or perhaps he was not as well served by his director of photography as he has been by people like Wong Wing-hang. In any event, the
fact is that the rack focus and close-up effects associated with Woo's
mature work are here given tryouts; Woo is feeling his way toward his
own highly individual film language.

We can see from *Last Hurrah for Chivalry* some of Woo's commonality with, or influence from, Chang Cheh. Like Chang, he uses rack
focus to highlight the importance of a particular character in a scene.
Chang often uses this technique to heighten the suspense in key scenes
by accentuating important figures: thus, in his *The Invincible Fist* (1969),
a scene set in Hung Lung Tavern is notable in its use of rack focus. The
villain Ma Wei Chia, sitting in the tavern, though known to the viewer
as the villain, is left unobtrusive and shadowy until the policeman begins
to notice him; the policeman becomes like the camera eye for the viewer,
and Ma comes into sharp focus. Woo uses the technique in similar fashion in *Last Hurrah for Chivalry*, but he seems less disciplined, either
because he is learning its use or because he is experimenting with it. (A
little of both, I suspect, since his employment of focal depth changes was
later to become masterful.)

Also in this Woo film are some clear borrowings from Chang Cheh:
lone or paired warriors battling multiple adversaries (also a feature of

other Woo films, including some of his early comedies), an emphasis on emotive or passionate heroes (compare Magic Sword and the One-Armed Swordsman) and, again, the central position of self-sacrifice and loyalty.

But Woo adds to the mix his own special touches, particularly some comic ones. Most notable is the strange and memorable battle between the Sleeping Wizard and the two heroes. The Sleeping Wizard is a swordsman who literally falls asleep during battle and then suddenly reawakens to attack—and he *is* lethal for all his buffoonery. Apparently a variation on the Drunken Boxing style (with a note of Harpo Marx), this swordplay technique lends a unique dimension to the film. This bizarrely comic aspect recalls the unforgettable battles staged in Woo comedies such as *From Riches to Rags*. So we can see that Woo is experimenting with a fusion of styles and genres. Incidentally, this interlude differs in its quaintness from the frequent comic scenes in Sammo Hung or Jackie Chan films. In *Last Hurrah for Chivalry*, the heroes seem to be confronted with a phenomenon which is nearly magical realist; they do not themselves contribute to the comedy of the scene, as Sammo or Jackie would: rather, they take the Sleeping Wizard as an annoying, not too serious obstacle keeping them from their real business, which at this point is killing Pai. If *Last Hurrah for Chivalry is* a tentative film, it is certainly one of Woo's more interesting early efforts because of its prominent employment of the "paired hero" motif and also because it features an early version of one of the most famous characters in Hong Kong movie history, Mark from *A Better Tomorrow*.

Chapter 5

A Better Tomorrow and A Better Tomorrow II: A Flawed Saga

*Mankind's common instinct for reality ... has always held
the world to be essentially a theater for heroism. In heroism, we feel, life's supreme mystery is hidden. We tolerate
no one who has no capacity whatever for it in any direction. On the other hand, no matter what a man's frailties
otherwise may be, if he be willing to risk death, and still
more if he suffer it heroically, in the service he has chosen,
the fact consecrates him forever.*

—William James,
The Varieties of Religious Experience (1902),
Lectures 14–15, "The Value of Saintliness"

Given Woo's earlier films, his *A Better Tomorrow* (1986) was somewhat of a surprise, if only because it represented a departure from his previous, primarily comedy and martial arts films. In another sense, though,
it was a continuation of certain aspects of his previous films. Its exaggerated melodrama recalls Woo's *Last Hurrah for Chivalry*,[1] and its emphasis on friendship and family relationships can be seen in Woo comedies
such as *From Riches to Rags* and *Plain Jane to the Rescue*. The comic ker-
nels of the story, in fact, were to be accentuated in *A Better Tomorrow II*,
which Woo seems to have understood in two apparently conflicting ways:
as a sequel like Coppola's *The Godfather Part II*, and as a comic strip
installment (Woo, personal interview, 8 November 1995). Taken together,
the two films certainly are not on the level of Coppola's twin masterpiece.
Woo had not yet found his footing as a mature director; the tone of both
films, especially the second, wavers between melodrama and comedy.
Additionally, the plot of the second film is murky and confused, but Woo's
original twin intent can be perceived clearly, as the film retains two distinct levels of treatment, one Coppola–esque, the other cartoonish.

A Better Tomorrow was the end of one stage of Woo's career and the

95

beginning of another, much more profitable one, both financially and artistically.[2] Although his earlier career features some interesting films, *A Better Tomorrow* broke new ground, both for him and for the Hong Kong film industry. In 1986, at the time of the making of Woo's film, some examples of recent Hong Kong films had been *Royal Warriors, Yes, Madam, Twinkle Twinkle Lucky Stars, The Protector, Righting Wrongs, Mr. Vampire, Hong Kong 1941* and *Police Story*.

Several of these (*Royal Warriors, Yes, Madam* and *Righting Wrongs*) were "lady cop" films, in which women take the buddy roles often seen in the West. Most were essentially light entertainments, with liberal dashes of humor, sometimes (as in *Yes, Madam*) including in the cast performers from the "Lucky Stars" series, such as Richard Ng and Sammo Hung, and with emphasis on the martial arts performances of their female stars (usually Michelle Yeoh [Khan] and Pennsylvania–born Cynthia Rothrock). *The Protector* and *Police Story* were two Jackie Chan films, with his patented and engaging style of comedy-action. *Mr. Vampire* was the first of many films reminiscent of Harold Ramis' *Ghostbusters*, but with a very special Hong Kong touch, starring master killer of vampires and ghosts Lam Ching-ying. *Hong Kong 1941* was a good example of Hong Kong drama, starring Chow Yun-fat.

Especially given the style of the police films mentioned, Woo's film would be a true departure. It generally eschewed humorous interludes, limiting comic moments to episodes revelatory of character instead of presenting little vignettes for their own sake; it concentrated on a group of male heroes; and it emphasized gunplay to the almost total exclusion of martial arts and the kind of stunts seen in Jackie Chan movies. *A Better Tomorrow* also adopted a tone of seriousness, frequently verging on melodrama, and it stressed especially character and family relationships, in contrast to the "lady cop" films, in which character and friendship revolve totally around work and are kept on a superficial level. While it would be some time before he attained a sure footing artistically and commercially, *A Better Tomorrow* was the watershed film in the process of Woo's becoming a director known worldwide for his mastery of action filmmaking. This fame has not been an unmixed blessing for Woo, as he has become typecast as an "action director," a designation he does not readily accept. But without *A Better Tomorrow*, Woo would probably not have developed as the artist we know.

As we noted in the Introduction, *A Better Tomorrow* is a remake of a 1967 film of the same title (that is, the same Cantonese title, *Ying hung boon sik*, or *True Colors of a Hero*).[3] Woo's arrival at the point of making this film in 1986 had involved a long career of making comedies and occasional action films. Most recently, he had undergone a difficult period in Taiwan. Woo's business partner Terence Chang recounted that, after Woo had gone to the newly formed Cinema City, he was assigned administrative work in Taiwan by the studio heads. His administrative stint did not go well, and he began to run short of money. So he was allowed to make two nugatory films, *The Time You Need a Friend* (1986) and *Run Tiger Run* (1986). He returned to Hong Kong in desperation, but the Cinema City studio was not supportive.

While in Taiwan, according to Chang, Woo had visited with Tsui Hark, who "at that time became a major director, because he did a couple of comedies which were very successful." The subject of a remake of *True Colors of a Hero* was discussed, and plans were now made:

> I don't know who came up with the idea of remaking *True Colors of a Hero*, which is a black-and-white film. Tsui Hark wanted to make it a film about the friendship of three women. But John wanted to do a film about guys. At that time Tsui Hark set up his own shop, Film Workshop, as a production entity for Cinema City. And so Tsui Hark said, "I'm going to help you. I'm going to produce a film for you and for Cinema City" [Chang, personal interview, 2 March 1996].

Despite the creative disagreements over the film, specifically the issue of male as opposed to female emphasis, Woo was allowed to proceed with the project. The film was constructed around male leads. Two casting decisions are particularly important to the film: the choice of Ti Lung for the elder brother role (Ho) and the decision, pushed by Woo, to hire Chow Yun-fat for an important supporting role.

Ti Lung's presence in the film is not usually given the emphasis placed on Chow's, and understandably so, with the great fame achieved by Chow following his appearance here. Nevertheless, Ti Lung is important for the film in several respects.

One of these concerns his importance in Hong Kong film history. Ti Lung began in films with Shaw Brothers Studios, where he appeared in many of legendary director Chang Cheh's martial arts productions, becoming a major star. His career hit a downturn in the 1980s, at least partially because of the changing fashion in Hong Kong film away from the kind of martial arts and swordplay movies in which Ti Lung had specialized.

A Better Tomorrow tells the story of two brothers, Kit (Leslie Cheung Kwok-wing) and Ho (Ti Lung),[4] who live on opposite sides of the law. At the beginning of the film, Kit, the younger brother, is finishing his studies at the police academy. We have already been introduced to

Ho, who is a member of a Triad group controlling counterfeit money distribution. Kit's existence and relationship to Ho are then presented, leading us to view his graduation from the academy with some apprehension, as it will place him into conflict with his brother's way of life. Ho is shown to be the more mature and competent of the two; the point is made clearly when Ho teases and hazes Kit about his graduation from the academy. Kit is shown with very short hair, a boy's haircut, and is awkward and defensively adolescent, protesting Ho's ribbing with a youth's laughter. Woo thus neatly poses the conflict early in the film, with the added note that Ho's enterprise is counterfeit by extension. He will prove to be unsupported and needful, and the vaunted loyalty among Triad members to be sometimes as false as the money they print.

The viewer's unease is deepened when Ho goes to visit his ailing father in the hospital.[5] The father tries to convince Ho to leave his criminal career and reminds him that Kit doesn't know what Ho does for a living. With this piece of information, we become aware that the film is in part an initiation story and that a painful *anagnorisis* for Kit is in the offing.[6]

Thus, the seemingly simple gangster plot is revealed as dramatically layered. Woo's concentration on Confucian relationships is again evident from the outset. Ho is shown as a concerned son, although his obedience to his father's wishes is at best dubious, given his criminal activities; and he is presented as a *dailo* at least interested in his brother's aspirations and affectionate towards him.

This familial structure is counterposed to a structure within the Triad. Ho goes to the leader of his Triad, the fatherly but corrupt-looking and harsh Mr. Yiu,[7] who asks Ho to go to Taiwan to meet with some potential business partners whom he does not fully trust. He sends along with Ho a callow apprentice, Shing (Waise Lee Chi-hung), in Triad parlance, a younger "brother." We have, then, Ho acting as an "older" brother or mentor to a younger "brother" who will be initiated into the ways of the Triad; the "father" commends a mission to them and trusts Ho to see it through.

Ho therefore becomes the pivotal point of trust and maturity in two family structures, with one, his natural family, being counterposed to his adopted family in the Triad. Ho will soon discover that his adopted family's ethic is based on values other than trust.[8]

When Ho and Shing go to the meeting in Taiwan, Ho cautions Shing to be careful, that something is amiss. We fully expect that Ho and Shing will be ambushed or betrayed, and so they prove to be; they escape the ambush, killing the rival gang members, but are forced to elude the

Chow Yun-fat (left, as Mark Lee) and Ti Lung (right, as Ho Sung-tse) clown with shot glasses as Waise Lee (center, as villain Shing) watches in amusement. From the set of *A Better Tomorrow* (1986). (Courtesy John Woo.)

police. Wounded in the gun battle with the gang, Ho suspects that Shing, who joins him only belatedly in his hiding place, may have betrayed him. Shing offers the plausible rejoinder, "If I had betrayed you, why would I be here?" But he manages to escape, while Ho is led away handcuffed.

Woo cuts to a sinister-looking man reading an address from a slip of paper; we soon see that he is a button man sent out to threaten Ho's family (or at least his father), to warn Ho off revenge; and, if necessary, to kill Kit and his father, on the pretext that Ho tried to have Shing and Mr. Yiu killed. Kit and his girlfriend Jackie (Emily Chu) manage to disable the attacker, but Kit's father is killed. Thus Kit will blame Ho for the wrong reason, but not totally unjustifiably, for their father's death. Kit, the younger brother, will see his older brother as a traitor to his family; while Ho will soon learn that his "younger brother" Shing has actually betrayed him.

Woo has established, then, a balanced "mirror image set" of families, one based, as we shall see, on loyalty masquerading as betrayal, the other based on betrayal masquerading as loyalty. To this parallelism he will add an element that will serve as a focal point for resolving the conflict between appearance and truth.

The focus here is on Mark (Chow Yun-fat),[9] a very capable gangster who is a buddy of Ho's. The ethical stalemate between the "good" and "bad" families (or, if one prefers, the entropic state existing between them) is broken when Mark avenges Ho by killing the gang members who had set up the attempted hit on Ho. But Mark is crippled in the battle, becoming thereby a sacrificial figure.

The scene shifts to three years later, when Ho is released from prison.[10] He soon encounters Kit, who is now presented as an accomplished policeman and as now quite capable of physically besting Ho. Woo thus signals that the dynamics of the family have changed, that Kit has begun the maturation process.

Ho finds an honest job as a taxi driver, attempting to leave his past behind, belatedly following his father's wishes. He is surprised to land this job, given his criminal record, but his new boss[11] tells him that everyone working there, including himself, is an ex-con.[12] Meantime, he encounters the partially crippled Mark, who has become a very subordinate member of the Triad now headed by Shing. Mark and Ho are reunited in a scene not untypical of Woo in its unapologetic sentiment. The two even embrace tearfully, an event which should normally have taken place between Ho and Kit. Mark again becomes the focus for the positive emotional content in the film; by contrast, Kit's relationship with his fiancée is strained and unconvincing.

While Ho works at the taxi agency run by Ken (Kenneth Tsang Ko), who serves as his mentor and a surrogate father-figure, Shing becomes the new "son" for the retired Mr. Yiu. Shing, frustrated at not being able to recruit, or co-opt, Ho, has the car agency attacked. Ho's "father" stands by him and attempts to calm him; contrasted to this genuine scene are Shing's later betrayal and murder of Mr. Yiu and his beating of Mark.

Mark goes to Shing's offices after the attack and beating and forcibly removes a tape with incriminating evidence. He and Ho blackmail Shing for $2 million for its return, but Ho demonstrates that he retains (or has rediscovered) his integrity by informing Kit where the drop will occur. In the final gunfight, Ho is wounded and is trapped with Kit by Shing and his gunmen.

Now Mark's role in the story becomes clearer. Instead of leaving with the money as he and Ho had planned, he dramatically returns to rescue Ho and Kit. Ho had stayed behind from loyalty to Kit, and now Mark presents to both, but especially to Kit, a lesson in loyalty and self-sacrifice. In a key shot, Mark brings Ho and Kit together, berating Kit for not understanding that Ho's recent actions stem from his fraternal loyalty. Woo poses Mark between and above the two brothers, in a perfect analogue of his role as the apex of a triangle of oppositions. He is viciously gunned down by Shing and his men as he finishes his harangue of the brothers. The film ends with Kit lending Ho his gun, in an illegal but peculiarly moral act, allowing him to avenge Mark by shooting Shing, who has tried to turn himself into the police. Ho then handcuffs himself to permit Kit to arrest him and thus to advance his career and restore their relationship.

A Better Tomorrow reworks generic conventions into a brash, black-humored mix. Though recognizably a generic crime film, with typical iconography—guns, cars, large sums of money and of course Chow's emblematic trenchcoat[13]—*A Better Tomorrow* displays Woo's characteristic tendency to cross generic lines.[14] One example will illustrate this penchant. When Kit accompanies his fiancée to her long-awaited cello recital, she becomes flustered, totally flubs the recital and then breaks a taxi window accidentally with her cello case. McDonagh criticizes this inset as an instance of Woo's "crude comedy" (47), but its admittedly broad handling of quasi-slapstick elements and its bordering on farce actually fall into line with Woo's interest: the highlighting of relational dynamics. Kit must be shown, by association with Jackie, as ingenuous and clumsy, wet behind the ears, and furthermore as an awkward fit into the world of music and art inhabited by her.[15] That is, his callowness is stressed even as his potential as a cop is adumbrated; he does not fit well into her world, as his preoccupations intrude too heavily. The farcical aspect points up the absurdity of his assumption of a normal, student-like life until the deeper questions concerning his family are resolved (and probably not even then).

The music audition scene appears merely jarring or heavy-handed, but in fact it functions centrally within the language of *A Better Tomorrow*. Woo establishes the orientation of the film from the outset, with a striking opening shot, unexplained and unmotivated. We see a sequence in which a shadowy character is pursued down a tunnel, falling after the sound of a gunshot. Our suspicion that the sequence may be a dream (because of the unreal visual tone, lent by using gauzy lens filters) is confirmed when a man jolts up in bed, sweating, and screams, "Kit!" We next see this man as the credits roll, entering an office building with a companion, and we gradually learn that the man is Ho Sung-tse. The dream at the beginning concerns his brother Kit, whom we will soon meet, and about whom, we now know, he worries.

But at least as important as the narrative significance of the dream (communicating to us the information that Ho has a brother about whom he frets) is its position in the film. We are not told when the dream occurs, so we cannot orient it within the narrative, other than as an informative piece or as a tone-setting device. Perhaps the dream is a flash-forward or a premonition, as Kit is shot later in the film; but if so, it is misleading, as it seems to imply that Kit is killed, when in fact he is not (at least not until the sequel, which presumably was not yet composed at this time). The dream thus fits into the category of an atemporal narrative device; that is, its function is other than a purely narrative one, since it does not fit precisely into the plot.

The importance of this dream would appear to be thematic and tonal. It introduces the major conflict within its focal character, Ho, whose ethical dilemma about leading a life of crime in the Triads stems from his Confucian loyalty to his father and brother. The dream serves as a foreshadowing of a possible disastrous outcome resulting from Ho's allegiance to the Triads. It also sets the film's often violent and nightmarish tone.

Such scenes may seem jarring, but Woo is criticized in much the same way that Sam Fuller and Douglas Sirk were: Their taste did not seem to fit accepted norms. It wasn't "even" enough, or it was too quirky, or it was too "primitive." In fact, directors such as these—and to the list I might add Joseph H. Lewis and Edgar G. Ulmer—are stimulating in their brashness, or perhaps, in their readiness to experiment and to violate norms. Despite the polished technique often found in Woo's work, and the frequent brilliance of shot composition and editing, the viewer often feels that the director is almost rashly "pushing the envelope."

But Woo's work is in fact quite carefully worked out, although this is often the result of seemingly spontaneous decisions.[16] (This virtue, of course, is precisely what allows him to be *outré* at times.) A good example of methodical treatment of scene composition appears in Woo's presentation of two of the important father-figures in respective encounters with their sons or protegés. In the first of these scenes, we see Ho visiting his real father, who is in a hospital bed. Ho is therefore shown in a relationship of relative physical strength compared to his father. When Shing meets with his "father," Mr. Yiu, similarly Shing is normally shown standing while Yiu is seated; or, in one important scene near the end of the film, they are shown standing and facing each other, and Shing's height points up the contrast between his new position of dominance and Yiu's shrinking in importance. When Shing treacherously shoots Mr. Yiu, again Yiu is shown seated and Shing as standing. While both Shing and Ho are shown as physically dominant with respect to their elders, Woo only emphasizes by means of this parallel the sharp contrast between Ho's conscience-stricken relationship with his father and Shing's opportunistic exploitation of the trust vouchsafed him by Yiu.

The well-made *A Better Tomorrow* is a very flashy gangster film with some of Woo's best scenes. Mark's revenge on the gang members who tried to kill Ho is visually innovative—Mark hides automatics in flowerpots so as to be able to reach them as he exits—and a quintessential Woo gunfight, with paired automatics blasting, clips dropping, shell cases popping onto the floor, bodies contorting, and hairbreadth escaping from death by the hero. Still, *A Better Tomorrow* does not totally transcend its material or its genre. It is rather in its exaggeration of generic elements that this movie succeeds.

The film also flirts with autobiographical allegory. It contains references to Woo's then-recent career history. In fact, the film might be read as an allegorical text into which Woo inserts his own frustrations and personal concerns. This kind of critical approach meshes with Woo's own declarations about his films and characters, as he has claimed that he "sees himself" in Chow's heroes and that he has injected his own life history into films such as *Bullet in the Head*. By examining the allusions to Woo's life in *A Better Tomorrow*, we will see that the film is something other than a straight action movie.

The film concentrates on family and personal relationships, emphasizing the Confucian hierarchy of loyalty and service. On one level, *A Better Tomorrow* can be read as a straight gangster picture in the post–*Godfather* mode—that is, as a rather melodramatic romanticization of life among the Triads, with "good" bosses (Mr. Yiu) and disloyal and loyal "sons" (Shing and Ho). Or it might be seen, as we have noted, as a latter-day version of chivalric or romance novels such as *Water Margin*, with the knights replaced by gangsters and policemen, on opposing sides of a war in which justice must prevail. But a third level of interpretation is also possible, and it is this level which helps give Woo's films their peculiar depth and allure. This is the autobiographical, allegorical level, in which the film's plot and characters are actually surrogates for the director's own preoccupations.

How does this level of meaning operate in *A Better Tomorrow*? First, we must bear in mind that the structure about to be examined is not a rigorous analogy. The film does not precisely mirror Woo's career. But it does have enough teasing similarities to draw our attention.

The most important clue to the autobiographical or confessional nature of the film is the reference to Taiwan in the script. Taiwan plays an important role here. Ho and Shing take an ill-fated trip to Taiwan to close a deal for Mr. Yiu, Shing betrays Ho there, and Ho is captured to

spend three years in prison. These incidents, of course, can be read on a
straightforward level as part of the action plot. If we consider, though,
that the bad deal could just as well have taken place in Hong Kong, or
Macao, or perhaps even Japan, we might question why Taiwan was chosen. Perhaps the choice is related to Woo's own biography. Woo had
been sent to Taiwan by the producers at Cinema City. He was shunted
into an administrative job there and became very frustrated. Pleading to
be allowed to direct, he was given two minor projects, *Run Tiger Run* and
The Time You Need a Friend; these became two films of which he is still
rather ashamed. Finally, he returned from Taiwan and was given the
opportunity at another production company, Tsui Hark's Film Workshop, to direct *A Better Tomorrow*.

Like Ho in the film, then, Woo was sent to Taiwan on a project. He
found himself "betrayed" by his bosses (here the analogy is not exact, since
Ho is not betrayed by Yiu but by Shing, his junior) and "imprisoned" in
work on two dead end films; his stay in Taiwan, like Ho's, was about
three years. Woo also plays a significant role in the film as the Taiwanese
policeman who captures Ho and who follows his case. If we accept the
Ho character as a Woo surrogate or double, then the cop in the film
becomes a doppelgänger figure for Ho-Woo, a "second self," in C. F.
Keppler's terms, who functions as a psychic censor. He admonishes Ho
on his release not to come back to the prison, as if Woo were telling himself not to return to his severe difficulties in Taiwan after leaving there
(as, in fact, he did not).

When Ho does return to Hong Kong, he decides to go straight,
avoiding the Triad contacts he had once maintained, and of course
eschewing involvement in their counterfeit money operation. (Would it
be too much to say that, according to our reading, Cinema City, the
Triad's "real" counterpart, was making artistically counterfeit films?) He
gets a job working at a taxi service run by and staffed by ex-convicts. The
character of ex-con Ken (Kenneth Tsang Ko, Woo's friend in real life)
gives him a break, hiring him under a "tough love" regime. Here we might
see a parallel with Tsui Hark's extending a hand to Woo by giving him
the project to direct which became, of course, the very film in which these
parallels are to be found.

Ho eventually runs across Mark, his former friend who had avenged
his betrayal and his father's murder. Mark was partially disabled in the
revenge hit, having lost full use of one leg, and has come down from his
former position of prominence in the Triad to a very lowly job as a car
washer and janitor at the garage where Shing keeps his car. The roles at
the beginning of the film have been reversed: Shing is now Mark's "senior,"

and he treats him quite badly. We might draw an analogy to Chow's hiring by Woo for *A Better Tomorrow*. Woo went to bat for him (as Ho does, in a different context, for Mark) with a true flash of intuition, perhaps seeing within him the potential for real stardom. And, of course, Chow did go on to become a huge star. Mark, not so fortunate, dies after saving Ho and Kit from Shing's men. But even he achieves a kind of stardom, becoming a hero for a younger generation of Triad members and hangers-on, as we see in *A Better Tomorrow II*.

The parallels between Woo's career and *A Better Tomorrow* are extended by Tsui Hark's appearance in the film. He plays a dismissive, bored-looking music director who suffers through an awkward, failed audition by Kit's fiancée, and, with injury added to insult, is nearly brained by her cello when she swings it accidentally, breaking the window of the car in which he is leaving the audition. Although here the character played by Tsui is not directly counterposed to the Woo character, Tsui's presence in the film represents another "censor" or authority figure, given our knowledge that he not only produced but may have actually initiated *A Better Tomorrow*.

After the huge success of *A Better Tomorrow*,[17] Woo was encouraged to make another film of this type. He had written a prequel to the first film, detailing Mark's life in Vietnam and Hong Kong. But he was convinced by Tsui Hark, who had written a *roman à clef* script about producer Dean Shek's ill-treatment at the hands of his Cinema City partners, to direct a sequel. So *A Better Tomorrow II* was filmed. While the original intention may not have been to treat the material in a tongue-in-cheek fashion, this sequel, though mixed and muddled in tone, does deal with the heroes of the previous film as pop heroes or culture idols.

Woo's heart appears not to have been totally in this project. He did not like the concept, which uses Shek's "exile" to New York by his callous partners as a subtext for the film's story of the betrayal of Mr. Lung, an erstwhile Triad leader, by his "friends" (Woo, personal interview, 8 November 1995). Lung, played by Dean Shek, leaves Hong Kong for New York only to suffer the grief of his daughter's murder by Ko, his "friend" and partner. Descending into catatonia, he is placed in an asylum, rescued by Ken (Mark's heretofore unknown twin brother) and, with Ho and Ken, takes revenge on Ko and his men, who have meantime also killed Kit.

The film is hardly an artistic success. David Chute exaggerates only somewhat in remarking that "[t]his is a film that knows no shame" (Chute, *The Killer* 40), and tries to apologize for this quality by characterizing it as part of the film's appeal. But not much can be said for the film as a whole, although it does work part of the time, and even contains some of Woo's better moments. Much of the reason for this failure may be the fact that it was released in a severely and hastily cut version. As Woo explains,

> [The] original cut was two hours and 40 minutes, which was pretty long. You know, the original concept was pretty close to *Godfather Part II*. [There was] more story on Chow Yun-fat and Leslie Cheung—because while I'm shooting I realized that Dean Shek's part wouldn't work. But Tsui Hark insisted on having him, and after we shot the whole film, we got the release date [as] one week. So we were forced to cut—we cut about one hour of footage, so we had to separate into six or seven groups, I cut, Hark cut the first two reels, and I cut three or four, and the editor cut another two or three reels, and I never had the chance to put it together and look. I saw it in the theater—I was shocked—why was the movie so choppy? Some of the story didn't make sense [personal interview, 8 November 1995].

The film simply should not have been released in such a butchered state. Nevertheless, even as it stands, we can see glimpses of what it might have been as well as moments when it functions on a level worthy of its director and stars. And, though it was not the hit that *A Better Tomorrow* had been, it was not a financial failure either:

> And so the film turned out to be a box office disappointment. I think it only made 22 million [HK]. The first one made 34, this one only did 22. But the film did very well overseas, it did not lose money, it's still making a lot of money. It's not a flop in any sense [Chang, personal interview, 2 March 1996].

A Better Tomorrow II features some of Woo's more elaborate set pieces. The battle in the Victor Hotel is one of Chow's best, and the closing fight stands apart as one of the bloodiest and "over-the-top" in all of Woo's films. This battle, fought with a real ferocity that only briefly lapses into comedy, when Ken throws grenades hidden in his coat, is a revenge killing which leaves little space for heroism. It is not a fight for survival, as in *The Killer* or *Hard Boiled*. The motive is vengeance for the deaths of loved ones, and so the killing is done with a particular anger and coldness to suffering that truly make this a shocking scene. Ho even uses *kung fu* and a samurai sword, in more than a nod to actor Ti Lung's career as a martial arts star. This scene, incidentally, was quoted in Tony Scott's *True Romance* (1993), in which one of the two main characters (Patricia Arquette) watches it bemusedly on television.

The scene also includes a signature face-off between Ken and Chong, the hired killer for Ko. One of the rare moments in the film when the viewer experiences that special frisson, the eerie tension that signals Woo at his most intense and otherworldly, the scene is both an opportunity for Chow to display his strangely magnetic animality, dropping his character's mask of charm to reveal the snarling Triad killer, and a clever recasting of samurai elements. The two gunmen, in a gesture which will reappear in *Hard Boiled* (in the final confrontation between Mad Dog and Tony), lower their guns, touching the barrels to the floor, recalling samurai movies whose duels often begin with swords at a tense rest.[18] Here, the two men signal their mutual professional respect by making the contest into a kind of quick-draw, sliding their guns across the room in a curious trade, thereby underlining the opponents' essential similarity, and then rushing to pick them up (one might be reminded as well of the last gunfight between the Richard Dysart villain and the Eastwood avenger-hero in Clint Eastwood's *Pale Rider* [1985]).

Despite some fine Woo moments of this kind, though, the movie falls flat, partially because its tone is uncertain and mixed. Woo says that he wanted the film to be "like a comic book," functioning as a serialization of already worked-over material (Woo, personal interview, 8 November 1995). This explains the odd and intriguing scene in mid-film when Ho talks to a character whose appearance seems unmotivated: a cartoonist who has apparently made a comic strip from Mark's adventures with Ho and Kit. Who the artist is, and why Ho talks to him, are questions not answered in the film.[19] Still, the concept of these reluctant heroes' becoming characters in a comic strip, as pop legends in their own time, is promising and could, if anchored more solidly in the narrative, have lent a self-reflexive quality to this film. The characters could have been shown more convincingly and extensively as being conscious of their own status as pop heroes.[20]

But the major problems of *A Better Tomorrow II* were caused not by inattention or indecisiveness on the part of its director, but by the usual bane of creative artists in film: the budget. Woo, as we have seen, recounts that the studio wanted a release print ready in about seven days, and that the movie as it stood was over two hours, 40 minutes long.

Woo had reason to be, as he says, "shocked" at the film's disjointedness. In the existing cut, the transitions, for a Woo film, are extremely rough (for instance, between the New York episodes and the Hong Kong ending). Some scenes are difficult to understand, for example Ken's presence in the sanatorium where Lung is confined. How did Ken learn of this confinement, and how did he gain access to the hospital? I suspect also that, if Woo had been given more time to edit, he might well have cut some of Dean Shek's grosser and sillier displays of madness. And further editing could have tightened up some scenes, such as the confrontation with the Mafia in Ken's restaurant, which Woo said was "too long" (personal interview, 8 November 1995).

Woo also regretted that large parts of the plot had to be excised. He pointed especially to the film's detailing of the undercover investigation by Kit and Ho, now reduced to some interplay between Peggy (Regina Kent), Lung's ill-fated daughter, and Kit. One of the more incisive and promising scenes in the film, when Kit brings Peggy home to protect her and faces his pregnant wife without being able to tell her the truth, is not followed with any meaningful denouement. The tension between Kit and his wife is not resolved, nor does it build to an explosive head; it is simply not dealt with at any significant length.

A Better Tomorrow II is an artistic failure for Woo, but not one totally, or even chiefly, of his own making. He may fairly be criticized for a repeated reluctance to trim his movies, thus leaving the first cut overlong and giving the studio an excuse to intervene and snip injudiciously. This happened not only on *A Better Tomorrow II*, but also on *The Killer* (though not as severely) and on *Hard Target*.

In personal terms, the legacy of *A Better Tomorrow II*, and the production problems associated with it, concern Woo's friendship and professional association with Tsui Hark. Woo had written a prequel to *A Better Tomorrow*, recounting Mark's activities in Saigon and Hong Kong, and was planning to direct it, with Tsui producing, as *A Better Tomorrow III*. He learned that Tsui was going to direct the film himself. Woo was summarily out of the game; Tsui had apparently cooled towards Woo pursuant to the production problems on *A Better Tomorrow II*. Woo later turned his own prequel script into *Bullet in the Head* (Chute, supplements text, *The Killer*).

Woo's next film, *The Killer*, built on the generic emphases of *A Better Tomorrow* and its sequel, and concentrated these elements into a cultish mix of near-camp and riveting stylistic brilliance. We will examine this central film in Woo's *oeuvre* in the next chapter.

Chapter 6

The Killer:
Heroism Defeated

*I love the man that can smile in trouble, that can gather
strength from distress, and row brave by reflection. 'Tis the
business of little minds to shrink; but he whose heart is
firm, and whose conscience approves his conduct, will pursue his principles unto death.*

—Thomas Paine

*The drying up a single tear has more
Of honest fame than shedding seas of gore.*

—Lord Byron,
Don Juan (1823),
canto 8, stanza 3

The Killer is for many followers of John Woo's movies his most poetic
work. It may seem that Woo was destined to make this uniquely cross-
generic film, but the facts are otherwise. Its gestation was difficult; as with
many movies, its appearance as a final product, much less a work of art,
is nearly miraculous as a fact.

When Woo proposed the story for this film to his producer, Tsui
Hark, he had most recently come from the mixed results and contro-
versy surrounding *A Better Tomorrow II*. According to Terence Chang,
Woo was urged by actor and friend Chow Yun-fat to make another
film. Chow signed for the film as a work overload but took responsibility for doing so out of friendship for Woo (Chute, Supplement text, *The
Killer*; Chang, personal interview, 2 March 1996).[1] So, Chang said, Woo
"came up with the story of *The Killer*." Woo and Chow "proposed it to
Tsui Hark and Tsui said no." Tsui did not believe in the commercial
potential of the script, contending that "[n]obody wants to see a film
about a killer."

So Woo proceeded with the film that would, more than any other,
gain him fame overseas. With Chow already cast as the killer, Woo needed
especially to fill two other lead roles: the cop who would pursue and come

to understand the killer, and the unfortunate torch singer whose fate would be tied to the killer's.

For the cop, Woo preferred Danny Lee (Lee Sau-yin), who already had played numerous cop roles and was more or less identified with the type.[2] Woo had also known Lee since 1971 (Lee, telephone interview), when they had both worked for Shaw Brothers. For professional and personal reasons, Lee was a logical choice—and, as things turned out, a very fortuitous one. But, as with so much else with this film, an obstacle had to be overcome—a minor and tractable one:

> John wanted Danny Lee to play the other part. Danny Lee said, "I'm under exclusive contract as an actor to Cinema City. The only way for me to get out of this is [if Magnum,] my company, [is] involved in it. Then I can be in the film." So the film was financed 90 percent by Golden Princess, 10 percent by Magnum. Magnum is owned 51 percent by Golden Princess and 49 percent by Danny Lee. It was a Film Workshop production [Chang].

For the singer, Tsui preferred Cantopop singer and actress Sally Yeh (Yip Sin-man), who had appeared previously in his own *Peking Opera Blues* (1986). Woo went along with the choice, a decision that would cause him some headaches because of Yeh's later uncooperativeness, but nevertheless a choice that was also fortuitous for the film—Yeh's beauty and dramatic expressiveness, as well as her soulful rendition of the film's two "torch songs," added significantly to its emotional effect.

Even after the film was finished, its shooting having been challenging in itself, there were disagreements about its release. As Terence Chang recounted, Tsui expressed reservations about the finished film, objecting to its seeming campiness and melodrama:

> He wanted to cut out the Chow Yun-fat opening—to start the film with Danny Lee—and only use that part as a brief flashback, you know, Chow blinding the singer. John disagreed. He said, that's crucial for the story. It sets the mood for the whole thing.

But Woo prevailed, and the film was released. After its release in Taiwan, Chang said,

> It was cut to its present length. The new cut was much better.[3] It was down to about 110 minutes and it was released in Hong Kong in July. But unfortunately it was on the tail of the Tiananmen massacre, and people were very very sick of people shooting at each other, so it did not do too well in Hong Kong.

But the film "did well" for Woo's critical reputation, and ultimately for his career. The film's English title, we might say, implies its impact while encasing its complexity. The progression of Woo's work from the seemingly soapy pulp fiction of *A Better Tomorrow*, with its Sicilian Mafia undertones, is here replaced by an emphasis on the main character as defined by his profession. Evocative not only of Robert Siodmak's *The Killers* (1946) because of its title,[4] but more importantly of Jean-Pierre Melville's *Le Samouraï* in its privileging of the *métier* of the hero—and he is to be a peculiar kind of hero—the film centers on the effects, moral and physical, of the profession of contract killing on its practitioner. In a twist on the police procedural film, the methods used by the killer are depicted, including his choice of weapons. His business arrangements (receiving the contract and payment) are also shown to us, but we come to see that the "business" no longer appeals to this hit man. John (Chow Yun-fat)[5] is burned out, having become morally sensitized in a profession that cannot admit or afford sensitivity or compassion.

Woo keeps the film centered on John's dilemma from its opening shot of John receiving his putative last contract in a church. The near-blasphemous tension of sacred and profane is established here, as is the strangely vulnerable nature of the killer.

The title, though, is both ambiguous and ambivalent.[6] "The Killer" evidently refers to John (Chow Yun-fat), the assassin-for-hire. But the surface reveals other layers: John is, of course, a killer by profession, but he also "kills" indirectly, blinding Jenny (Sally Yeh), a cabaret singer, with the blow-back from his gun. And he "kills" morally, destroying his self-respect and spiritual core by leading the life of a cold-blooded murderer. Furthermore, the title may refer to the profession itself as a killer: the murderer of the soul and of friendships, his and Sidney Fung's. (Fung, an assassin whose gun hand is crippled, is played by Paul Chu Kong, who happens to be one of Chow's personal friends.) Finally, the title is ambivalent. It points in two directions—to John and to his double Li, the policeman played by Danny Lee.[7]

This Woo film, as much as any other, brings to the foreground the double motif, an element also present to varying degrees in *A Better Tomorrow*, *Bullet in the Head*, *Once a Thief* and *Hard Target*. *The Killer* is so effective precisely because the opposition between John and the policeman is so clearly established. Woo has noted his preference for triangular relationships between characters, and certainly one again sees the kind of triangular structure established in *A Better Tomorrow*. The difference here is chiefly in the importance placed on the woman. In *A Better Tomorrow*, the female lead is important as support and as a moral corrective for

Kit; Jackie serves as a bridge between Kit and Ho. In *The Killer*, Jenny is little more than an emblem or a projection of John's guilt feelings. Her blindness is the accidental result of one of his amoral acts. She is a helpless victim character much like Mr. Lung during part of *A Better Tomorrow II*, a catalyst for the moral regeneration of John, as is Lung for Ken. She is less a character than a surface, a plot device rather than an active element. Her blindness functions as a kind of displaced projection of John's moral condition. When Jenny is blinded, John can "see" at last. He finally can find meaning for his formerly useless and pernicious life, and he sees clearly what has become of him as a human being.

The relationship between Jenny, surface character that she is, and John is nonetheless artistically quite intriguing. Since John sees a picture of Jenny before the gunfight, and also hears her sing, the ties between them are one-sided at the outset, with the male as privileged viewer (or listener).[8] The treatment here echoes films such as *Laura* and *Portrait of Jennie*,[9] but Woo does not focus on Jenny as is the case with the women in these two films—or, in another sense, with *Vertigo*. Jenny, unlike Laura, is not an enigma to be unraveled, or, like Jennie in the eponymous film, a lost love to be rekindled. The emphasis here is shifted almost totally onto John and his spiritual regeneration or *crise de conscience*. Jenny's functional status is signaled in part by her association with symbolic imagery, seen usually in an ironic way—her dress, during the scene of her blinding, carries imprints of card designs (diamonds, normally a symbol of good fortune and permanence—also, of course, of commitment); she has a cat, but many less than nine lives; and she is repeatedly shown singing nostalgic, near-campy songs of loss.[10] She is rarely shown without either John and/or the policeman Li present, thus underscoring her lack of independent existence and importance.

Jenny, as a hinge between John's and the policeman's worlds, is also the interface between their two Janus heads. John and Li gradually discover that they have a peculiar and combative spiritual link. Before discussing their relationship in more detail, it will be necessary to present each one as a character. This presentation will do much to illuminate Woo's development of character in his films and his treatment of venerable motifs like the double.

John is first shown in a church, apparently praying or meditating. The camera tracks from the rear, focusing on the altar, with its modernistic crucifix. The viewer is at first unsure of the import of this shot; only slowly is the figure of John revealed, and then he is shown talking to another man (Sidney) whom we discover to be an agent of his employer. John is being hired to do a "hatchet job," a contract hit. Asked by Sidney if he believes in God, he professes disbelief, saying, "No, but I enjoy the tranquility here" (ch. 2). We now gain our first insight into John, thanks to Chow's subtle facial expressiveness. We somehow do not quite believe his denial, sensing rather that he protests too much and that we are in the presence of a conflicted spirit. (This is communicated as well by his hesitancy at taking the contract.)

Li is first introduced fully to us in an unmarked police car, in plainclothes, heading for a rendezvous with gunrunners. He is accompanied by his partner. Woo has thus established a parallel between the two characters. Both John and Li are first identified for us in connection to their professions, one a contract killer, the other an undercover cop. While John is presented as a somewhat anomalous killer (taking contracts in a church, preferring tranquility), Li is given a "crazy" aspect. His partner Chang (Kenneth Tsang) cautions him to settle down, or they'll think he's from the "nut house" (ch. 6). This remark could be interpreted as merely a throwaway rib at Li, but in fact, as we will discover, Li is something of a misfit in the police department. He speaks his mind a little too freely and is more interested in results than in procedure—a hothead, in other words. Later, Chang asks him if he is "nuts." Like John, Li is provided with no real back story. We know nothing about his family or friends. Both are totally creatures of their work, and it is only when they begin to step outside their roles that they will meet with real trouble.

These two characters, and their professional partners, revolve around Jenny. The pivotal figure in the film, she has been introduced in the nightclub scene, when John inadvertently injures her. In the released version of *The Killer* in Cantonese, John meets Jenny only indirectly until after he has blinded her. Woo originally wanted to open the film with their having a prior relationship.[11] The existing Cantonese opening, though not the director's first choice, does serve to establish a connection between John and Jenny and to set a lyrical tone for the film.

One of the special appeals of Woo films, a facet that makes them different and unique as genre works, is the way they tie into film history.[12] Woo is not just a plunderer of film tradition, or an alluder for allusion's sake. He states often that he is conscious of working within a tradition, whether it be of martial arts films, Chinese historical romance or Hollywood genre. This type of appeal, naturally, is easy game for film buffs, but Woo's films are not just mines for trivia-hunting or self-reflexive cuteness. Instead, Woo is a director who works with a serious consciousness of film history; his movies cause us to re-evaluate and study that history.

The Killer, then, echoes other films. The movie is indeed a sustained homage to *Le Samouraï*, and may also contain other assimilated and thus less than consciously employed imagery. For instance, the way Inspector Li takes his gun out when chasing a killer in the tram always recalls for me Bullitt's similar action at the airport; but the scene also comments freshly on the subway chase scene in *The French Connection*, providing the viewer with a new canvas filled with cinematic action. And the scene *is* a deliberate allusion to *All That Jazz*, a reference that we will soon consider. Furthermore, Woo is so imbued with film culture and technique, film imagery is such a part of his natural language, that he appears to echo other films even when he is not conscious of doing so, or when the echo is a mere coincidence.[13] Woo, as it were, discovers imagery independently and inserts it into his work; to many critics, this process appears to be little more than imitation.

What is the effect of all this? Some would certainly say that Woo is nothing more than a camp artist, or that his films lack originality.[14] Neither of these assertions is accurate, but of more interest here is the placement of Woo in generational terms. Woo lists among his "top ten" films only two movies prior to 1960: *Citizen Kane* and *Seven Samurai*. The rest are films from the 1960s and 1970s: one, *West Side Story*, stands out from the list because it is not usually thought of as a "director's film": instead, it represents for Woo, as for many of his generation, an epitome of a certain type of youth sensibility. The others are, strikingly, all products of the "American New Wave": Coppola (*The Godfather Part II*), Scorsese (*Mean Streets, Raging Bull*), Kubrick (*Dr. Strangelove, 2001: A Space Odyssey*), and Peckinpah (*The Wild Bunch*). Two of these directors, Coppola and Scorsese, are products of American film schools and consciously engage in film allusion, much as Woo does; the other two are "maverick" directors, although not similar to each other in their approaches and concerns.

Woo is quite consistent in noting his favorite films. They are of a piece with his avowed "romantic" outlook. By "romantic" Woo appears to mean "redolent of romance," that is, deriving from the romance form. He uses the term repeatedly in conversation about his movies, but almost never in the popularly accepted sense of "love-oriented." Rather, he emphasizes values associated with early European Romanticism:[15] individualism, sentiment, violation of accepted norms in art, subjectivity and open form. Without exception—save perhaps *Seven Samurai* and *2001*, almost classically disciplined films—the movies in Woo's list have very Romantic structures. *Mean Streets* and *Raging Bull* both depict Byronic or Shelleyan hero-figures battling lone and futile struggles against indifferent power-structures. *The Wild Bunch* features a band of outlaws—a supremely romantic plot kernel—sacrificing themselves as a gesture, from loyalty to a friend and outrage at the image of what they could have become (Gen. Mapache, the Mexican leader). *Citizen Kane* is more cynical, questioning the ethics of its antiheroic title character, but nevertheless noting loss of love as his motivation. *West Side Story* romanticizes and musicalizes gang members and the immigrant experience. And *2001*, though classically told, is basically a narrative emphasizing the futility of scientific overreaching, a theme found in Romantic works such as Mary Shelley's *Frankenstein*.

So, Woo's choice of a character like John (or Sidney, or Inspector Li) in *The Killer* is not solely commercial nor due only to his interest in pulp narrative. It is deeply anchored in his fascination with romanticism. He stresses this point, referring not just to movie history but to his sources in Chinese narrative. For Woo, film stories about heroic figures should reflect characters such as the bandit or military heroes of *Water Margin* or *Romance of the Three Kingdoms*. In *Water Margin*, a group of outlaw-heroes flee to the mountains to combat unjust government.[16] *Romance of the Three Kingdoms* romanticizes the doomed struggle of pro–Han forces against the vicissitudes of history (see Chapter 1, n. 2).

With such a perspective, *The Killer* is not merely—or at all—an exercise in pulp sensationalism. Nor is it only a brilliant display of directorial fireworks. It is essentially an homage to romanticists such as Scorsese, Jean-Pierre Melville, Kubrick (the early Kubrick of *Killer's Kiss* [1955]), Coppola, De Palma and, of course, Peckinpah. The film fits solidly into this brand of movie tradition as well as into the progression of movies that Woo has made since *A Better Tomorrow*. *The Killer* also fits well with the "swashbuckling" tradition in Hollywood as represented by many of the films of Errol Flynn, Douglas Fairbanks and Tyrone Power. Woo celebrates the chivalric virtues of such films in *The Killer*, with his two seemingly invincible (but not invulnerable) heroes who best legions of often indistinguishable villains.

The heroic or chivalric content of *The Killer* is more ramified than a first inspection would indicate. Of course, the two leads (and also Sidney) are "heroic" in their loyalty and selflessness. They are indeed like the *Water Margin* "knights" who shoulder the burden of fighting injustice.[17] But these characters are linked in another sense. They are knights, yes, but vassals too. They have all "betrayed" their masters: Inspector Li by not accepting authority, John by giving his identity away, and Sidney by not killing John for his mistake. The film is usually discussed in reference to its paired heroes (reflecting its title), but it is really better understood by examining its three main agonists (Li's partner serves to balance Sidney but is not nearly as realized or important as a character). These three are not precisely knights in our Western sense; they are more akin to *ronin*[18] or ninjas or the assassin societies of Chinese novels. Indeed, they are very much like *ronin* who rebel against or kill an unjust *daimyo* (master). At one pole is Li, who ignores inflexible orders (as does Kit in *A Better Tomorrow* or Tequila in *Hard Boiled*), at the other is John, who pursues his "*daimyo*" (Johnny Weng) after Weng has tried to kill him. Sidney falls in between the two, as he tries to respect both the code (an assassin who betrays his anonymity must die) and his friend John, and tries both to ignore his "*daimyo's*" duplicity and, indeed, psychosis, and to follow his orders legalistically.

The *Killer* highlights the relationship between authority figures and "subjects." Even John must follow authority in a sense, or at least he does not have the independence that his skill and his status as a contractor— have gun, will travel—would seem to grant him. None of the heroic characters is an independent agent. By resisting authoritarian structures or, as Woo puts it, trying to "beat the system," they gain moral and spiritual stature.

More than this is involved, though. Underpinning *The Killer*, and the chivalric novel, is the Confucian ethos. Though subjected to adaptation during the "neo–Confucian" era of the T'ang, Sung and Ming dynasties (c. 950–1550), still the Confucian ethic prescribes a compact of mutual respect between the just ruler and his subjects or subordinates.[19] The police, Li's superiors, violate this compact by their too strict adherence to "the book"—a common feature of "rogue cop" films (from *Bullitt* to *Lethal Weapon*), but relevant here nonetheless—and thus by not tempering their discipline with tolerance. Their violation of Confucian prescriptions is not as extreme as Weng's: he fits the paradigm of the unjust, grasping ruler who should be overthrown. Of course, Johnny is not exactly John's ruler, but he does have a proprietary or contractual relationship with him. John's killer character is placed into a parallel status with other heroic figures like the Duke of Chou and Robin Hood, who see another loyalty than that owed to a master who has not merited that loyalty.

All three characters, as well, bear heroic markers. As Kehr notes in respect of Tequila in *Hard Boiled*, a wound or injury is the mark or badge of a hero ("the red badge of courage"), the evidence of his passage through a trial (Kehr, Commentary, *Hard Boiled* ch. 21): as a mythographer might say, the secular version of stigmata. John receives his scars in the battle that injures Jenny (thus, his heroism is flawed and shown to have too high a price). Li's wounds come later, during the final battles, but he only becomes a "true hero" for Woo when he understands and empathizes with his prey (John) and throws in his lot with him: or, expressed another way, when he comes to understand himself and stops seeing John as his enemy. Sidney's old scar, his disabled hand, is a badge, a liability and a disqualification. He does not belong to the heroic cadre until he can rediscover his true friendship and loyalty to John. He can then ignore or compensate for his crippled gun hand and die in a just cause. His scars of battle eventually prove fatal, but, like Lancelot returning to help King Arthur in his last battle, he has rejoined his erstwhile friend.

All this discussion of heroes and chivalric myth in *The Killer* may seem exaggerated or overblown. (Perhaps, in a sense, it is; the film itself is exaggerated and overblown.) But Kehr is quite right in saying that critics or viewers who see Woo as a camp artist are missing the point. Kehr (Commentary, *Hard Boiled* ch. 23) claims that Woo is totally "sincere"; perhaps we could amend the evaluative "sincere" to "straightforward" or "transparent" (though not in a negative sense). Woo is a thorough romantic who does not engage in ironic parody in films like *The Killer*. As Woo himself has written, "I often feel that I have to hide the romantic side of my nature because people—even friends—would regard me with suspicion if I showed it. So I put all my romance in my films" (Woo, "Chinese" 61). Those who perceive such a man as a parodist (in the usual sense) are feeding his films with their own prejudices. Probably they see the Tarantino in Woo instead of what they *should* see, the vestiges of Woo in Tarantino. Woo is not Tarantino; he does not appropriate only to parody.

If parody or camp statement were Woo's goal, or if his films were nothing but nests of influences, one would expect his allusions to be both numerous and easy to tease out. They are neither as numerous nor as easy to discern as many have assumed. In conversations with me about *The Killer*, Woo repeatedly downplayed the role of influence, although he was not slow to admit or even to volunteer its presence when justified. I soon concluded that my "allusion-hunting," like that of some critics who have written about Woo's films, was leading me down a stony path. I could only extract from Woo a few admissions or claims of strong influence and borrowing. He mentioned a few films such as *The Shining, Butch Cassidy and the Sundance Kid* (1969), *Le Cercle rouge*, and of course *Le Samouraï* and a Ken Takakura film whose title he could not remember at the time.[20] But my attempts to find references to *Bullitt* and *The Godfather Part II*, for example, usually were met with an expression of kindly bewilderment, a friendly chuckle or, if I insisted, a shrugged, smiling "Maybe a little bit." And both Woo and Terence Chang have pointed out that Sirk's *Magnificent Obsession* (1954), the putative model for *The Killer*, could not possibly be that model, as Woo had seen no Sirk films before making *The*

Killer. He does not recall, either, having seen the earlier version of *Magnificent Obsession* (John M. Stahl, 1935; with Irene Dunne and Robert Taylor).

We should examine here one of the references to which Woo especially drew my attention in *The Killer*, for here we will discover some of the truth about Woo's allusions to other films. *The Shining* is the source for this allusion.[21] This reference, to the blood deluge from the elevator during one of the boy Danny's "shinings" (paranormal visions) is placed near the beginning of *The Killer*, after John has carried out his contract and has blinded Jenny. In both cases, the outflow of blood is the emblem of a terrible, nearly repressed incident: the murder of the family in *The Shining*, casting a penumbra of guilt and horror over the almost deserted hotel; and, in *The Killer*, the awful occasion of Jenny's blinding. In Woo's image, Jenny literally "sees red": her damaged corneas have shut off external reality from her, but her memories and fears are projected onto her internal mindscreen. That the image is less powerful than Kubrick's is in no small part due purely to technical factors (Woo, Commentary, *The Killer* ch. 4). Probably the less-than-successful results were due to budgetary limitations, causing the filming method used (see n. 23) not to be well executed.

The image, as Woo constructs it, also demonstrates that his borrowing from other films is not simply copying; neither is it parody in any usual sense of that word.[22] In Kubrick's film, the deluge was an undifferentiated mass which suggested some natural force, overwhelming in its elementalism. But Woo shows Jenny's visualization, that is, her subjective perception and memory of her blinding, as a melding of the blood splash or visual effect that she might have seen when the blow-back hit her, and her only clear memory of John, standing posed with gun in hand and wearing an enigmatic expression. His body is dissolved by the red splash, as if his reality were tenuous for Jenny, and also as if her visual field were breaking up.[23] The image both denies and affirms his reality. Like an image immersed in film emulsion, he shudders and deliquesces, but he is, more importantly, the subject of a strong statement about his status. Woo's image shockingly expresses John's identity with the effects of his trade as well as his rigid, mannequin-like insensitivity to those effects. Again, though, his unreality is demonstrated. He has no content, being a hollow vessel—morally speaking—who has but one dimension.

Such a complex image is not the product of a filmmaker "shamelessly" borrowing from others' work. Nor is it campy, comic book or pulp indulgence. It is the work of a director who has matured artistically so that he can assimilate others' images and ideas, using them as raw material for

his own creativity. Of course, Woo also pays tribute to Kubrick by borrowing his concept.

In *The Killer*, Woo acknowledges influences but is not dominated by
them; nor does he drop their names in throwaway fashion. The film is of
course an extended gloss on *Le Samouraï* and, to a degree, on *Le Cercle
rouge*. Contrary to critical commonplace, it has nothing to do with
Magnificent Obsession. It does derive some ethos and imagery from *The
Wild Bunch*. Typically, though, Woo's allusions are unexpected and rather
quirky. Though, for instance, it is true that the final gunfight is indebted
somewhat to *Butch Cassidy and the Sundance Kid* (the back-to-back pose
of the heroes about to endure martyrdom), it is also a fact that the context for the image has very little to do with the George Roy Hill film.
John and Li are not on the run; more importantly, their friendship is not
of long standing. (In fact, such friendship is difficult in Woo films. Both
The Killer and *Hard Boiled* feature quickly established friendships between
men, evolving so much like romances that some critics have jumped to
label then homoerotic.) In any case, the imagery here is quite distinct
from that of *Butch Cassidy and the Sundance Kid*; only the sense of doom
or futility is similar. But even here Woo borrows with a difference—what
really interests him is the image of the two back-to-back, and of course
the romanticism of their courageous stand, and not so much the need to
refer to some film model. And we should note that when John and Li set
themselves back-to-back, neither they nor the audience (unlike that of
Butch Cassidy and the Sundance Kid) conclude that they are sallying forth
to certain death. On the contrary, they appear nearly invincible, and the
viewer almost expects both to survive. Thus, the scene of John's death
becomes poignant, and justified, in a way that the rather tinnily rendered
end of Butch and Sundance—not really very interesting people, after all—
does not.

Again, a part of what interests Woo here is the look of the two characters back-to-back, or the appearance of heroic masculine solidarity
against overwhelming odds. Although, as Michael MacCambridge has
perceptively noted, the gunfight at the end of *The Killer* might well look
like what Butch and Sundance would have met if Hill had shown the fight
after they went out the door (MacCambridge 7), the comparison ultimately falls apart because the back-to-back shot in *The Killer* appears
after most of the assailants have been dispatched. As with some of Woo's
appropriations from other sources, the reference is not as broad or as con-
tent-filled as we might expect.

Of a different nature is the legitimately pop reference in the famous
pistol dance in *The Killer*. Woo says that he got the idea for this setup

from *Spy vs. Spy*.[24] And though the similarity may seem rather esoteric, other than the general physical identity of Li and John, rather like the comically opposed double figures of the *Mad* strip, in fact the allusion fits neatly into Woo's universe.

Recently, the Cuban–born creator of this strip, Antonio Prohias, died in Miami at the age of 77. *Mad* editor Nick Meglin, who hired Prohias in 1960, told Noah Adams of *All Things Considered* that the characters were not "good" and "bad": "We thought of it as cold war. The white spy didn't win. The black spy didn't win. Both won and both lost. Every issue that we had an episode, two episodes, one would win in one and the other would win in the other" (Meglin, Interview, *All Things Considered*, 26 February 1998). The thematic similarity to Woo films is clear. His villains and heroes are neither all good nor all bad, and they both win and lose (that is, even when the hero "wins" he loses in some respect). The villains and heroes also exchange places in Woo's best work—as with John and Li, neither of which is totally "black" nor totally "white." And, as Woo comments, the two birds in the comic strip are not really mortal enemies (neither are John and Li): "The black bird and the white bird, they are always against each other, but deep in their heart they are friends" (Woo, Commentary, *The Killer* ch. 20).

Sometimes Woo's allusions are even richer in content. So it is with the tribute to *Le Cercle rouge* in *The Killer*, because this tribute is quite emotionally charged for the director. It points to a kind of moment that deeply inspires Woo, and not just to a nice touch in a film (the kind of allusion we see in the camerawork from *The Shining*).

Woo has referred to this tribute in the laserdisc text for *The Killer*. He also elaborated on it in discussions with me. The scene in *Le Cercle rouge* concerns an attempted robbery for which a marksman ex-cop, now down on his luck, is recruited:

> The scene is about Yves Montand's character. He's a loser. So Alain Delon, he comes to do a job, [there's a] security lock, it's quite a distance from the gate to the other side of the wall, and there's a keyhole on the lock. Delon knew Yves Montand was a great man, so Delon brings him back, and he will do the job for him. So [Montand] cleans up and dresses like a gentleman. It's very close to our Chinese chivalry, they appreciate each other and usually will do anything for a friend, will die for him. Well, when they do the job, Montand, he looks at the keyhole, he takes a tripod, he sets the gun on the tripod, and then he adjusts the sights and the distance and the height. And then, he's very well set, and through the telescope you can see the keyhole. So, he looks at the keyhole, and [he says to] Alain Delon, take a look, and he looks. Good. Yves Montand looks a while and smiles, suddenly he picks up the gun and fires! That

shot means he really comes back. That kind of moment always impressed me. If you set the gun perfectly, there's no emotion, but if you pick up a gun without any support, without any help, there's passion [personal interview, 8 November 1995].

Woo paid tribute to this extraordinary scene in the Dragon Boat scene in *The Killer*, when John shoots Tony Weng with three freehand rifle shots from a considerable distance, and in an important scene in *Hard Boiled* (titled, on the Criterion laserdisc, "The Red Circle") when Tequila detonates one of his .357 shells with a quick-draw shot.[25]

What especially interests Woo about the Montand scene is its motif of the resurgent hero. As Woo told me in the same interview, "This kind of thing always amazes me. It must be a comeback moment." We see this element, or this moment, in several of Woo's favorite films: Borrachón (Dean Martin) in *Rio Bravo*; Bennie (Warren Oates) fighting off the Mob in *Bring Me the Head of Alfredo Garcia*; Jake La Motta (Robert De Niro) rousing himself to defeat an opponent in *Raging Bull*. Woo is transfixed by the tension between the down-and-out loser, or potential loser, and the triumphant hero—even if he only triumphs for a moment. This is unmixed romanticism, right out of Liszt's *Les Préludes* or Hugo's *Les Misérables*, and is one of the keys to Woo's own neo-romanticism.

Also present in scenes such as these is a very Eastern element, or if one prefers, an intuitive one. Zen and its related disciplines in martial arts all emphasize the necessity of freeing oneself from one's own mind, allowing natural instinct and intuition to merge with physical training and discipline so that body and mind come into harmonious potential. In Woo's films, a good example of this is Tequila's .357 shot. When he tries to aim—that is, when he consciously thinks the shot through—he cannot execute. Only when he breathes deeply, relaxes and acts in an intuitive fashion is his shot effective. Although this scene is not comic, it does bring to mind the humorous scene in *Butch Cassidy and the Sundance Kid* when Sundance is asked to demonstrate his prowess for the old miner (Strother Martin) in Bolivia. He misses when trying to aim (that is, to think and plan), and only when he asks "Can I move now?" and draws from his holster does his full skill come into play.

Woo enjoys these moments in film and tries to include such elements in his own work. So, for example, one can see the Woo touch even in a compromised film like *Hard Target*, as we will see in Chapter 9. We might mention, for now, another such moment, from *The Killer*. This concerns Sidney, whose hand is now crippled. He is thought, like Dean Martin's Borrachón (a drunken ex-sheriff in *Rio Bravo*,) or like Wang Yu's Kang in Chang Cheh's *One-Armed Swordsman*, to be useless as a fighter, having lost his nerve and his physical capability. But he finds new purpose and resurgent ability after he rediscovers his friendship with John. In a sadly predetermined scene—we know that he will probably not escape— he rouses himself and kills several of Weng's gunmen who are holding him captive. Finally, he is overpowered and beaten so badly that he soon dies.

A very memorable instance of intuitive, Zen-like hand-eye coordination occurs soon after John's hit on Tony Weng, when he shows up at the beach for his rendezvous to collect the money. Johnny Weng has sent killers instead. We first see John get out of his powerboat and stroll up the beach. He waves to a little girl playing there; then we notice a puzzled expression on her face. The camera follows her eye-line, and we see a gleam in the trees above.[26] John, watching her, takes off his dark glasses and uses one of the lenses as a mirror, thus avoiding any signal that he has noticed anything amiss; he sees the gleam in the lens. Woo cuts to a close-up of the trees, and we see that a gunman is sighting in on John. John continues to walk forward slowly and then suddenly leaps, draws and fires repeatedly after the gunman misses him because of his sudden movement. Having killed the gunman, he whirls and kills another assailant, then another.[27]

Lastly, a strange such motif occurs in *A Better Tomorrow II*, a film that suffered serious damage due to time constraints and studio interference. One of the heroes, Mr. Lung (Dean Shek), has been rendered nearly catatonic because of his daughter Peggy's murder. Ken (Chow Yun-fat) takes him from a sanatorium and tries to rehabilitate him. Ko, the Triad boss who ordered Peggy's assassination, having learned of Lung's whereabouts, sends killers to New York. Ken fights them off in a spectacular gun battle in the appropriately named Victor Hotel. He literally has to drag Lung along with him. When Ken is wounded in the street, Lung suddenly comes to life, shouting Ken's name and returning to his old form (according to Ken, "The Lung of yester years [*sic*] could face anything"). He kills the remaining assassins and even causes their car to explode, while Ken laughs in relief.

Earlier we noted the presence of the double motif in *The Killer*. One of the great strengths of this film is its integration of such structural elements directly into its style. Woo uses editing, one of his most important tools, to underline the doubleness, the mirror-imaging, of the two main characters here. The editing serves to foreground the symbolism, and helps to make *The Killer* among the most self-reflexive of Woo's films. *The Killer* insists on bringing its double motif to the forefront, again and again. So, in two of the richest examples of doubling in the film, Woo violates continuity, or the 180–degree rule, of classical Hollywood style, in order to indicate that John and Li are substantially interchangeable. One of these scenes takes place in Sidney's apartment, at the beginning of a ferocious gun battle with Paul Yau and his men. John and Li end up temporarily on the floor, pointing their guns at each other in a scene often noted as a Woo signature. The other scene takes place after the gunfight with Yau, by the river, when John and Li finally begin to converse as friends. In both cases, instead of alternating with angle-reverse angle, that is, from the left shoulder of one subject to the right of the other subject, Woo edits from angle to identical angle, or from left to left, as if the characters were simply exchanging places or supplanting each other.

This type of device is a good example of "art-film narration" (the term is David Bordwell's), but Woo does not thereby slide into full-fledged art-film mode. It is not coincidental that Woo admires Coppola, Kubrick, Penn and Scorsese. All these directors fall more precisely into the category of artists who employ art-film technique but who remain grounded in more traditional narrative practice (see Bordwell 232). Much the same can be said of Woo, but his choice of techniques indicates quite clearly his pronounced sympathy for editing as a primary tool of filmmaking.

The doubling motif is melded in *The Killer* into another characteristic Woo procedure, namely, as Zigelstein says, his rehearsal of masculinity as performance. The combination of these elements is very clearly signaled in the *Spy vs. Spy* scene in Jenny's apartment when the two adversaries engage in a little dance, changing places visually with each other as they "waltz" through the room. The two even speak in performance terms, with Li claiming to have come "well prepared" (to "have his act together," so to speak) in order to avoid an encore of his prior failure to catch John after the beach battle.

This dimension of performance art is in fact an inherent aspect of *The Killer*, as it is of *Hard Boiled* and especially of *Once a Thief*. Though more explicitly detailed in *Face/Off*, as Zigelstein notes (10), where acting is itself the subject of the screenplay, certainly acting and performance are central to the presentation of masculinity in *The Killer*. When John plays his role as the killer, at the beginning of the film, he passes Jenny performing one of her Cantopop ballads. When he "goes on," that is, performs the hit on Weng's partner, Jenny is seriously injured, and her performances afterward are significantly limited—she sings while seated, as if restricted in her movements due to her poor vision, and seems almost to be singing for alms, taking in tips in a large mug. Also, her singing has become tied to John (that is, to his masculine force). She tells Li that she only sings, gives private performances, for John. Thus, the feminine performer's star declines as the masculine one (or ones, if we include Li, Sidney and their partners or enemies) is in the ascendant.

John's strategy as a killer is founded upon his performance of roles. He wears disguises, once for the hit on Tony Weng, and then to try to escape from Li and his associates at the airport. In the latter instance, he is aided by Sidney, who plays first the role of John and then of a drunken casting agent for movie companies, as he says facetiously to the police.

John's and Sidney's performances are complemented by Li's and Chang's. As with the airport escape, where Jenny is present and in fact first betrays John and then alerts him, Li's important "roles" are played either with Jenny (the feminine force in the film) present or intervening by proxy. Thus, after John dispatches Weng's killers in his apartment, Li comes to the scene and senses his presence ("It was him," he tells Chang). He sits in the chair we know to have been occupied by John and plays one of Jenny's songs on a tape deck. Her music, and thus her spiritual presence, forms a bridge between the two men, and furthermore enables Li to "become" John, to perform as John, so that he is shown by editing to occupy the same physical space as had John (in a series of matching cuts) and to appear to shoot one of Weng's killers (though he really only draws on Chang, who then asks him if he is "nuts").

Li's other performance occurs in the *Spy vs. Spy* scene in Jenny's apartment, when he is arrested by Chang. This scene is peculiar in that it contains two female figures, Jenny and an old woman who lives in another apartment. The presence of two figures tends to confirm Zigelstein's assertion of the feminine "threat" to the male role in Woo films such as *Face/Off* (11). Here, though comic in some respects, the threat is made explicit. Chang, pretending to be a janitor, is upbraided by an old woman for throwing garbage bags down to the foot of the stairs, thus blocking the fire escape. She even says that she "can't fly away like a phoenix" if a fire starts (ch. 20). (Her phoenix statement may seem purely comic but takes on a sad quality later, since it is connected to Chang, who dies tragically: apparently he isn't a phoenix either.)

This apartment scene provides, as well, the most explicitly rendered example of role-playing in *The Killer*, as John and Li try to hide the truth of their identities (that is, their true roles in the drama) by playing false roles. The two pretend to be old friends who grew up together, and they take on nicknames (Ha Tau and Ah B, respectively).[28] The curious fact about this scene is that the deception, which fails, actually becomes the basis for true communication between the two men. Their nicknames also become terms of endearment as the narrative progresses. Near the end of the film, when Li asks John for his real name, John prefers to be known as Ha Tau, that is, his new stage name is more real to him than his given name, because the stage name has contributed to creating a bond of friendship with Li.

As Zigelstein notes, *The Killer* was not the only Woo film to feature the performance motif. He cites, among others, *Hard Boiled*, whose plot revolves around the concept of role-playing, since Tony/Alan is an undercover cop pretending to be a Triad. He complains at one point that he no longer knows which he is, and Tequila also complains to Chief Pang about the confusion of roles in society: "You'd better tell us who are the cops and who are the thieves, and why you want us to kill each other?" (ch. 21). And Tequila seems to understand his job as a performance. He refers to being "kitted out for tonight" (ch. 14)—that is, properly costumed in Kevlar armor and combat gear for a raid on Hui's warehouse. He is also a jazz performer, and he seems to play a certain role in the station house, as the big uncle to the junior officers. Additionally, in a revealing little scene, he offers joss sticks and prayer to the statue of Kwan Yi outside Teresa's office door, asking him to give his girl back. This performance is comically executed, as if Tequila does not take the prayer seriously, or as if he were acting out a part without quite believing in it.

Narazumono and The Killer

The Killer is in no sense a mere remake. It does, though, have antecedents and inspirations. Woo often credits *Le Samouraï* with providing him much of the inspiration for *The Killer*, and its influence is visible, though not determinative. He has also mentioned a Japanese film whose title he could not recall for many years, as a strong influence on him.

This film, Woo said, starred Ken Takakura, the famous Japanese star of *yakuza* and swordplay films. I quote Woo's summary of it here:

[Takakura, playing a mob hit man,] discovers that he has been used by a gang to kill a good person.... So the killer tries to [take] revenge [on] the whole gang. And somehow he met a Japanese woman, a prostitute, who had TB and wanted to get back to Japan. He promises that after he takes revenge, he will take her home. [But, he is killed, and the girl is left] still waiting on the dock, and the hero never comes... [Woo, supplement text, *The Killer*].

The film, as Woo and I discovered almost simultaneously, was *Narazumono* [*The Outlaw*], a 1964 Toei production (see n. 20, above).

Here, as elsewhere in his work, Woo gains inspiration in curious ways. While *Narazumono* is an interesting film, it is certainly not in the league of *The Killer*. Woo was, by his account, powerfully inspired and moved by the film's motif of the killer's becoming emotionally attached to a tubercular prostitute. While this is a noticeable element of the film, it is not the central one. That Woo would have noticed and elaborated on this motif to the extent of fitting the plot of *The Killer* around it, bespeaks his innate romanticism and the patent vividness of his "inner life." Further evidence of his intensity of perception and empathy can be seen in his reaction to the closing scene of *Narazumono*, which is somewhat less poetic than his mnemonic recreation of it.

Perhaps the most interesting development by Woo of the iconic "tubercular prostitute" motif (found often in Romantic narrative) is his transformation of the disease from TB to an injury resulting in blindness. No longer, in *The Killer*, the result of societal neglect, malnutrition or simply one's own way of life as is the TB of *Narazumono*, Jenny's injury is taken totally out of the realm of her personal responsibility. The onus for the injury is, of course, the killer John's, and this fact has important consequences for the narrative. Not only does the Killer become a more strongly focused figure than the Takakura character, but the shift of blame will also allow Woo to concentrate insistently upon the moral crisis faced by John and to place his further decisions about killing, leaving Hong Kong and so forth, into entirely another dimension from the one in *Narazumono*. In short, Woo tightens the existential screws, turning *The Killer* into a very personal and intense examination of the social and moral consequences of one's actions.

The change from TB to blindness is also important because it touches upon a concern often apparent in Woo's films. Jenny is significantly the only person in the movie whose vision is impaired. Or rather, her vision impairment is highlighted by the extent to which the other major characters *see*. These characters undergo important life experiences as a direct result of their faculty of vision. Seeing is integral to Woo's work, and nowhere is it more emphasized than in *The Killer*. It is no accident that the only really innocent person in the film (besides the child and other uninvolved bystanders who suffer) is also the only one who is prevented from seeing the reality around her.

Vision, perspective and clarity are important aspects of *The Killer*. We first clearly notice this point in the hit scene when Jenny is injured. Before her injury, the camera lingers for a brief moment on her face, which looks shocked at the violence she sees around her. When she believes that John, whom she does not know, is about to kill her, she closes her eyes to shut out the horror of her impending death, a reality that of course she does not wish to face. Then she is injured and her sight clouds. From this point on, until the end of the film, she is shown to have progressively worsening vision, though paradoxically she can "see" the truth of John's love for her and of his hopes for a new life for both of them.

The notion of the person who loses a sense and becomes specially sensitized in compensation is nothing new. What is unusual here, though, is the emphasis placed by Woo on the sight sense in other characters. The camera frequently dollies in to a close-up of a character's eyes, and then switches to a POV shot from that character's perspective. The characters, like us, are viewers of a spectacle. But more importantly, their eyes—the locus of the soul, for the Neoplatonists—become their most important asset for survival as well as for revelation of truths that they would rather not confront.

Thus, in *The Killer*, John begins to face the reality that his actions have harmed an innocent. This self-awareness is presented in recurrent imagery: John's face is shot from slightly above, looking downward in anguished contemplation of inner scenes. We see this most clearly in Jenny's apartment, when John's eyeline becomes the dominant factor in the scene. His attention is first caught by a picture of Jenny in tennis garb; Woo establishes his eyeline, matched by the picture, as the organizing principle of the scene. The viewer is led to expect John's point of view to dominate and guide the narration of the scene. And in fact, the next object of focus for John is the scarf with which he wrapped Jenny's eyes after her injury. Even the music that Jenny plays on tape for John—suspiciously intradiegetic, being her "theme song"[29]—acts not only upon his auditory faculty but also upon his vision. We are shown yet another eyeline match to the tape deck playing the song, and John begins to "see" images from his recent past. As does Jenny's mind when she tries to remember John's appearance and can see only the *Shining* image, so too John's mental plane becomes a kind of theater screen on which flashback images are projected.

So vision is an important, actually the most important, means of self-awakening in *The Killer*. The visual faculty is also used in a Neoplatonic sense. When John and Jenny first meet, they do not speak, because Jenny is singing. All their communication is effected through their eyes. They alternately make contact and break off that contact, but the overall import is to recall the Renaissance formulation of the "optics of love."[30] Ironically, during the rest of the film, it will be Jenny's near-blindness that allows her to fall in love with John, and that causes him to love her because of his guilt and his recognition of her value.

Woo also uses vision to point to offscreen space, but not always in the traditional manner, as when a character looks offstage and we are led by direct eyeline matching to the position of another character. Again, the scene in Jenny's apartment is one of the best examples of Woo's masterful and original use of point of view. As John is shown looking into other reaches of his memory, he seems at the same time to be staring offstage, out of the frame. The camera executes a 180–degree turn and swings toward a transition to another location. It tracks slowly toward Inspector Li. We see him sitting on a bench, also, staring at an angle analogous to John's. The characters are set up from the beginning as doubles. Significantly, this is accomplished in part by a play on vision, a *trompe-l'oeil* shot in which John appears both to "see" Li and to "see" what Li "sees." The match is effected by means of the 180–degree track and by the analogy between the gaze of both characters, as well as the transitional music track, with overlapping lyrics. It is a brilliant and memorable scene which encapsulates Woo's preoccupation with the visual.

The narrative kernel or *topos* of vision as revelation and self-awareness, or in classical terms, *anagnorisis*, is repeated throughout Woo's work, but with most insistence in *The Killer*. Since blindness is a kind of benchmark for the film, with the characters generally approaching this state or distancing themselves from it, all the major characters (John, Li, Jenny, Sidney, Chang, Johnny Weng) are shown insistently "seeing" or staring. Whether or not they learn anything of moral or emotional importance depends both on their function in the narrative and on their basic nature, as well as their willingness to face themselves. Thus, we can understand part of Woo's repeated use of doubles in his films. In the richer instances of doubling, such as John and Li, one appears to "see" himself in the other, or, more particularly, to see his "shadow." So, Li comments, staring off into space, but implicitly "seeing" John's image, "He doesn't look like a killer" (ch. 13).

Clearly enough, Li sees the killer in himself, and we are prepared for this by the incident on the tram, when Li kills a fugitive. Like John, he is just doing his job, but an innocent is harmed there—in fact, she dies of a coronary. Li fiercely defends himself against his superiors' accusations of recklessness, but such an incident must leave its mark, and the parallel with John and Jenny is surely not accidental. Woo, then, carefully prepares Li to accept the essential kinship between himself and John. In similar fashion, John is prepared to accept Li by a series of incidents, including Jenny's injury, which cause him to question his moral position. All the incidents center on questions of betrayal and justice: Sidney's betrayal of John; Weng's betrayal and assassination of his uncle; the unfortunate injury of the little girl in John's fight on the beach. As John later tells Jenny when he promises not to kill again, "I thought the people I killed deserved to die. Now I believe everybody has the right to live" (ch. 26). That he cannot keep his promise is due to no current moral failing of his own but rather to the trap into which he and his two friends, Li and Jenny, have now fallen. They cannot avoid the consequences of John's past way of life.

This point brings us back to *Narazumono*, which, like *Le Samouraï* and *The Killer*, contains the motif of the man unable to escape his past. Actually, *The Killer* is a synthesis of the two earlier films, since Woo uses elements particular to one or the other: from *Le Samouraï*, the killer (the Outlaw [Ken Takakura]) who falls for a singer; from *Narazumono*, the killer who harms an innocent or who kills the wrong person because of a setup. Woo recasts these elements, and others, to fashion *The Killer*. All three films feature a professional killer who in some sense kills himself as if expiating his own sins. John seems to decide that he will sacrifice himself for Jenny, since he tells Li to remember their agreement about using his contract money to pay for new corneas for her, and he knows that his next action, drawing fire from Weng, will very possibly result in his own death. *Narazumono*, like Chang Cheh's *Vengeance*, places its killer in a position which is nearly suicidal. Like John, the killer in *Narazumono* goes back to kill his former employer to try to get money to leave with his lover; but, like David Chiang's character, he has the additional motive of vengeance for his closest male friend, his partner, who died as a result of the employer's treachery. So, like the Chiang hero, he deliberately enters a situation from which he has little possibility of escape. The killer in *Le Samouraï* is perhaps the most suicidal of all. Entering the bar where the singer who has in fact betrayed him is performing, he points his gun at her and appears to be ready to kill her, but the police enter and kill *him*. When his gun is examined, it is found to be empty.

Of the three killers, Jef in *Le Samouraï* seems to have the least to live for; John and the Outlaw, the most. Their deaths are the more poignant because the potential for a better future is undermined by their karmic destruction. Jef seems almost willful and is certainly cynical and manipulative, using his girlfriend as an alibi while himself being fascinated by the singer. Although Woo has used both films as sources, he has swung more to the Outlaw's side, discarding the unromantic and Sartrean overtones of Melville's film and highlighting the pathetic and romantic elements of *Narazumono*.

Manhunter and The Killer

A seemingly unlikely source of inspiration for *The Killer* was Michael Mann's 1986 film *Manhunter*, one of the precursors of Jonathan Demme's 1991 *The Silence of the Lambs*. (*Manhunter* is based on the novel *Red Dragon* by Thomas Harris, to which *The Silence of the Lambs* is a sequel, and the novels share important characters, especially the imprisoned serial killer Hannibal Lecter.) Woo paid high tribute to director Mann in an onstage appearance in Seattle:

> I loved *Heat* very much. I thought we have something in common. It's something about friendship, and loyalty.... I've admired him since *Manhunter*. I really loved the movie. I got some inspiration from that film for making *The Killer* [Woo, onstage appearance, 7 July 1996].

What did such a seemingly contrasting film as *Manhunter* lend to Woo's creative process when planning *The Killer*? Besides its intriguing visual style, certainly attractive to Woo, the film contains some material that can be seen submerged or commented upon in *The Killer*.

An important focus of Mann's film is the symbiotic relationship between the investigator Will Graham (William Petersen) and the serial killer Hannibal Lecter (Brian Cox, in the role later to win an Oscar for Anthony Hopkins). Graham goes to Lecter for help in catching a serial killer dubbed "The Tooth Fairy" because he leaves tooth-marks on some of his victims. Thus, the cop-killer relationship is split, with Lecter forming the central axis and himself acquiring the dual function of killer and detective, while Graham takes on some of the aspects of the killer, at least psychologically. (Lecter even tells him that he understands the killer because he is just like him.) The duality between cop and killer, entailing their shifting roles as well as their confused identities, surely was of great interest to Woo.

The film also concentrates on the destruction of the family by the killer. He preys on families, but he also indirectly affects Graham's family, as Graham's obsession with serial killers, stemming partially from Lecter's serious injury of him when he captured Lecter, interferes with his relationship with his wife (Kim Greist). Lecter also learns Graham's address and terrorizes his wife. Perhaps even when making *Face/Off* Woo was not unmindful of the precedent here: Castor's intrusion into the Archer family is just as unwelcome as Lecter's into the Grahams' marriage.

The Will Graham character is akin, too, to Inspector Li, and to other Woo heroes, in his obsession with the killer, and even more strongly, in his obsession with setting right a wrong. Near the end of the film, he refuses to leave the case, insisting that the killing must stop. He risks his life and his family's to end a scourge on the lives of other families. It is crucial that his whole involvement in the enterprise is voluntary; he comes out of retirement, or convalescence, to confront his own demons. His experience with serial killers is more than academic and even extends to the point that he is able to intuit facts about the killer that other investigators miss. Like Tequila, and like the villain Pik in *Hard Target*, Graham communicates intuitively with the killer, sensing his presence and his psychological nature.

Graham also becomes the rescuer of Reba (Joan Allen), a blind woman who has entered into a brief relationship with the serial killer. Acquainted with the killer from her work, she has become intimate with him but does not sense his evil. He is surprisingly gentle towards her until he suspects her, wrongly, of seeing someone else. She fails to comprehend him, the film implies, because she cannot see him; or more precisely, her blindness becomes a metaphor for her trust and lack of insight into his true nature.

As we have noted, the visual plays an important role in *The Killer*. Jenny's impaired vision prevents her from knowing the truth about John, although in this case her lack of vision is actually a metaphor, or a gateway, for her intuition about his deep nature: a basic decency and gentleness hidden below the surface of the professional killer. And Jenny is the only character in *The Killer* who maintains her innocence, a status expressed by her lack of sensory input,[31] while John, Li and the others are conspicuously shown to "see" or to visualize on several occasions. Li, like Graham, tries to visualize John (before he has met him), using his intuition to fill in the gaps in his knowledge about his target. *The Killer* features a scene when a police artist provides sketches based on vague descriptions of John. Li is shown studying them alone and seemingly "seeing through" them. He intuits John's nature from the sketches.

In *Manhunter*, Graham points out that one key to the killer's makeup is his obsession with seeing. The killer wants to organize his victims into tableaux that simulate grotesque visions of acceptance of him by family units. His victims are chosen by his viewing of their home movies (he works at a film darkroom), and his clearest evidence of their "acceptance" of him is through their seeing him as he comes to torture and kill them. Perhaps this accounts for some of his interest in Reba. She cannot see him and so cannot trigger his obsession with this participatory ritual. So, she is "safe" for a time. In *The Killer*, Jenny is "safe" in emotional terms until later in the film because she is unable to see John clearly and thus cannot connect him with the man who carried out the killings at her nightclub and who inadvertently blinded her. Perhaps it is coincidental that both films feature a blind, or impaired, woman who enters into a relationship with the hunted killer, but the parallels between the two films are certainly clear enough in this respect.

Woo was also very impressed with Mann's *Heat* (1995), an epic crime drama set in Los Angeles. While there is of course no question of influence on *The Killer*, it is instructive to examine this Mann film because of its own borrowing from Woo, from Hong Kong film, and from American film genres. We will see that Woo's positive reaction to Mann is even more understandable when the parallels between Woo's approach to filmmaking and Mann's are taken into account.

Heat, which tells the intertwining stories of Detective Vincent Hanna's domestic difficulties and of Neil McCauley's organization of a series of big "scores" (robberies), strongly echoes two important films from the 1950s: *The Asphalt Jungle* (John Huston, 1950) and *The Killing* (Stanley Kubrick, 1956). As in these two films, a strong leader recruits a professional group of heist artists to pull off a big score, but personal factors and fate intervene to cause the plans to go awry, ending in disaster for the participants. Mann accentuates an element not as important in the earlier films: the kinship between the cop and the criminal, who are brothers under the skin.

Vincent (Al Pacino) is obsessed with the hunt, living only for his career and thereby losing a series of wives. Neil (Robert De Niro) is restless when not engaged in a job and forms no lasting relationships (much like the characters in *Le Cercle rouge*). Both undergo crucial character development in the course of the film. Vincent's stepdaughter tries to commit suicide, and Neil meets Eady (Amy Brenneman), a beautiful young woman who changes his set notions about commitment. Besides the set piece heist and action segments, the cynosure of the film is the meeting between Vincent and Neil, a showcase for Pacino and De Niro and an opportunity for the film's themes to coalesce around the mutual kinship of the two characters. As do Li and John, the two men show their mutual respect, even their grudging affection, but do not hide the truth about their divergent calling. Mann's film is less romantic, more uncompromising here than is Woo's: Vincent and Neil affirm that neither will hesitate to kill the other if necessary. And, in fact, Vincent kills Neil at the end. Neil dies grasping Vincent's hand in a last gesture of human contact.

Between their meeting and the final shootout, Vincent has come to an ambiguous reconciliation with his wife Justine (Diane Venora)—he in fact tells her that he isn't right for her, but they both seem closer than before—and Neil has convinced Eady to go to New Zealand with him. Neil shows a streak of nobility worthy of a Woo character in the last scene, when he sees Eady waiting for him in the car and backs away from her, knowing that he will be killed or will have to kill Vincent, and not wanting to involve her. (In fact, Neil has demonstrated his loyalty to his friends and his integrity, within his peculiar code, repeatedly during the film.)

Like the hero of *Narazumono*, Neil dies because he cannot overcome his desire for revenge. He is about to leave for the airport with Eady but turns the car around to go back and settle accounts with Waingro (Kevin Gage), the man who had betrayed him and his friends to the police. After killing Waingro, Neil is spotted by Vincent; this leads directly to the final reckoning. A character defect in Neil's makeup simply prevents him from getting past his old life. He differs in this respect from John in *The Killer*, because John stays behind to get his money to try to help Jenny: it is John's attempt to leave his old life behind which results in his undoing. As Woo has said, John has done too many bad things to escape his fate.

Woo had just made the film that was to bring him to the attention of many Western viewers. After making *The Killer*, Woo turned to a project that expressed some of his inner preoccupations. This was the film that he considers his most personal to date, *Bullet in the Head*.

Chapter 7

The Move to Independence: *Bullet in the Head* and *Once a Thief*

Woo had a big critical success with *The Killer*, although the film was not at first so popular in Hong Kong as it was abroad. This was due to the massacre at Tienanmen Square in June 1989 and the consequent distaste of the Hong Kong public for violent films.[1] But he was still not an independent force in film, nor did his name carry the kind of cachet that it would later in Hollywood, especially after the release of *Face/Off.* He was still essentially a contract director for Film Workshop, and so he passed through a period of some difficulty, at least in terms of getting his projects approved. Nevertheless, during this time he shot one film, *Bullet in the Head*, which, though flawed, is one of his strongest works, and another, *Once a Thief,* which set an alternate course for him along the line of light comedy-action, much as films like *Foreign Correspondent* and *North by Northwest* provided Alfred Hitchcock with a diversion from heavy works like *Vertigo.*

Bullet in the Head: Heroism Denied

> *You cannot have power for good without having power for evil too. Even mother's milk nourishes murderers as well as heroes.*
>
> —George Bernard Shaw,
> *Major Barbara* (1905),
> Act 3

The genesis of *Bullet in the Head* goes back to the time after *A Better Tomorrow*, when, due to the film's unexpected success, a sequel was discussed by Woo and his colleagues, including Tsui Hark (Chang). A

135

sequel was difficult to do, because the "real" star of the film had been killed off.[2] So, "John suggested doing a prequel, which is the story of *Bullet in the Head*" (Chang).

But Tsui had a story of his own ready for a sequel, revolving around studio politics concerning one of the Cinema City partners, Dean Shek, who plays the character "based" on him in the film (Woo, personal interview, 8 November 1995). As Chang said, "It was Tsui's story. And he asked John to do it." So the prequel idea was shelved for a time.

After *A Better Tomorrow II* was completed, Woo had proposed two projects. One was *Once a Thief*, the other, the prequel, *Bullet in the Head*, for which he wanted to use Chow Yun-fat. But, as we have seen, Chow could not then appear in these films. *The Killer* was made instead, after Chow did a little maneuvering so that he could appear in it.

Tsui also commented that a film about Vietnam would be of no interest to anyone, but, unbeknownst to Woo, he was planning his own prequel, which became *A Better Tomorrow III*. Woo learned of this from the press (Chute, Supplements text, *The Killer*). Tsui's *A Better Tomorrow III* was released in November 1989. A dismayed Woo now made plans to do *Bullet in the Head*.

The project was very ambitious, demanding a rather large budget (Chang). Chang had not yet decided to become Woo's business partner, and besides, he was still under contract at Film Workshop, so this affected the production history of *Bullet in the Head*. Concern was also expressed about making the film profitable without Chow's star power:[3]

> It was a very expensive film, you know. The line producer at that time did the budget, it was about eight million [Hong Kong] dollars, and I added four to it. 12 million, they said, without Chow Yun-fat, how can you expect to recoup that kind of money, with Tony Leung, and Jacky Cheung? They're not big stars. And so I presold a couple of territories to convince them that it could bring in that kind of money. John asked me to join him. I said, "I'd like to but I can't." I was bound by contract, you know, it takes six months to leave. So he became the producer himself, and the film ended up costing $28 million. Instead of 12 [Chang].

The film also had problems not unknown to a Woo project. It had to be cut, and its length contributed to another problem:

> We had a premiere at the Convention Center. At the premiere, the film ran 2 hours and 35 minutes. You know how the theaters in Hong Kong operate. If the film's over a certain length, either they throw away some reels in the middle or they speed up the projector [laughs]. So I said, "You have to cut it down." I mean, the film was opening the next day.
> We had no solution, finally some guy from Golden Princess said to

cut the final scene. So we had to cut the prints. So we ended the film, in Hong Kong releases, in the boardroom. There's a fade to black, you hear a gunshot and that's it.

The editing process was quite an adventure:

All of us went with John to the lab, and we had ten editors standing by to cut the prints. We'd cut one print and the other editors would conform to that print, and so forth, and in the morning three guys would deliver the prints to the theaters.

To add insult to injury, the film did not do well with the critics. This is understandable, given their probable expectations for a "John Woo film." *Bullet in the Head* is indeed a very dark and unusual film. But it also happens to be a masterwork, even if it shows flaws; and some of its problems might well have to do with the hasty surgery that had to performed upon it. In any case, Chang's opinion of it is, as usual, judicious:

And then the film got bad reviews. It's very strange, except for some people saying negative things about it. I said, I don't think so. It's kind of heavy-handed, but it's a very good film. It's very emotional. It's his most personal film.

Bullet in the Head has not received the critical attention accorded *The Killer*, nor the wild popular raves given *A Better Tomorrow*. *Bullet in the Head* is, as McDonagh argues, a more "uncompromising" work than any of Woo's other films. For this reason, some critics have found it difficult to evaluate and even to accept (48–49). But it is precisely a work such as *Bullet in the Head* that demonstrates Woo to be more than just a commercial action director.

Bullet in the Head follows the lives of three gang members from Hong Kong who emigrate to Vietnam in 1968 to try to make their fortunes in smuggling. They are plunged directly into a confusing and violent crime and war milieu, and their loyalty to each other, as well as their courage and spiritual resources, are severely tested. At the end of the film, two of the three friends are dead, one having betrayed the others and having shot one of them in the head. The last of the three kills the betrayer, as well as the crippled friend (this in an act of compassion), and appears himself to be dying of his wounds. McDonagh correctly states (see 48–49) that this is the most bleak of Woo's films, as it leaves no room for facile romanticism (it is nevertheless very Romantic, as we shall see).

Bullet in the Head is not a genre picture like *A Better Tomorrow* or even *The Killer*. It is arguably a melodrama, or it could be termed a "gang" picture, but it really comes closer to being a "horrors" film, as *Coriolanus* is a "horrors" play.[4] It relies on repeated shocks or Grand Guignol effects— Sally's futile death, Frank's bullet in the head, Ben bringing Frank's skull to Paul's board meeting—to drive home points about loyalty, honor, and the cruelty of war.

Woo sees *Bullet in the Head* as his own favorite among his films. Certainly, this is the most personal of his works, referring as it does to various autobiographical occurrences. The most apparent is that Woo participated in anti-war protests in Hong Kong and witnessed police violence against demonstrators. And, like many of his characters, Woo grew up poor and perhaps, for a time, gang membership seemed attractive (although it certainly came to frighten and disgust him).

Again in this film the Woo triangular structure appears, although made more complex by the addition of a fourth male friend (Luke). The female characters alternate between Jane, Ben's wife, and Sally, a Hong Kong torch singer who has been enlisted forcibly into heroin addiction and prostitution in Saigon. Both these characters pivot around Ben as axis; he is the member of the male group who insists on saving her. But she is killed, and her importance in the film is more as a reflection of Ben's and his friends' morality than as a full-blooded representation of a female character. Her death makes the objective of the friends' desperate escape attempt from Vietnam seem pointless and hollow, since they were trying to rescue her from the clutches of a mobster.

The emphasis on morality in *Bullet in the Head* is part of its formal nature. The film is an attempt at modern allegory. Allegory has fallen into some disrepute in the twentieth century (see Honig, especially 3–9), probably as much for its artificiality as for its frequent connection to medieval hagiography and Christian didacticism. But for John Woo, essaying a very personal statement about morality, and possessing a background in Christianity as well as in Chinese philosophy, the allegory form seems an obvious choice in which to set *Bullet in the Head*. If in *The Killer* the heroes and villains are certainly modern versions of traditional Chinese characters—the knight, the villain, the virtuous maiden—the heroes in particular are not starkly delineated from each other in moral terms as are the four heroes in *Bullet in the Head*. John, Li and Sidney are all representative of loyalty, integrity and courage; their morality is somewhat outside the normal social pale—John and Sidney are, after all, killers, and Li is certainly unconventional and rebellious. But in *Bullet in the Head*, the four friends, Ben (Tony Leung), Frank (Jacky Cheung), Paul (Waise Lee) and Luke (Simon Yam), display distinct moral characteristics which lend the film the quality of allegory.

Bullet in the Head is challenging generically, as a hybrid of the escape film, the Vietnam film and the caper film. This latter aspect of *Bullet in the Head* is perhaps not immediately apparent, but the tragic error that leads to the destruction of Sally and the three friends is the theft of a box of gold leaf, belonging to the CIA, from the headquarters of a Vietnamese gangster. The film does not emphasize the procedure of stealing the gold as in caper films like Jules Dassin's *Rififi* or Kubrick's *The Killing*, but the heist does become the central engine of destiny in the film as well as a metaphor for the war's robbing of human decency.

The tragic error is not so much attempting to steal the gold as it is not being willing to forsake it to save one's own, or another's, life. Thus, the friends repeatedly urge Paul to leave the gold, but to no avail; it becomes, like the gold that drowned many of Hernán Cortés' men in Tenochtitlán during their flight from that Aztec capital, worth more (or less) than its value to the holder—a kind of Ring of the Nibelungs that leads to revenge and hatred among erstwhile associates.

Frank becomes the pivot of the deteriorating friendship. He is the least strong-willed and ambitious of the friends, as we see especially when Paul suddenly pulls a gun in a store in Saigon. Frank is surprised into following him in the robbery but clearly wonders how he got into such a mess with these people; Jacky Cheung's strong performance lends to our sense of his bewilderment and fear. His pivotal role is signaled early in the film when Woo shoots him in a group: he is placed between Ben and Paul.[5] Frank's troubles also cause the trio to leave Hong Kong; Ben, playing a brother's keeper's role, leads him to avenge his injury by Ringo, a gang leader whose turf he had crossed. Ringo is killed, and the three friends leave Hong Kong for Saigon.[6] Significantly, Frank's injury was caused by a bottle blow to the head; later, he will become deranged due to brain damage from a "bullet in the head" inflicted by Paul.

Bullet in the Head is only one of Woo's films in which tragic error plays an important role. As in the films of Scorsese, Coppola and Kurosawa, Woo's characters normally make decisions that lead inevitably to their demise or disgrace. This penchant of his heroic figures is but another trait of their romanticization; they are made pathetic (in the original, Romantic sense) by their stubborn insistence on duty, integrity or love for another.[7] Thus John accepts one more contract to earn enough money for a corneal transplant for Jenny; Mark avenges the attempted hit on Ho, thereby setting the whole dark plot into motion; Ken, in *A Better Tomorrow II*, helps Mr. Lung; and Tony agrees to help to destroy Johnny Wong in *Hard Boiled*. Woo's liking for the work of Coppola, Scorsese, Kurosawa, Peckinpah and Welles is understandable in this respect. All these directors emphasize such errors or decisions by their protagonists as leading them into a romantically charged outcome.

If the narrative structure of Woo's films is generally romantic, stressing a fateful decision taken by one or more of the heroes, and ending with one of the heroes being forced to live with the consequences of that decision and its fatal effect on his friend, *Bullet in the Head* is the most exaggerated version of this narrative. We are not even assured of Ben's survival at the end of the film. This kind of denouement is only to be seen elsewhere in *A Better Tomorrow II*, but the probable death of all three heroes from their wounds in the latter film is clearly ironic and comic in its treatment: the heroes' comments about their wounds are humorous in their detachment. Critics have been right in calling *Bullet in the Head* the most uncompromising and personal of Woo's films; it is also the most visibly *"Nouvelle Vague,"* with its noticeable recourse to jump-cutting and obviously "artistic" editing.[8]

But this film, like Woo's other work, is essentially classical in its basic style, with some innovative use of certain devices to "dress up" its surface. Like Fuller or Peckinpah, Woo does not simply throw out Hollywood editing canons; he departs from them, building on classical continuity, lighting and pacing to forge his own very personal style. Thus, while influenced by New Wave directors, Woo (like his models Scorsese and Coppola) is no Resnais or Godard. His films do not seriously question narrative logic or present themselves as deeply self-reflexive. They rely for their power upon the effective display of editing, lighting and image in order to advance a basically traditional narrative.[9]

Bullet in the Head is instructive for Western, and particularly for United States, viewers because it deals specifically with Vietnam. A Vietnam war film, during its second half, *Bullet in the Head* presents the Vietnam experience from a perspective unfamiliar to viewers and critics of the Vietnam film as cultivated in the United States. Though akin in its search and rescue structure to films like the *Missing in Action* series, in which the hero Braddock (Chuck Norris) returns to Vietnam to rescue American POWs, the film does not deal with such issues centrally. The visit to Vietnam by the three is not a rescue initially, but rather an attempt to get rich quick by connecting with the HK Triad society in Saigon and becoming more important in the smuggling profession.[10] Only after the three arrive in Saigon and find that a singer-prostitute named Sally (Yolinda Yan) is being grossly mistreated by the mob leader Mr. Leong, do the three decide to attempt a rescue for her. The "prisoner" rescued will not be a POW kept by the NVA but a woman enslaved and addicted to heroin by a transplanted HK gangster. The war becomes in this sense a backdrop against which a conflict between HK elements is played out. Like Mexico in *The Wild Bunch* and *Bring Me the Head of Alfredo Garcia*, Vietnam is the setting for a morality play with foreigners as the main players.

Bullet in the Head in fact seems to owe some important characteristics to the two Peckinpah films. In both *The Wild Bunch* and *Bring Me the Head of Alfredo Garcia*, the protagonists are hired to do a certain job in Mexico and end up rebelling against and killing their employers, much like the situation in *Bullet in the Head*. Furthermore, both the Bunch and Bennie (Warren Oates) act chiefly from outrage at the treatment of a close acquaintance, Angel (Jaime Sanchez) in the Bunch's case and Anita (Isela Vega) in Bennie's. All three situations involve the mistreatment or murder of a vulnerable third party by the heroes' employers or as a result of their actions. Thus, the heroes (or antiheroes) act against their own interests because of an affront to their principles. Woo often values such morally transcendent activity (even when effected by less than morally pure people), as for example in the cases of Ch'ing Ko, Inspector Li, and Ben and Luke in *Bullet in the Head*.

The moral subtext of *Bullet in the Head* shows a streak of pronounced populism, in the sense that the efforts of the "little men"—small-time gangsters, mercenaries—are valued over and against those of the big corporation, whether represented by Leong or later by Paul. Here, as well, Woo is in the company of Peckinpah and of Leone. All three directors dislike, or in Peckinpah's case, cordially hate big corporate enterprises because of their dehumanizing effects. It is no accident that the villains in Woo films are either established corporate (Triad) bosses (Leong, Lung in *The Young Dragons*) or men on the make (Mr. Ko in *A Better Tomorrow II*, Shing, Johnny Weng), although it must be noted that Woo actually values the old-fashioned bosses like Mr. Hui in *Hard Boiled*, who have their own moral code and are the exceptions to the norm. Woo's villains are usually dehumanized or depersonalized, corrupted by greed (even in his comedies: *Plain Jane to the Rescue*, *From Riches to Rags*); perhaps here we see his closest approach generally to social criticism, as he implicitly attacks the fast money mentality in Hong Kong.

Bullet in the Head can easily be read as a morality play on the theme of greed, but more than simply this, it comments bitterly on the corrupting influence of accessible and quickly made money. Significantly, it is American gold, stolen and hoarded by Leong, that corrupts the susceptible Paul, whose character flaw has been introduced to us early in the film. Admittedly, when we first see Paul, his childhood ambition to escape from his father's fate of poverty seems only natural and laudable, and we should draw the conclusion that Paul is not really different from any of us in being a mixture of good and bad traits. We only later see his ambition as pathological.[11] This neo–Confucian critique of money's corruption of youth and innocence, the future hope for Hong Kong, is directly in line with Woo's earlier films, surprisingly enough in the grim context of *Bullet in the Head*: comedies like *Money Crazy*, *From Riches to Rags*, and *Plain Jane to the Rescue*, where poverty is to be preferred to the ruthless money chase.

A similar contrast is apparent in Woo's comedy-drama *Once a Thief*, and rather unexpectedly, given their divergent tones and subjects, *Once a Thief* and *Bullet in the Head* share some other important features. Both contain nostalgic recreations of the youth of their protagonists. And though *Bullet in the Head* has much more autobiographical content (probably even more in the original full-length version) than does *Once a Thief*, still the implicit conservative nostalgia about the virtues of poverty (certainly as opposed to criminal greed) can be tied to the director's own early life of poverty and hardship, which was difficult but in some respects positive, as Woo learned the value of hard work, charity and family solidarity.

Some of the most poetically rendered scenes in each film concern the youth of the protagonists. In *Bullet in the Head*, much of the original material was lamentably cut. Woo had included more scenes showing Ben (his surrogate in the film) teaching dance classes, as Woo once did, and hanging with the street gangs (a clear allusion to *West Side Story*). If what remains of the beginning is fleeting and rather "murky," to borrow the term of my colleague Michael Anderegg, the scenes at the film's opening still evoke in an impressionistic fashion (an impression perhaps unintentionally enhanced by the montage effect forced by the extensive cutting) the early lives of the three friends.

Similarly, in *Once a Thief*, an uneven film because of budget problems, some of the best scenes show the three friends as children, learning first from their "bad father" Mr. Chow (Kenneth Tsang) how to steal and then being "reformed"—especially, fed adequately—by their "good father" (Paul Chu Kong). Charity, an activity dear to Woo because of his own experience with the Lutherans, is highlighted here in contrast to unrestrained acquisitiveness as practiced by Mr. Chow and his associates.

Bullet in the Head, though a "Vietnam film," is distinctive in its approach to the Vietnam conflict, since it really does not deal directly with the war. The Vietnam War is, as we have seen, a backdrop for the foreground story, and the war additionally functions as a surrogate setting for allusions to political events concerning Hong Kong, specifically the Tienanmen "incident," and for general moralizing about war's cruelty, or more broadly, about the inhumanity of governments and armies. Like *The Wild*

Bunch, one of Woo's canonical influences, *Bullet in the Head* employs a displacement strategy, with the setting serving mainly or partially as referent for another scenario. The Vietnam setting is a conveniently violent and venal milieu for a morality play and an implicit commentary on 1997, while Peckinpah's use of Mexico during the 1910–17 Revolution is easily interpreted, and so it has been, as an allegorical scenario for the war in Vietnam. If Peckinpah's treatment is metonymic (Mexico = Vietnam, Revolution = War), Woo's is metaphorical, since no direct equivalence but rather a symbolic restatement is being made.

In any case, *Bullet in the Head* owes a good deal to Peckinpah, although not in a derivative manner. As we have seen, Woo transposes some of the dramatic situations, especially the "rescue" motif, from *The Wild Bunch* and *Bring Me the Head of Alfredo Garcia* to his own film. And *Bullet in the Head* does not allude only to Peckinpah's films. *Mean Streets* and *The Deer Hunter* (Michael Cimino, 1978) have also served as palimpsests for Woo's most unusual mature film.

The Deer Hunter might seem only too obvious a precedent for *Bullet in the Head*, given the similar Russian roulette scenes, and Woo's use of it only too derivative. But merely at first glance does *Bullet in the Head* appear unduly imitative of Cimino's film. Woo actually puts the most famous (or notorious) scene from *The Deer Hunter* to an original use. The shocking Russian roulette scene from the Viet Cong prison camp, in *Bullet in the Head*, becomes even more horrendous than in the Cimino work, as Woo's prisoner characters are forced to kill not themselves, but each other.[12] The wager element is eliminated, since the guns appear to be fully loaded. The element of chance or fortune is transferred to the question of which prisoners will be forced to participate in the killing game.

And, unlike Cimino, Woo injects an explicitly political dimension into the scene. In *The Deer Hunter*, the roulette game is a cruel form of betting, in which the Viet Cong soldiers bet on the men's luck with the partially loaded revolver. But in *Bullet in the Head*, Woo eschews the game motif, moving the United States–Vietnam conflict into the foreground. The Viet Cong place the Hong Kong people into the "game" because of their suspicion that the Hong Kong men are CIA agents (they have found CIA papers in Paul's stolen gold). They are forced to kill American soldiers and suspected Vietnamese collaborators or spies, and then to attack each other, with Ben nearly forced to kill Frank.

The scene acquires an allegorical structure, too, because of the Viet Cong's forcing Frank and Ben to kill U. S. soldiers. One might read this dramatic situation as an allegorical treatment of the difficult position of Hong Kong, caught between the United States, or the British, and mainland China. Or, if one prefers, the scene might refer to "young" capitalistic Hong Kong—the Hong Kong men on the make being pushed by the Communist Viet Cong (read, mainland Chinese) to "kill" or reject the "older" capitalistic United States (or Britain). In any event, the scene is richer than Cimino's in its relevance to a social and political dilemma, adding to its focus on character and loyalty.

During the scene, Frank, the gentlest member of the trio, is forced to kill (he protests frantically, "I don't kill!") first a Vietnamese accused of CIA contact, and then a U. S. soldier. As Frank becomes increasingly incapacitated with shock, Ben volunteers to kill people—we suspect, especially if we've seen *The Deer Hunter*, that he wants to get his hands on a weapon. He kills Americans, finally going berserk in an image that Tony Leung would reprise in *Hard Boiled* when Alan shoots Hui's boys. Then, to Ben's horror (effectively concealed but sensed by us), he is shoved toward Frank. He reassures Frank that all will be well, and that he had sworn not to go home to Hong Kong without him (that is, if Frank doesn't go home alive, he won't either). Then he tricks the guards and shoots some of them, giving the three the chance to escape with the help of the serendipitous arrival of Luke accompanying a rescue force of Americans. (Here Woo uses his own films as a device for suspense: we may expect Ben actually to shoot Frank to save him, or both of them, as Ho shoots Kit in *A Better Tomorrow II* to prove his loyalty to Mr. Ko.)

Ben does not have to carry out an act totally repugnant to him, and his obvious revulsion at killing his "brother" is to be contrasted sharply to Paul's treatment of Frank not long afterward. Faced with the wounded Frank's disclosing their whereabouts to a Cong patrol after the escape from the camp, Paul shoots Frank in the head (the "bullet in the head"), admonishing him, "Don't blame me." He then callously kills innocent villagers to get their boat. Though Paul, like Ben, had previously been frightened—horrified, indeed—at the cold shooting of a suspected VC in Saigon by an ARVN soldier (the first "bullet in the head"), their eventual reactions to Frank illustrate the growing gulf between them in moral terms. Additionally, Woo chooses to put Ben and Frank together in the "roulette" scene; significantly, Paul is shown meantime lying to his captors about his (nonexistent) knowledge of the CIA's location in Saigon so as to survive and escape with his gold. Not only his greed and deceit but his separation from the other two men are thus neatly highlighted.

Frank barely survives his ordeal but becomes a heroin-addicted psychotic prone to murderous rages (rather like a physically more pronounced version of Cagney's Cody Jarrett in *White Heat*). The bullet lodged in his head causes his physical pain and adds to his mood swings; it also serves

On the set of *Bullet in the Head* (1990): Woo bearing arms between takes of the POW scene. Tony Leung (as Ben, right, in jacket and white shirt) stands by. (Courtesy John Woo.)

as a reminder of Paul's treachery and as a metaphor of the effects of Vietnam. Luke, who survived though with some disfigurement and crippling, and Ben, go to see Frank. In a fiercely emotional scene, Frank seems to signal to Ben that he wishes to die at Ben's hand. Ben, agonized, kills him and then goes to seek out Paul, who has parlayed his gold into a vice-chairmanship in a major "corporation"—actually a Triad operation.

In Woo's own version of Bennie's return from his mission for the *patrón* (Emilio Fernández) in *Bring Me the Head of Alfredo Garcia*, Ben is shown barging into a meeting of the board at which Paul is about to take over everything; Ben has with him Frank's skull, complete with bullet hole. Paul, of course, reacts in horror and then tries to escape; a car chase in a parking garage and a wild gun battle ensue. Paul attempts to exorcise his guilt by shooting the skull again, and Ben finally kills Paul with an eponymous bullet in the head.[13]

Bullet in the Head is, though, especially effective in its use of certain devices to assist in its storytelling. One of these is the score, important as always in a Woo film. In this case, the team of James Wong and Romeo Diaz has fashioned an evocative combination of pop tunes and variations on themes. Woo uses this music as a bridge between characters and situations, much as in *The Killer*, but in a rather more subtle way.

One of the themes used in *Bullet in the Head* is the Monkees' standard "I'm a Believer," appropriate for the film's time period (1967–70). The tune is very apropos in two senses: the line "I saw her face / Now I'm a believer" is to be applied both to Jane and to Sally; and the song's title is severely ironic, given the fact that no one in the film can believe in anything, or at least in anything good, most of the time. Jane becomes disillusioned with Ben (although there appears to be some hope by film's end); Ben loses faith in himself; Ben and his friends can no longer believe in, that is, trust Paul; no one can believe in the Hong Kong government's or the Saigon government's good intentions, as we see from similar scenes of crackdowns on demonstrators, and furthermore from a chilling scene in which the ARVN robs a jewelry store, killing all inside; Sally has lost hope, only to regain it, and then to be killed. The only dependable people in the film are Ben and Luke; both of them stand by their friends. Although Jane, Sally and Frank are positive characters, they are either sidelined (Jane) or become undependable in the sense of being helpless or conflicted.

Furthermore, the song "I'm a Believer" undergoes a significant narrative transformation which parallels the process of Ben's *anagnorisis*. When first introduced, the song accompanies a dance class, with Jane and Ben as participants; that is, it backs up a happy occasion. Later, though, in Saigon, it is played in the bar run by Mr. Leong, the cruel and exploitative criminal who has forced Sally into addiction and concubinage. The song's movement from an essentially positive mirror of youth to a totally ironic and distorted reflection of betrayal and viciousness is a neat but subtle (because understated and backgrounded) summation of Ben's trip through the Inferno. Similarly, a melody based on the "Happy Birthday" song recurs throughout the film, extradiegetically. It is typically used in seemingly inappropriate or jarring places in the narrative, as for example when Ben kills Frank.

This film contains some very clear examples of Woo's use of the camera, and of editing, to highlight character relationships. Major characters are repeatedly shown in triangular setups, a favorite Woo technique. One such setup is used in a scene after the John Woo cop comes to Jane's apartment looking for Ben. We have a complicated shot that ends with Frank against the wall, almost parallel with Ben, and facing Paul. In the triangle, Paul is symbolically placed in opposition to the other two

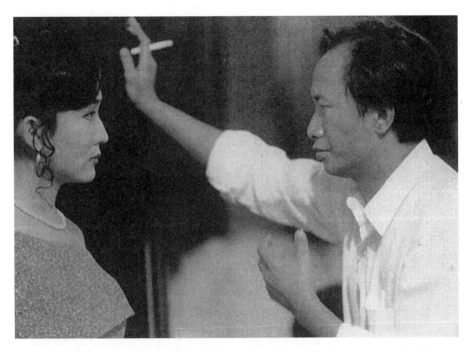

Woo explains a scene to Yolinda Yan (as Sally) on the set of *Bullet in the Head* (1990). (Courtesy John Woo.)

characters. Later in Leong's hangout, Woo also uses a triangular structure in close-up. Ben is shown to the left, Paul to the right, facing each other. Frank is in between in close background; Paul moves out of the shot toward the camera after discussing the need for looking out for Number One. Such foregrounding of technique, as well as the intensity of the acting and the extreme violence of *Bullet in the Head*, contribute to making it a very personal and idiosyncratic film that expresses a vision of the world which is unusually dark for John Woo.

Once a Thief: A Comic Respite

> *The moment we indulge our affections, the earth is metamorphosed; there is no winter and no night; all tragedies, all ennuis, vanish,—all duties even.*
> —Ralph Waldo Emerson,
> *Essays* (First Series, 1841),
> "Friendship"[14]

In this instance, Woo recurs to an earlier part of his career, but with quite a difference. Some of his early films, much cruder in their technique and script (*Follow the Star* leaps to mind), are nevertheless contributors to the type of film represented by *Once a Thief*. Critics have not been very comfortable with this movie, perhaps because it doesn't fit well into received categories: not exactly a pure caper film, it combines slapstick, a loopy love triangle (based on Truffaut's *Jules et Jim* [1961]), and the elements of violence associated with Woo's more operatic pieces. It clearly refers to Hitchcock's *To Catch a Thief* (1955) as well. Terence Chang says that the script of *Once a Thief* "is an original idea conceived by John" but that the title was taken from a film with Alain Delon and Ann-Margret called *Once a Thief* (Ralph Nelson, 1965) (Chang, e-mail 2 February 1999; personal interview, 4 November 1995). In any case, it has some notable characteristics, including a Dickensian Fagin character ("Mr. Chow," the trio's "bad father"), and some clever allusions to other movies. Thus, it both departs from and continues Woo's career, and in so doing it demonstrates just how much Woo has matured as a directorial talent since the seemingly unpromising days of some of his early comedies.

The three thieves here are played by Chow Yun-fat, Cherie Chung and Leslie Cheung. In an obvious reference to *Jules et Jim*, they form a good-natured love triangle, but actually comport themselves more like three siblings. This shows how Woo departs from his models and influences, shaping his material to fit his own perspective. Rather than emphasize the emotional tension and conflict found in the Truffaut film, Woo highlights the good-humored competition between the three, their practical joking and their bittersweet love contest. But the film is not, like *Jules et Jim*, tinged with sadness and introspection.

Ethically, the film avoids the tricky question (especially for either a Lutheran or a Confucian) of the morality of thievery by the simple device—used in another way in *To Catch a Thief*—of having the thieves steal from worse thieves. They are also presented, as in *Oliver Twist*, as offspring of a criminal community. As in other Woo films, the protagonists are not severely criticized even though their pursuits are immoral, unethical or illegal by society's ruling standards.

Thus, the retrospective scenes showing the three thieves as children are important to the film not merely because they serve as back story for the characters. They also illuminate for us crucial qualities of these three that distance them from the evil, grasping world of Mr. Chow. Specifically, when they are shown plying their trade, stealing bread from a baker, they do not keep all the proceeds for themselves. We discover that one of the chief reasons for the theft was to give the bread to an old woman and her family—thus, we find, these are again Woo heroes with a conscience. This fact explains their growing loyalty to the cop who befriends them and their eventual solidarity (the parallel with *The Three Musketeers* is clear enough). In contrast, Mr. Chow's world features betrayal and total self-concern: Chow has his French partner killed (in an unfortunately too-obvious reference to the garroting scene at the end of *The Godfather*, when Carlo, the victim, kicks out the windshield of the car where his execution occurs); and, perhaps even worse in moral terms, he uses Jules (Chow Yun-fat) and then turns on him, brutally pushing him down a flight of stairs in his wheelchair.

Once a Thief also parodies the caper and adventure film. The sophisticated gadgetry and intricate gymnastics, which we don't really take too seriously, in the art museum remind us of Jules Dassin's *Rififi* (1955) or of the James Bond films. The characters confirm the film's light treatment of such motifs when they "limbo" under the laser beams at the museum. A clear antecedent of *Once a Thief* is Hitchcock's *North by Northwest* (1959), itself a parody of the international espionage film. Perhaps Woo was paying tribute to Hitchcock by including a conspicuous art auction scene, echoing the memorable scene in *North by Northwest* when Roger Thornhill (Cary Grant) creates a disturbance to force his ejection from the auction house and thus to foil the attempt of Van Damm (James Mason) and his henchmen to kidnap him.[15]

Woo appears also to be recasting his earlier work, almost in an homage to his own past style. His comedies often featured exaggerated Jerry Lewis mugging, Three Stooges fisticuffs and absurd parodies of martial arts films. A good example would be the donnybrooks in *Follow the Star*, featuring a card-wielding martial arts expert like the one in *Once a Thief*, and especially in *From Riches to Rags*. The difficulty with *Once a Thief* is that the film tries to be too many things: a *Jules et Jim* homage, a *Rififi* parody, and a rehashing of elements familiar to Woo *cognoscenti*. The tones simply do not mesh, and this helps to explain the difficulty many viewers have had with this film.

The film's lack of structural unity is substantially due to budget problems and some studio pressure. Woo could not sustain his vision of the film as a "French," Truffaut-like comedy of manners. The first parts of the movie, shot in Paris, do have this flavor, but the latter ones, shot in Hong Kong, become an uneasy combination of Cantonese action, parody and slapstick. As Woo himself says,

When I shot *Once a Thief* [I was] thinking of elegance, very much French style. And also I sort of used the film as a tribute to François Truffaut. In my original thinking I tried to play their relationship, Chow Yun-fat [and Leslie Cheung] the same as *Jules and Jim* but to make it lighter. In Paris I got the mood, but when we moved back to Hong Kong everything changed. [We had a] very tight schedule, and the script had to be changed. So the second half is a different kind of movie. The first half of the movie is more French and more myself. The second half—it's a comedy but pretty much Hong Kong style, because in postproduction we only had two and one half months [personal interview, 8 November 1995].

Once a Thief was, according to Terence Chang, a project that Woo had proposed soon after *A Better Tomorrow II*. But it was temporarily shelved because Chow Yun-fat was not available for contractual reasons (see above, Chapter 6). Tsui suggested instead that Woo employ George Lam for the role, but Lam's asking price was much too high, according to Chang (1.6 million HK, "a huge amount of money" at the time). So Woo gave up on the project for the moment and was convinced by Chow to do *The Killer* instead; Chow agreed to appear in this film.

So *The Killer* was released and did quite well, especially outside of Hong Kong; and Woo went on to make *Bullet in the Head*, which did not do so well. Chang had meantime decided to form a partnership with Woo: "By that time I had decided to join him and form the company, John Woo productions, with another partner, Lynda [Kuk], and she came up with the name Milestone" (Chang). Their financial angel, Mr. Ng, had been impressed with *Bullet in the Head* despite its lack of draw and "still wanted to support John," so *Once a Thief* again came under consideration. "And so [Mr. Ng] wanted to do *Once a Thief*, but he wanted to do it as a comedy, because he gave [John] a Chinese New Year slot, which is one of the best times of the year."

Leslie Cheung was hired for the sum of "two million dollars, which was an outrageous amount of money at that time." Woo was beginning to gain recognition by now, with the success of *The Killer*, and Chang went with him to Cannes that year (May 1990). So, now in France, they began shooting about November 11. The shoot took about two and a half months, according to Chang. In France, the shooting alternated between Paris and Nice.

One of Woo's minor films, *Once a Thief* nevertheless featured some nice comedy and some appealing ensemble acting and provided some light relief from the extreme heaviness of *Bullet in the Head* and the romantic pathos of *The Killer*. Next, Woo was to make one of his most intense and demanding, but also most visually exciting, films: the police epic *Hard Boiled*.

Chapter 8

Hard Boiled:
Heroic Cops

*Ultimately a hero is a man who would argue with the
gods, and so awakens devils to contest his vision. The more
a man can achieve, the more he may be certain that the
devil will inhabit a part of his creation.*
                                        —Norman Mailer,
                                    The Presidential Papers,
                                            Preface (1963)

Hard Boiled (1992) has been characterized as a much more "straight"
action film than *The Killer.* Terence Chang observes that most Americans prefer *Hard Boiled* to *The Killer* because the later film is "more accessible" (Wu and Chang, personal interview). Not only a more straightforward
action movie than *The Killer, Hard Boiled* is a more technically accomplished work and one that seems to explode the action genre from within
by carrying the hyperbolic "super-action" set piece, now identified closely
with Woo, to nearly incredible extremes.

Thus, *Hard Boiled* may be the *ne plus ultra* of the action genre for
Woo. I express this observation in such a contingent fashion because one
really cannot say for certain whether Woo will return to this style or
whether his work will evolve into something rather, or even quite,
different. The reason for this doubt is that *Hard Boiled* was his last film
before his relocation to Hollywood, and his Hollywood projects, with the
outstanding exception of the recent *Face/Off,* were generally adulterated
either by studio interference or by his own reluctance not to fit into his
new ambience. So the progression in Woo's development was interrupted
after *Hard Boiled,* and his viewers and critics are only now beginning to
see the outcome of his recent career move.

Additionally, Terence Chang downplays Woo's identification by
critics with "macho bloodfests" and the like. Chang has said that Woo
"doesn't want to make violent films any more, according to him. I remember one morning he came to work and he was very disturbed. In Orange

County, three Vietnamese kids tried to rob a big appliance store and they were eventually killed in the store. And they were all fans of John Woo's movies. He was very upset about that" (Chang, personal interview, 4 November 1995).

In any case, *Hard Boiled* rewards examination in several respects. One of these is its unusual variation on the "buddy" film. Many so-called "buddy" films have recently concerned policemen or detectives. A partial list would include *Lethal Weapon* (Richard Donner, 1987), *48 Hours* (Walter Hill, 1982), and *Red Heat* (Walter Hill, 1988; with Jim Belushi and Arnold Schwarzenegger). The formula of a pair of male heroes who usually begin by disliking each other and grow in friendship is derived in part from such films as *The French Connection* and *Bullitt*. The major difference between the two generations of films is that the relationship between the two heroes is essentially preformed and static in the earlier examples. There is no real development in their understanding of each other, nor does there need to be, since their focus is on the crime and the apprehension of the criminals. In the newer films, the criminal search is either a pretext for antics by the pair of heroes (*48 Hours*), or the criminal is an exaggeration of the negative features of one of the pair (*Red Heat*, *Lethal Weapon*) and so must be suppressed for the two heroes to become and remain friends, or the apprehension of the criminal provides the stage on which the growing friendship of the two pro-antagonists is played out.

In most of these movies, the two heroes are "open partners"—that is, they function together publicly, riding in patrol cars, entering bars to arrest suspects and so forth. Their bickering and banter are usually extended, occurring during or after chases, fights and the like. They may even have public disagreements, fighting with each other, and arguments with their superiors about being forced to work together. One of the pair is usually the "straighter" or more serious, objecting to the other's flakiness—*Lethal Weapon* is a good example. But in most cases, these pairs who function as law officers (some are themselves outlaws but work on the "right" side) are pressed into service by a superior, normally against their will.

Hard Boiled works both within and against this schema. Tequila is a tough cop with principles, very much in the Bullitt mold, who has no patience with messy bureaucratic entanglements: "a man who would argue with the gods," in Norman Mailer's words. In the course of an investigation into gunrunning, he inadvertently discovers that one of the Triad's main killers is actually an undercover cop. The two almost kill each other in a typical Woo face-off and then begin to work together secretly. They

eventually destroy the gun ring, and the undercover cop goes into protected retirement.

We can see several differences here with the formula previously out-
lined. For much of the film, the two characters are not publicly linked;
they do not even know each other for the first third of the film; and they
pair off *against* orders. Why the variations here? I think that this devia-
tion tells us something about Woo's films which helps to account for their
unique appeal.

The buddy movie's public display of friendship or companionship
between the two lead characters finds little place here. The interesting
point about *Hard Boiled*'s development of the buddy motif is that the two
cops only converse in private, in enclosed rooms, until the closing scenes
of the film.[1] This is rather unusual for such a movie, which is otherwise
(*Lethal Weapon* again) a sometimes public display of macho fireworks,
temper and so on. But after their initial encounter, when Alan saves
Tequila from killing Johnny Wong—or from being killed by Wong's
men—and Tequila does not know who Alan is, these two cops meet on
only two occasions before the final sequence in the hospital. One of these
is a brief contact, when Tequila singly breaks into the garage where Johnny
has just taken over Mr. Hui's operation. The two cops nearly kill each
other, with the scene ending in a moment of *anagnorisis* for Tequila. The
second meeting occurs on Alan's boat.

In both cases, the meeting is initiated by Tequila's injecting himself
into Alan's life; that is, Tequila is the unwanted intruder. Tequila is placed
in the odd position of being the "open" or public half of the pair, the visible and official, established policeman, who intrudes on the invisible,
unofficial and extralegal cop's affairs. This is a peculiar reversal of the
Lethal Weapon paradigm, in which Sgt. Murtaugh (Danny Glover) is the
sober, established cop who does not want to be associated with the
drunken, unpredictable, disreputable Martin Riggs (Mel Gibson). In *Hard
Boiled*, the tough cop seeks out the semi-outlaw. And their meetings, even
their pairing in the big hospital fight against Wong's men, have a curious intimacy normally lacking or underexpressed in buddy films.

Woo seems here to understand these two as descendants of the warrior class, and as such he places them apart from the society of others. To
put the point in Japanese terms, they follow the "way of the warrior."
Tequila and Tony are updated versions of Li and John, of Ho and Mark,
and of Brother Kin and Fan Ming (from *The Young Dragons*). Like these
earlier Woo heroes, they are "secret sharers," participants in a nearly ritual working-out of a code that only they, or those like them, very few in
any case (like Sidney in *The Killer*), understand and practice. *Hard Boiled*

is the last film, so far, in which Woo uses this formula. Some of the relative weakness of his early Hollywood efforts is directly attributable to the absence of the "paired hero" element.

Hard Boiled is also an intriguing film because, while it appears to be a straight action film, just a cop movie, it in fact fuses action film conventions with martial arts choreography and with some very Asian iconography. If *A Better Tomorrow* was a *wuxia pian* in modern dress, an updating of Chang Cheh's films about intra-clan disputes, and if *The Killer* was a gangster epic with strong admixtures of the Western and the *jidai-geki*,[2] *Hard Boiled* is a direct fusion of the straight action film from the West, the tough cop movie (*Dirty Harry, The French Connection*), and the buddy film, with the martial arts movie. That is, *Hard Boiled* is not primarily a recasting of familiar elements in modern dress; it is a fusion of several currents from movie history into a very unique mixture.

An important shift in the film from Woo's previous work is its self-assured, straight-ahead lead character. Tequila is a later-generation Inspector Li, but without that character's crippling romantic vulnerabilities. If Li's loss of Jenny is tragic for him, Tequila's difficulties with Teresa (Teresa Mo Shun-kwun) are part of his eventful life and are even an occasion for whimsy.

Woo has said that the Tequila character was modeled on Dirty Harry and on Popeye Doyle (Gene Hackman from *The French Connection*), and he does have Harry's toughness, insouciance and impatience with bureaucracy. He has Doyle's tenacity, but not his coarseness and brutality. Chow brings some added qualities to Tequila: a soulfulness expressed in his love of jazz music; an easy rapport with his fellow officers, making him especially popular with his subordinates, which Harry and Doyle are not; and, contrastingly, a kind of calculated but heated, almost out-of-control viciousness, seen when he kills the "undercover cop" in the opening teahouse scene.

Tequila is an original character in his own right; to call him a Chinese Dirty Harry is much too limiting. He resembles Mifune's samurai heroes in Kurosawa's *Yojimbo* and *Sanjuro* in his basic integrity and compassion masked by a show of indifferent callousness. The scene when Tequila jokingly discusses his single status with some of the junior officers is particularly reminiscent of *Sanjuro*, which has several humorous scenes showing the adulation of the young samurais for the experienced Sanjuro (Mifune). Not much is usually said, in connection with Woo, about Chow's contribution to character studies, but his efforts in *A Better Tomorrow, The Killer* and *Hard Boiled* have created at least three memorable and distinct characters who are yet all of a piece, men of an essential integrity and heroism who rediscover or reaffirm their humanity in struggles with evil.

Tequila represents as well an interesting counterpoint to the tough female cop seen in many Hong Kong films of the 1980s and 1990s, beginning with *Yes, Madam* (1985) and *Righting Wrongs* (1986), and continuing through the several *In the Line of Duty* films with Cynthia Khan (Yeung Lai-ching). In these films, the female cop is repeatedly displayed in situations requiring her to be tough and ruthless, as well as physically competent.

Cynthia Khan in particular derives much of her screen interest from the viewer's surprise (mirrored in the frequent skepticism of her male colleagues and criminal adversaries) that such an attractive woman could be at least as competent as the men on the force, yet maintain her femininity. The male police team up with her, but there is only rarely any hint of romance; the relationship is kept professional, with Cynthia playing the role of the first among equals. Her competence and her willingness to kill, when necessary, are not in question.

It is instructive to compare this image of the female cop with the one presented in *Hard Boiled*. The only policewoman presented at any length in the film is Teresa, Tequila's on-and-off girlfriend. She participates in the action as an adjunct, placed into positions usually reserved for women, for example, clerical work (she maintains the code contact with Alan). Furthermore, in the big hospital scene, she becomes the protectress of the babies in the infant ward, charged with evacuating them from the hospital; the SWAT team cops must guard her while she assists the nurses. She only uses violence on two occasions. She slaps one of Wong's men for making too much noise and scaring the babies, and she shoots another of Wong's men in self-defense. Teresa does not lack courage—slapping an armed man is certainly risky—but Woo does not really allow her to escape her gendered role. Perhaps, in fairness to Woo, this is closer to the real situation in Hong Kong, where policewomen generally are relegated to the types of roles usually thought of as "feminine." In any case, Chow's extremely tough and often callous cop is perhaps a response to the *Yes, Madam* type of character, which, in hands less talented than Cynthia Khan's (or Michelle Yeoh's), often slides into unintended caricature (as in 1994's *Satin Steel* with Jade Leung Ching).

Although *Hard Boiled* is a rather straightforward cop story, it is, like many of Woo's films, more subtle than a first viewing might indicate. Woo says that he made this movie to encourage the police in light of the serious crime problem in Hong Kong, so he did simplify its narrative for message purposes. Still, though not as difficult as *The Killer* and *Bullet in the Head*, it is not simplistic either. Tequila's violence is not uncritically approved; he suffers guilt and fear throughout the film because of his unthinking murder of a police witness[3] and his failure to protect his partner. His lone wolf attitude gets him into trouble; he very nearly kills Alan in a confrontation that would not have taken place had he followed Pang's orders. Even if audience sympathy is enlisted in his favor when he argues with Pang (Phillip Chan Yun-kin) about orders, the narrative clearly shows that he must learn to work as part of a team. Tequila has also begun to question the division between "thieves" and "cops," as he says to Pang in a particularly heated exchange (ch. 21). Like "Dirty" Harry Callahan or Wes Block, the Eastwood cop in *Tightrope*, Tequila is in danger of becoming his own enemy, of turning into the worst of what he pursues.

Woo's treatment of Tequila as separated from the group works on levels both literal and symbolic. On a literal level, Tequila is isolated because of his refusal to obey orders. This also contributes to his disagreements with Teresa. The point is underlined symbolically beginning with his killing of the "undercover cop." Woo has indicated that the flour on Tequila's face in this scene, when he shoots the "cop" and blood spatters into his face, gives him a ghostly appearance (he reminds one of the white-faced vampires in Hong Kong vampire movies). At this point, the film's narrative bifurcates into a literal realm of cops and gunrunners and a symbolic plane of death and rebirth. With his killing of the "cop," Tequila enters the realm of the "dead." He is "dead" to his colleagues in that he becomes a loner isolated from the group, and he is also tainted with death-dealing. He has contact with his policemen subordinates, but indicatively is posed not in two-shots with them, as at the very beginning of the film with Ah Lung and at the end with Tony, but as one man surrounded or faced by many. When he does appear in two-shot scenes, it is with Pang and Teresa, with whom he hardly agrees, and with Alan/Tony, whom he is only beginning to trust. (Also, he talks with "Mr. Woo," the bartender ex-cop played by Woo—but both men are isolated from the force; and with Foxy, an informer who belongs to neither world.) Tequila "goes it alone" in attacking Wong and his men. He appears in this instance (after the big garage battle) in an opposed two-shot with Alan; this is a signature Woo encounter in which they nearly kill each other—hardly an instance of successful resolution of communication problems.

After this scene, he begins to draw closer to Alan, going to his boat to find out the real truth about his work as an undercover man. From this point, he starts to work towards re-integration into the community, going to the Maple Group Hospital to see Foxy (who was nearly killed by

Wong's men and was only saved by Alan's clever intervention) and being shown in three-shots—a favorite Woo setup—with Tony and Teresa.

It is scarcely accidental that Tony and Tequila go into the hospital morgue to search for Wong's arsenal. Of course, the plot requires this, but the choice of the morgue is significant, as Tequila and Tony pass through the underworld on their way back to the world of the living.

Tony and Tequila enter the morgue by finding out which codes refer to empty receptacles for bodies—in other words, they find the password to cross over into the other world. When they enter through the "secret door," they are eventually sealed in with the underworld's guardian—Mad Dog (rather like Cerberus in Hades, or, in pop culture terms, a little like Oddjob who stayed behind in Fort Knox in *Goldfinger* to stop 007 from dismantling a nuclear bomb)—but not before they effect an escape from the first chamber, in the "Red Circle" scene, when Tequila causes the electronic seal to explode. When the seal does not fully release, Tony completes the circuit and is shocked into insensibility. Fearing that he is dead, Tequila revives him—brings him back to life, as it were. Tequila has now re-entered the world of the living. He has come from life-taker (killing the "cop") to life-giver. Woo underscores the point by inserting Tequila's memory of his partner Ah Lung's being killed by the "cop," thus tying the two scenes together.

Now Tequila again has a partner to replace Ah Lung, and together they go to fight first Mad Dog and then Wong and his other men. And, importantly for Tequila's recovery by the living, he becomes the savior of a baby in one of the film's most famous scenes.

As Tequila and Tony emerge from the morgue, they exit the way they entered—through the receptacles for the corpses. Now, though, instead of using the door, they actually lie on the pallets and emerge popping out in sequence like the dead springing from their graves. Now both have rejoined the group and will eliminate Wong and his men,[4] whose threat of death menaces not only the cops but also the hospital patients and personnel.

Tequila and Tony have finally seen eye-to-eye, and it is in fact Tony's role as undercover cop within the Triad to counterbalance Tequila. If Tony did not exist, Tequila would have no check on his excesses; and if Tequila did not exist, Tony might well lose himself within the life of the Triad. Each man complements the other, in a Taoist yin-yang opposition: Tequila is a near-criminal in the eyes of his chief Pang; his violent excesses cause problems for the force. Alan/Tony exercises a positive influence within the Triad, restraining Johnny Wong's worst excesses.

For Wong and his henchman Mad Dog (Philip Kwok Chun-fung), Alan is a shadow cop; for Pang, Tequila is a shadow criminal; he operates outside the law as often as within it.

In this respect, *Hard Boiled* is a lighter mirroring of *The Killer*, since that film had an "outlaw" or maverick policeman and a legalistic (principled, "ethical") outlaw. The structure of *The Killer* contributes here, too, in the triangular relationship between Tequila, Teresa and Tony. The passion and romantic weight are, to be sure, drawn off from this structure in *Hard Boiled*, but again we see Woo returning to his preferred plot geometry. As in *The Killer*, a woman becomes the axis of the relationship between the two heroes.

Here, Teresa is Tequila's ex-girlfriend, and she is shown receiving flowers from an apparent suitor. Tequila does not know that these white rose bouquets are part of an elaborate code by which Alan communicates with Pang, and Teresa does not mind letting Tequila think otherwise. Thus she reveals her actual interest in him, as she would not care to tweak his jealousy if she had no feelings for him. While it cannot be said that Alan has any serious feelings about her (we have no indication that he has even met her), later in the film, some banter takes place when the three are put together in one scene. A clear indication of the relative flattening of personal relationships in this film is to be seen in the fact that little is made of the possible love triangle. It is treated rather offhandedly. Unlike *The Killer*, *Hard Boiled* is concerned mainly with the professional, public environment of police and Triad. There is little room here for private display. Contrast the rather forced exchanges between Tequila and Alan (on the yacht, in the morgue) with the heavily emotional displays between Sidney and John and between John and Li.

Still, I would maintain, as does Dave Kehr, that *Hard Boiled* exhibits characters with "rich interior life" and features subtle rhythms (Kehr, commentary, *Hard Boiled* ch. 14). The film's surface brilliance is deceptively superficial. It conceals complex tensions and conflicts. Certainly, for instance, Alan's anguish at being forced to kill Mr. Hui (Kwan Hoi-shan), and his subsequent berserker attack on Hui's sons, are not light matters. Neither is Tequila's self-recrimination over the death of his partner. And for that matter, neither is the death of Mad Dog. When Wong kills him after Mad Dog resists his murder of patients, Woo's camera tracks in over his supine figure, curiously small and doll-like, given his prior displays of ferocious physicality. *Hard Boiled* is not at all a flippant or light treatment of serious matters but rather a professionalized, rather Hawksian treatment of them. A job needs to be done, and no one has time or energy for overemotionalism. Thus, Tequila reproves Tony for his self-pity and self-doubt: "Up there are hundreds of people in trouble, so drop the self-pity" (ch. 34).

The professionalism manifested in this film is, despite tonal differences, similar in emphasis to the status of the heroes in *The Killer* and of the group of protagonists in *Bullet in the Head*. In all these films, Woo shows a preference for a small, tightly joined group of men[5] resisting the evil influence of a large organization. Woo professes to detest politics (commentary, *Hard Boiled* ch. 31), but he does try to convey, as it were, anti-political messages in his films. So, he says, the "uniforms" and "fancy shirts" worn by gangs like Weng's in *The Killer* indicate military or dictatorial organization (Woo, personal interview, 2 March 1996). It is not difficult to see all three films as, on one level, metaphors for the struggle of Hong Kong people to retain their identity against the takeover by Beijing. This might help to clarify Woo's repeated recourse to small, unified groups of highly accomplished professionals—that is, outnumbered but very disciplined underdogs, winning out on a fantasy level against the super-organized forces of dictatorship. One of the problems with Woo's Hollywood films may be that this political subtext has been displaced. Thus, the troubles of Chance in *Hard Target* and of Hale in *Broken Arrow* become little more than standard good guy versus bad guy heroics.

Hard Boiled seems indeed quite far from the universe of *Broken Arrow*. From the earliest scenes, it is clear that we are not dealing with just another hero cop story, nor are we watching one of those "Triad glorification" films that became so popular by trivializing the content of *A Better Tomorrow*.

Tequila and some of his cop buddies, including his partner, joke as they head for a rendezvous at the Wyndham Teahouse in Hong Kong. Tequila and his partner Ah Lung have a quiet conversation over a dim sum breakfast, but we see that they are waiting for a bust to take place. The waiters are not all waiters—some of them are police. The scene unfolds before us, and we hear snatches of conversation among some men observed surreptitiously by Tequila in the mirror on a birdcage at his table. They are discussing gun shipments, and our anticipation becomes tense. Then, a prearranged signal, and one of the "waiters" throws a hot teakettle at a group of the men. Tequila follows suit, and an incandescently ferocious gun battle begins.

The innocent are killed as well as the combatants; bodies and bullets fly and land everywhere. The police and the criminals both seem surprised, as if the genie were out of the bottle and could not be put back. They hadn't bargained on this much chaos and death. Woo shows us here, as elsewhere, the falseness of "screen violence" which often seems so antiseptic: many people suffer and die in this scene, which neverthe-less is beautiful in its horrifying energy.

The scene is fascinating, and corrosively violent, but also confusing, at least after the fact. One important character does not act in a consis-tent fashion; when Chief Pang later explains to Tequila that one of the men he killed—spectacularly and grotesquely, his blood spattering on Tequila's flour-covered face—was a witness, this is perhaps acceptable dramatically. The man had deliberately shot innocent people in the restau-rant, had in fact killed Tequila's partner: maybe a witness would do even this last in an attempt to cover himself from suspicion. But later in the film, Pang and Tequila argue because Tequila killed *a policeman* in the restaurant. Do they mean his inadvertent killing of his partner by not protecting him enough, or do they mean to refer to the man he had killed? Pang appears to hint at the latter interpretation.

Any viewer looking for consistency would certainly have a complaint. And, in fact, when I brought this subject up to Terence Chang, he reacted almost with relief, mentioning an "earlier story" (see n. 3).

What was "the earlier story" to which Chang was referring? Woo clarified this for me in an interview. As Chang had explained, the tea-house scene was shot in some haste, since the building was scheduled for demolition (Woo just speeded up the process!). Woo elaborated on this point and on the conflicts in the script:

> We shot the teahouse scene before we had a script—because the teahouse is very historical—so we shot the scene before they tore it down. The original idea is that Tony Leung was playing the psychopath. He killed a baby, put poison in [its food]—like what happened in Japan about six years ago. He also cooperated with the gun smugglers and tried to black-mail the city. So I really didn't want to give the young audience any bad influence. So I changed the story.[6] Tony Leung is an undercover cop, and he has been sent to kill people—and he feels guilty about that. And I also tried to build a new kind of relationship with Chow Yun-fat and Tony Leung. So we made up a story—one of the bad guys was undercover. And Chow Yun-fat, he didn't know that and he killed him by accident. So Chow Yun-fat had a good relationship with Tony Leung, and he didn't want to have the same thing happen again. Also, I can build Chow Yun-fat's character, and also build his point of view, and he does the job but he also doesn't want to kill the people [Woo, personal interview, 8 No-vember 1995].

As Terence Chang had commented, the scene is indeed a little difficult to follow: "You don't know who's shooting whom. It's a little bit confusing because it's from another story." The man killed by Tequila did not fit well into the story because, as Chang said, "He was not supposed to be a cop."

Perhaps such inconsistencies do not ultimately vitiate *Hard Boiled*, since its effect depends on other factors—kinetic bloodletting, relationships of loyalty and so forth—but they do contribute to its falling short of a film like *The Killer*, which though made on a lower budget is still quite consistent on its own terms and also emotionally additive. The viewer experiences a constantly growing dread about the probable outcome for John, Jenny, Li and Sidney; somehow, though, we never have the same suspense in *Hard Boiled*, chiefly because the cop formula is more strictly followed here. We have little doubt that Tequila, at least, will win out in the end.

Tequila will survive, and will rejoin the social group of policemen, but not before he undergoes a hero's trial of outsized proportions. He, and Tony, will survive a ferocious and protracted gun battle in the Maple Group Hospital. This battle, actually a complex set of running conflicts that succeed and interlock with each other, is justly seen as the highlight of the film. But, as critic Dave Kehr cautions, it is much more than a mere gunfight (commentary, *Hard Boiled*, chs. 32–33). The battle provides the occasion for Woo to interweave several threads of the plot and to examine his characters in the laboratory of a highly stressful situation.

A key to the artistic success of the extensive final gun battle sequences is Woo's reliance on suspense. He uses a technique like Hitchcock's in *Strangers on a Train*, deferring the audience's "gratification" by introducing factors into the plot and letting them develop while concentrating on other activities. Thus, in *Strangers on a Train*, tennis pro Guy (Farley Granger) must finish a match while we wonder whether Bruno (Robert Walker) will plant Guy's lighter at the scene of the murder of his wife; we are transfixed watching the tennis match while we know that Bruno is on his way to plant the lighter. Hitchcock tightens the screws by causing Bruno to drop the lighter into a storm grate; we must watch him groping and straining for it while we think of Guy pushing to finish the match in time to intercept him.

Woo uses a similar strategy in the gun battle. We are shown Tequila telling Teresa that she will receive flowers as a signal (his appropriation of Alan's code earlier in the film, and thus, implicitly, his resumption of his former role as Teresa's lover) to evacuate the hospital, and we are also shown some very vulnerable patients, including the inhabitants of the neonatal ward, totally defenseless infants. Now Woo cuts to Tequila and Tony's attempts to find Wong's arsenal; the scene shifts between these efforts and Teresa's anxious wait for the signal, which, unknown to her but vouchsafed to us in a prior insert shot, has already been placed in her pocket.

But Woo complicates the scenario further. While Tony and Tequila struggle to escape from a sealed chamber, Teresa and Chief Pang argue about the measures to be taken and about Teresa's feelings for Tequila. Pang realizes that Teresa still cares for Tequila; she discovers the flower. The action is thus advanced to the next level, which will be to inform the hospital administrator (a recalcitrant bureaucrat whom Pang crudely upbraids in a manner reminiscent of Tequila—it is not only Tequila who changes during the film) that all must be evacuated. Meanwhile, Tequila and Tony discuss their roles as cop and undercover man, and Tony complains that even when he tries to do good he ends up harming the innocent. As he says this, we see one of cops preparing a room for the expected assault by Wong's men. Later, we will understand the significance of this shot, since Tony will unintentionally kill this same policeman. Thus, Woo deepens the meaning of the parallel action tracks by adding moral and emotional dilemmas and complications to what could have been a routine storyline.

An added dimension to the layering of the battle scene is the focus on Mad Dog (Philip Kwok). The role of unredeemable villain is left here for Anthony Wong's character; Mad Dog, his factotum, is shown to be a killer with self-imposed limits to his criminality. Woo prepares us for Mad Dog's morally based rebellion against Wong by having him tell Wong that he should let the patients go. Wong asks him tauntingly if he's "scared," and Mad Dog responds tellingly, "I'm not scared. I've been around. But some things in life are out of line" (ch. 35).[7] So we are not surprised, indeed we are rewarded, when he comes to a tacit understanding with Tony after they have fought furiously. With a score of patients trapped between them, they lay down their pistols, and Mad Dog gestures to the patients to leave. Wong suddenly arrives and shoots the patients; this causes Mad Dog to attack him openly and to be killed.

The motif or trope of innocents threatened is introduced early in the sequence with a peculiarly placed shot of babies crying in their ward— the shot is oddly placed because it would seem contradictory in an environment of guns and gangsters. Teresa is soon linked to the protection of the infants in an admittedly conservative move (the lady cop as mother!), and Woo even creates a humorously exaggerated vision of a family unit by injecting Tequila into the little tableau. He quizzically asks Teresa if she wants this many kids, and she responds, "Sure, why not?" (ch. 37).

Both Teresa and Tequila will be placed as well in the position of "parent" to a single infant during the battle. In both cases, the parenting situation evokes a contragendered quality in the "parent." Teresa, holding a baby, reacts in nearly masculine fashion to a gangster's making noise by slapping him—a feminine, perhaps, but still a very assertive gesture.

Tequila sings a lullaby and cradles an infant to him in a maternal way to protect it from assailants.

Hard Boiled is a very nicely set-up film; the action sequences are particularly spectacular, and the production has a glossy look that belies its small (by U. S. standards) budget. Unlike *The Killer*, however, *Hard Boiled* is sometimes criticized for superficiality and cruelty (for example by Tony Rayns in his review). Although not as thematically complex as *The Killer*, *Hard Boiled* is more textually dense than many would maintain. A case in point, besides the already noted use of symbolism and parallelism, is its deceptively simple employment of musical elements.

Much of the music in *Hard Boiled* is scored to action and is quite kinetic. Some of the music is hauntingly effective, especially the orchestration (scored by Michael Gibbs) that accompanies Alan's yacht appearances; the ethereal quality of the saxophone background accentuates Alan's sense of insularity and unreality. Less obvious than such a foregrounded example, though, is the importance of the song tunes that Alan uses to communicate with Pang through Teresa. She partially decodes these tunes by putting the melodies into notation, and Pang enters the notation into the computer for final decoding. The neat little gimmick serves to obscure the relevance of the lyrics themselves.

The first of these songs, which Teresa receives with flowers (Alan's accustomed method) was "Hello," performed by Lionel Richie. The line used in the film is "Are you somewhere feeling lonely or is someone loving you?" The rest of the song, though, seems oddly apt (perhaps humorously so, in keeping with Teresa's comic approach to Tequila and later to Tony as a foil for her relationship with Tequila). In the context of Tony's anonymous connection to Teresa, with its use of flowers as communication, the song's references to being "alone with you inside my mind" and to "dreams" in which the lover has "kissed your lips a thousand times" are ironically pertinent to Tony's lonely undercover life.

The other song is the familiar standard "Mona Lisa," Nat King Cole's signature piece. Its lyrics are also situationally apt, especially the two verses preceding the ones quoted in the film. The code uses the line "Many dreams have been brought to your doorstep / They just lie there and they die there." The previous two lines are "Do you smile to tempt a lover, Mona Lisa, / Or is this your way to hide a broken heart?" Applicable either to Teresa or to Tequila, the lines could perhaps indicate that Alan "knows" something intuitively about Teresa and her situation. Perhaps not, but Woo has a penchant for creating "extrasensory" or intuitive links between his characters; thus, he told me, in *The Killer*, when, early in the film, Li does not know John other than as a suspect in the nightclub hit, he nevertheless "feels" him[8] (Woo, personal interview, 2 March 1996). In reference to the two songs in *Hard Boiled*, David Wu, the music editor, explained to me that Woo and he selected the songs deliberately for their lyrics, to indicate that Alan was sort of a "pen pal" to Teresa.[9]

Thus, the music, like so much else in this final Hong Kong project by Woo, enriches and comments on the film's text. With the complex action choreography and the melding of sound and visual elements in *Hard Boiled*, Woo had attained a level of skill and artistic sureness which was to become crucial for him in finding a niche in Hollywood.

Chapter 9

Woo in Hollywood: *Hard Target, Broken Arrow* and *Face/Off*

*They don't want you until you have made a name, and by
the time you have made a name, you have developed some
kind of talent they can't use. All they will do is spoil it, if
you let them.*

—Raymond Chandler,
Letter, 7 November 1951,
to editor Dale Warren (published in
Raymond Chandler Speaking, 1962)

Hard Target

Woo completed his first Hollywood film, *Hard Target*, in 1993. He had been brought to Hollywood both by his concerns about Hong Kong's transfer to mainland China and by his lifelong "dream" of working in the world's film capital. Assisted by business partner Terence Chang, he was introduced to Universal producer Jim Jacks. Jacks recalled, "[A]n interview was set up with William Morris agents for me to meet John and in passing I mentioned this Hong Kong movie. [A]nd he said, 'I directed that.'"[1] Woo had just completed *Hard Boiled*; perhaps, as Roger Avary says, "When John made *Hard Boiled*, he was ready to come to the United States. And I think actually, he probably imagined *Hard Boiled* as an American film" (Avary, commentary, *Hard Boiled* ch. 34). In any case, he was to find that even an "all-out action" genre movie like *Hard Boiled* would not prepare him for the Hollywood environment.

But the big problems came later. Initial difficulties had to do with selling the studio on a Chinese director known mainly for "over-the-top, melodramatic action movies" (Jacks, personal interview).

As Jacks said, the studio had a script, by former Navy Seal Chuck Pfarrer (*Darkman*, *Navy Seals*), and the project had been set up for shooting

in New Orleans with Jean-Claude Van Damme in the lead role of Chance
Boudreaux. The last major task, then, was to find a director—Andrew
Davis was interested, according to Jacks, but decided against it. Eventually, Woo's name became linked to the film.[2] This may be one of the
problems with the film. Movies in search of directors are not likely to
become auteur classics. One would prefer the reverse process—Hitchcock
looking for scripts and actors, for instance.

Woo was sent the script and liked it; a shooting schedule was set.
Woo did have some control once he signed on. He was able to cast some
of the secondary actors, to find a cinematographer, and so forth (Chang,
personal interview, 4 November 1995). The film's cinematographer, Russell Carpenter (whose most recent work is *Titanic*, for which he won a
1998 Academy Award), said that his hiring onto the film—a very positive
decision, in light of the final product—came as a result of an introduction by a mutual acquaintance:

> [A] friend, Darryl Kass, the UPM, [asked if I] would come in and meet
> John Woo. I went to a meeting [where] there were [about] twelve people.
> I had to admit that I hadn't seen any of his work—and I thought, well
> that's the end of that. But I immediately went out and saw *The Killer*.
> And at first I was repelled by the incredible amount of over-the-top and
> somewhat cartoonish violence. And yet twenty minutes into the film I
> knew that this was the work of a master. It was the choice of camera
> angles, how he was cutting his scenes—and also, in John's Chinese films,
> besides the mayhem there are stories about comradeship and loyalty or
> betrayal that I thought were very, very interesting. His films were little
> labyrinths; they weren't straight-ahead action-mayhem films like we often
> find in the United States. I really wanted to meet John again, and talk to
> him about his films. Luckily, another meeting was arranged, and we
> spoke for a short time. And I liked him very much. A little while later I
> found out that I was lucky enough to do the film [Carpenter, personal
> interview].

Hard Target, as we have noted, was assigned a director during its
planning stages. As Jacks recalled:

> *Hard Target* was a script that we were developing at Universal for Van
> Damme. And so I sat down with this writer Chuck Pfarrer. And we
> thought about both variations of *The Naked Prey* [and] *Most Dangerous
> Game*. And first we tried *The Naked Prey*, but that didn't really work, and
> we also had a kind of an *Aliens* which Chuck ultimately turned into a
> comic book called *Virus* for Dark Horse Comics. And the third thing was
> this *Most Dangerous Game* thing. And so we started playing with that and
> we decided to set it in New Orleans because it would give an explanation
> for Jean-Claude's accent—and off we went and started developing it.

Jim Jacks was instrumental in bringing John Woo to Hollywood. Although Woo was shuttling back and forth from the States to Hong Kong at the time, he had not decided to move to America, since he had no ties to a studio or even to a project. Jacks had met him previously and was quite interested in his style. Since Woo was back in Hong Kong, Jacks, Nina Jacobson, and Van Damme flew to Hong Kong to discuss the script with him.

When Woo accepted the project, Jacks was confronted with the problem of getting the studio to agree to hire Woo. He met with indifference or lack of understanding:

> [I]t became a process of trying to convince the studio to do the movie with John. They really just didn't want to hear about it. Every time I mentioned I was thinking about doing it with John Woo they said, "Well, gee, John would be great. Can he speak English?" I just couldn't get the studio to consider him because it was another Chinese director. [T]he drama in those movies tends to be somewhat over the top, and they were a little concerned about the language, and they had a lot of justifiable concerns. And also they just hadn't seen the movies. But finally Tom Pollock [chairman at the studio] looked at the movie and said, "Well, he certainly can direct an action scene. So if Jean-Claude will approve him, I'll do it with him."

In all these machinations one can discern the seeds of trouble for the film. Several factions within the production crew pushed and pulled at the film, as Jacks put it, "like a taffy pull." Having "a lot of cooks" on the film caused considerable problems and damaged the film's potential.

Hard Target simply does not realize its promise. Perhaps, too, the basic concept is a little too shocking or even exploitative. It was one thing, and bad enough, in the original Connell story "The Most Dangerous Game," for a man to hunt vacationers shipwrecked on his island. It is quite another for a crew of ex-mercenaries, rich eccentrics, and good ol' boys to hunt homeless veterans. The fundamental unpleasantness of the premise may cause the viewer to miss some of the film's stronger points and to dismiss it as a disappointing piece of genre work.

Hard Target does have its strong points, and we might pause in criticizing it to consider what it would have been without Woo at the helm. In fact, the high expectations—unrealistic ones, given all the negative factors in relation to this film—accorded Woo are precisely the reason that some critics are harder on this movie. It is in fact much better and more interesting cinematically than most movies of its genre. It does, though, illustrate for us some of Woo's vulnerabilities as a director, particularly and most noticeably his unfortunate tendency, understandable though it may be, to try to accommodate or please the studio in his new home in Hollywood. As Jacks put it, "I mean, he tries very very hard to please. He tries to please on one hand and since he really can't get everybody happy, at some point, he kind of shuts off and then he starts doing what he wants to do and it's neither fish nor fowl sometimes."

Despite all the studio interference and the participation of unsolicited "cooks," *Hard Target* is a John Woo film. It displays his distinctive touch, from the active camera and the use of signature transitions to the set pieces usually associated with Woo. The weaknesses of the film are attributable not only to interference but also to a script not totally suited to Woo's style—it lacks the opposed pair of male heroes—and to Woo's overeagerness to please the executives.

One of the most often-cited problems with the film concerns its star, Jean-Claude Van Damme. Van Damme has been severely criticized for his tendency to interfere in the film's shooting, as well as for his performance. The latter charge seems less justified than the former. Van Damme's performance actually deserves rather more credit than it has received. His interference in shooting decisions and in the scripting revision is more meretricious, although as a co-producer he certainly had as much right as anyone to make his opinions known.[3]

The greatest problem with Van Damme is the fact that he is not the best foil for Henriksen and Vosloo. Van Damme's screen persona is pretty straightforward (or simplistic, if one prefers): a physically impulsive, heroic figure. *Hard Target* needed a more complex character. The screenwriter, Chuck Pfarrer, had Armand Assante in mind when he created the role (Pfarrer, telephone interview, 8 December 1995). Assante's more intense screen personality and the sinister undercurrent perceptible in his work would have fit quite well with Henriksen's qualities.

All this is not meant to detract from Van Damme's appeal in the role. He does rather well at portraying a strong, tight-lipped hero who does not abide cruelty and who is even capable of displaying tenderness, as for example when he tells Natasha that her "daddy was murdered." Critics of Van Damme's work here were often expecting something else, a different kind of role; and admittedly it is not fine acting that has made Van Damme a star. Still, it is true to say, as Jim Jacks did, that "*Hard Target* really shouldn't have been somebody like Jean-Claude." The film would have worked better dramatically with a less straight-ahead action hero in the lead.

Hard Target would have been much more of a John Woo film if a complexly antiheroic actor had been cast in the Chance role—perhaps Armand Assante, as Pfarrer thought, or maybe Antonio Banderas. The reason for this is that Henriksen's villain, Fouchon, is much closer to Woo's ideal conception of an elegant, complex (romantic) criminal than are the rather one-dimensional criminals in Woo's Hong Kong films. A pairing of two opposed types, Chance as an antiheroic or somewhat villainous hero, and Fouchon as a somewhat heroic (tragic) villain, might even have given Woo the chemistry he has always sought.

Even with things as they were, Woo still made the best of it. He tried very hard—whether at Van Damme's insistence or from his own instincts as director—to give Van Damme added heroic status. While it is true that some of this was at the star's request, still Woo shows himself very much in character when he tries to romanticize his hero, to lend him larger-than-life stature. And it is also the case that probably no other director working in the action genre would have been capable of the kind of mythopoeia that caused one of the cast, Willie Carpenter ("Elijah Roper"), to claim:

> I just think as a persona, what John did lifted Jean-Claude quite a few levels up. John slows the camera down, and Jean-Claude suddenly looks like the biggest, baddest dude. I think he just raised him up, he made him bigger than life—talk about film magic, it was just absolutely wonderful stuff. What [Woo] did in that film made [Jean-Claude] look almost Arnold [Schwarzenegger]-size. I think John deserves credit for that [telephone interview].

In no Woo film before *Face/Off* are the villains quite so intriguingly sinister. Their characterization owes something to a jacking-up of the script from the relatively simple idea of a group of hunters with dogs pursuing homeless men to the high-tech, safari-leader-for-rent ex-mercenaries leading hunters with big pocketbooks on thrill kills, and, for dogs, using motorcyclists with high-tech MP5Ks instead of Dobermans. This technical element lends some interest to the film, not only on its own merits (flashy weaponry and so on) but also because it sets up an appropriate subtextual conflict: punkish, nouveau sophistication and urbanite decadence versus traditional, Old World integrity, loyalty, and self-sacrifice. That is, it replays American populist values: the country (Douvee) versus the city (Fouchon); morality (Natasha, Roper) versus decadence and deception (Poe, Morton); the New West or the frontier (Boudreaux, essentially a Natty Bumppo in New Orleans attire) versus the overrefined East or Europe (Fouchon again); and finally nativism or "old" immigrants (Boudreaux, Carmine [Kasi Lemmons]) versus "new" immigrants (Mr. Zenan).

Part of the dualism here between Europe and America, Old World aristocrat and New World "common man" can be teased out of a little

remark made by Fouchon after Pik (Vosloo) kills Dr. Morton. He tells
Pik: "Eastern Europe. We can work there for years" (ch. 17).[4] This, of
course, refers directly to the recent troubles there, but for movie audiences, the remark conjures up associations with Transylvania, Count
Dracula, vampires, and so forth.[5] And in fact *Hard Target* becomes rather
more intriguing if one considers it as a non-supernatural vampire film.
Fouchon and Pik are the leaders of a group of parasites preying off the
thrill-seeking of the moneyed class; their real work is at night; their dress
(generally black and flowing) even codes them as movie vampires. One
of Fouchon's lines stricken from the final film underlines the ghoulish
association: "I'm on every battlefield."[6] The film's structure is also reminiscent of vampire films with Chance and Nat acting the part of vampire killers.
Without overstretching the analogy, we should note that such resonances
lend weight to the film's contrastive structure and help to outline Chance
and Nat (and their associates, Carmine and Douvee) as "working-class
heroes" combating Old-World, aristocratic perversion, cruelty, and par-
asitism. Fouchon even has "only human" servants (that is, not endowed with
special training, in this context)—particularly Randal Poe, who is associated with a very perverse, sleazy ambience of sex shops and massage parlors.

Fouchon and Pik are, in Woo style, not really "villains" in the sense
of unredeemable, Scorpio-type psychos as in *Dirty Harry* or the Hammond brothers in *Ride the High Country*. They are, as Pik says, "professional": this is their work, amoral as it is.[7] Credit must go to Woo and to
Pfarrer for distinguishing Chance's opponents by humanizing them and
by providing individual characteristics for them.[8] That the finished film
is not as "John Woo" in this respect as one would like is due to production
interference and certainly not to the wishes of the creative team.

In spite of the production difficulties on *Hard Target*, it is an accessible film for studying Woo's working method. In the course of numerous interviews and communication with members of its cast and crew, I
was able to learn much about John Woo's working methods and the
atmosphere on one of his projects, as well as interesting details about the
making of the film.

Discussions with members of the crew only confirmed and augmented
what is known about John Woo: that his approach is always meticulous,
yet flexible and that he is always concerned about authenticity. Cinematographer Russell Carpenter provided insights both into Woo's general
working method and into the specifics of this particular production. Robert
"Rock" Galotti, the weapons wrangler for *Hard Target* and the armorer for
Broken Arrow and *Face/Off*, was very forthcoming with data about the
kinds of weapons used in the film and Woo's reasons for using them.

As Chuck Pfarrer indicated, the original script was considerably transformed before reaching its final version. The original script was technically quite akin to *The Most Dangerous Game*. A group of hunters with dogs were to pursue homeless men in New Orleans. By the time of the final shooting script, quite a technical change had taken place, with the simple hunter-hunted setup acquiring a glitzy and high-tech relief. Certainly to Woo's credit is the fact that he surrounded himself with technicians who brought high standards and personal qualities to what could have been a hollow commercial property.[9]

According to Galotti and others, Woo takes a direct hand in planning many details of his films. *Hard Target* was of course a new and often baffling experience for him, since he had to work not only with a new crew, but also in an unfamiliar language and a different setting—a setting made even more challenging by the many producers involved. But, as we shall see, Woo learns and adapts very quickly, although he does not simply reject his own preferences out of hand.

The weapons wrangler in a film might seem an odd choice for an extended interview, were it not for the nature of *Hard Target* and its director. Woo has said that while he has never fired a gun and is not in favor of harming anyone, nevertheless he likes to make movies with guns—as the counterpart of the sword in swordplay films—and that many times he uses the gun to "say something" (Woo, commentary, *The Killer* ch. 9). Even the most casual viewer of Woo's action films will see immediately the importance of guns for the narrative. They serve as icons, as props, as imagery within a particular scene, as narrative bridges and as plot elements. Woo even tries, like Peckinpah in *The Wild Bunch*, to link certain sounds of gunfire with particular characters.

Galotti noted that Woo has specific preferences regarding guns in his films. First, "he has one weapon that is in every show he works on— and that's a Beretta 92F, police issue type."[10] Galotti says that he has to have Berettas in his inventory "because if I ever do a John Woo movie, I know that I have to have Berettas somewhere in his films." Second, Woo is interested in taking a direct hand only in the choice of weaponry for the main characters. Finally, as Galotti put it, "John is big on noise and fire."

On *Hard Target*, Berettas certainly made their appearance. But also in the inventory, and appearing in the film, were an interesting variety of weapons, most firearms, some not.[11] One of the more unusual weapons featured in this film was the crossbow used by the actor Bob Apisa, who played Mr. Lopaki, one of the hunters. Galotti describes it as

an arrow gun that has been used by various military organizations. It's a pneumatic gun, basically. It forces an arrow with an aluminum shaft, rubber stabilizing fins and a very sharp broad tip on it. [I]t'll pump it up to 1800 psi.[12]

The "dogs," that is, the motorcycle riders who "spot" and chase the prey for the hunters, were stylishly outfitted. Their principal armament was the MP5K, a 9mm SIG machine pistol. Other characters used an assortment of handguns, M-16 based machine guns, CAR-15s, and shotguns.

Mr. Galotti said that the main discussion he had with Woo on the film was about Van Damme's Mossberg shotgun. Woo did not think that the "fire" was "big" enough from Van Damme's Mossberg. Galotti related this discussion as follows:

> The flash wasn't big enough—and he said, [imitates Woo] "I need the fire bigger." And I said, "OK," so I hand packed a few rounds and fired it and he went, "Uh——bigger." [I] packed a little bit more, and I thought, this isn't going to be much of a difference—so I went overboard. And he was standing outside, he was on the camera cart, right in front of everybody. "Mr. Woo, I need to do a test-fire for you, are you watching?" "Yeah." So I go, "Fire in the hole!" and I fire this shotgun round, and at about fifty feet away I hear people go "Jeez, that was loud!" And all I see is John smile. And I said, "OK, John?" And he's like, "Good, good, good." Big, big smile. And I thought, "That's it, OK." So everybody affectionately nicknamed the rounds Rock Loads for the show, but they were actually John Woo loads.

Another example of direct participation by John Woo in weaponry choice or style was the very important decision about the gun to be used by Emil Fouchon (Lance Henriksen). According to Galotti, Henriksen initiated the process by asking him for a weapon fitting his character's style:

> Lance came up and he said, "I need something really classy—you know, this guy wears Armani suits and he drives a Jag convertible. I got to have something that just shows *class*." So he says, "I want this," and, you know, kind of like the Contender thing—and I thought, a Contender would be pretty cool. So I went to John and John and I talked about it, and he said, a Contender would be very, very good.[13]

The Contender was a particularly apt touch for Fouchon. Not only did it fit perfectly with the character's upscale, pseudo–European image, but also it revealed or highlighted an important element of Fouchon's psychological makeup. The Contender requires reloading after every shot, and the process—the breech is broken, the barrel tilted downward, and a new shell dropped in—is visually sensual, especially under Woo's direction. This permitted Fouchon to express his "hands-on" approach to his profession and his dandified concern with style. Additionally, the single-shot weapon added an existential note to the "work" done by Fouchon. As a character living on the edge, he noticeably eschews machine guns, grenades, and even automatic pistols, as these weapons both distance the killer from his target and mechanize or automatize the process of battle, thus mitigating the danger of the hunt. The Contender fits well with a character who berates his second-in-command Pik for wanting to kill Chance from a helicopter. Pik, as a thorough professional without his leader's dangerous, corrupt romanticism, does not wish to take unnecessary risks. Fouchon dismissively and impatiently tells him, "Any pinhead can take him from the air. I want to take him from the ground!" (*Hard Target* ch. 27).

The art design for this film was also remarkable in its meticulousness and multi-textured qualities, culminating in the interesting set piece in the Mardi Gras warehouse. This is indeed one of the elements that differentiates *Hard Target* from run-of-the-mill action films. Much of the credit for the finished product should go to Phil Dagort, the film's production designer. And, of course, Woo must be credited with the overall visualization of the film; it is this "look," in part, that has led some critics to note the "Hong Kong" quality of the film (in the sense that it is somehow different from the usual Hollywood product).

Although one might believe that the New Orleans setting automatically creates baroque scenarios and lush landscapes, this impression is exaggerated. We have only to think of, say, *The Big Easy* (Jim McBride, 1987) or *Tightrope* to see how little a filmmaker might depend on New Orleans for baroque or grotesque effects. With the major exceptions of the bayou scene and (interestingly) the Mardi Gras warehouse and street scenes, *Hard Target* might have been shot almost anywhere. The evident (and noteworthy) point is that Woo simply has a different vision or perspective from the directors of the other two films.

Woo clearly decided to take full advantage of the odd aspects of New Orleans, not necessarily those appealing to tourists. This decision is almost immediately apparent in the scene with Natasha and her father's landlady. The landlady's house, an older dwelling in the city, has a cluttered and "lived-in" quality, but more importantly it "feels" right. The house seems very Southern, or perhaps Old World–like, with its antique furnishings, wall hangings, china, and pieces of art and bric-a-brac. Woo emphasizes the picturesqueness of the interior by shooting it from a Hitchcockian "god's-eye" angle and by tracking in onto the two women sitting in the parlor, as if we were entering a *tableau vivant*. The house also has an important Woo trademark or "signature" piece: a birdcage, which we first see prominently displayed as the dolly-in begins.

The birdcage was brought in by the set decorator, Michelle Poulik, who is an admitted longtime Woo fan. As Phil Dagort said, she "snuck" some things in (telephone interview). As usual, Woo was open to ideas: "He was very excited when I got the birdcage" (Poulik, telephone interview). The birdcage added a recognizable "Woo" quality to the film, one that a seasoned viewer would notice, given the fact that birdcages appear in *Hard Boiled* and are common fixtures in Hong Kong teahouses. Woo used the birds and birdcage, favorites of his, with typical flexibility: "What was interesting was John shot the scene and let the birds make noise— sound man be damned." Dagort explained that the house belonged to a woman who used it as a bed and breakfast: "The downstairs was her artist studio for her and the wall between the living room and dining room had been torn out, giving us the advantage of more space to work in. We completely redid the room, refurnished it, and used the missing wall and dining room as our camera port" (Dagort, fax to author).

Probably the most striking design motif in *Hard Target* was the Mardi Gras floats. Dagort was very proud of these (and Woo, Dagort said, saw the artistic value of the big face so prominently featured in the film). He stressed that they were not simply picked up or lying around at a warehouse:

> We did not simply go to an existing Mardi Gras storage facility. No, those spaces would have been very uninteresting visually. They have no windows and low ceilings. In addition, such a space would not be very practical for shooting. We could have barely gotten the camera equipment in, let alone have room to stage the stunts.
>   I found this wonderful old empty warehouse space with huge windows. In fact it had too many windows for the lighting budget—so the camera department ended up blacking a lot of them out. We brought all the floats and props into that space to create the set. We also constructed an entire two story building inside of the warehouse and dressed it as the offices and shop of our invented float company. This gave us more areas to stage a variety of action pieces.

The floats were in large part specially designed by a particular firm:

> Obtaining the floats we needed was a challenge because of the rivalry between the krews and float building companies. If we used floats from one krew or company we couldn't rent any from another one. We couldn't find any one place that had enough stock to supply what I needed to fill this huge warehouse until we found the Barth Brothers. We liked their work a lot. One brother was the business man and the other was the artist. He was a great sculptor. He did amazing things by treating brown paper with a sort of rubber cement and letting it get tacky. Then he would just sculpt away with it. They had some very wonderful pieces in

their stock we could use for the set, and I knew we could use them to build the dragon John wanted.

Dagort described some amusing incidents during the design stage that reflected tellingly on the setting in New Orleans. These incidents also tell us something about the improvisational quality that might not have prevailed on a bigger film, say *Broken Arrow*.

One of the incidents concerned the floats:

> On our search for floats we surveyed another float company, owned by a very politically influential man. I passed on them because I didn't like their work. Apparently they were not pleased. Later, the owner must have used his connections at the local paper to have an article published at the time of the film's release stating that *their* company provided all the floats for the picture. Then to make matters worse, the producers forgot to give the Barth Brothers screen credit as contracted in the theatrical release of the film. I'm still not sure that the mogul of the rival company didn't call in another favor and manage that little detail as well. The New Orleans old boy network at it again [fax to author].

In another case, the set-building for Chance's apartment ran into a major snag. Phil Dagort spent considerable effort trying to find a setting for Chance's quarters, since Chance was basically a wanderer and there was little indication about his living arrangements in the script. In any event, Dagort happened on a decrepit building in the Quarter and, seeing its possibilities for a "rundown" flop for Chance, began working on it:

> As soon as I saw it I could envision the set of the interior. From the outside of the building there was a shift of level and a funny kind of roof. This gave me the idea to do a split level garret set. And that's exactly what I did. I never went up into the real building to see what was really there. It simply inspired me from the exterior what the possibilities for the set on the stage could be. I was really proud of it. We did all the aged, peeling paint to make it look virtually abandoned, perhaps it was a place he didn't even own or rent, but he could just hang out there[14] [fax to author].

But, as Dagort related, local "politics," or lifestyle, intruded:

> We had started to build a set of the interior on our stage matching the doors and windows of the building in the French Quarter. Well, halfway through the construction the location manager comes to me and says, "You've got to stop building, we can't get this location." Apparently the guy he was negotiating with claimed to be the owner of the property but was really only the manager. So we stopped building the set while they tried to track down the real owner. I didn't know what we were going to do if we had to start all over. Well the owner was found, but he did not want anything to do with a film company.

It had been a difficult location to find and I wasn't about to start looking again, so the location manager persisted but it was not looking good.
They had the film commission on it. They even had the Governor on it.
I'm sure they would have loved for me to pick another location even if the
production had to incur a loss in construction. But John backed me up.
He knew the possibilities of the place both exterior and interior. So
finally by sheer will it happened, we had permission and we could con-
tinue building the set. Even the location manager never told me exactly
what they had to do to get that location. Some big palms had to be
greased, but that's the way it is there [fax to author].

Dagort was similarly amused about the shooting schedule in "Detective Carmine Mitchell's" office. This set was part of a historic building in
the Quarter, which the *Hard Target* people used because they wanted a
"forties" feel, like the setting in Randal's office and home.

Woo didn't want a modern police station. We wanted something with
lots of old wood paneling—a forties detective kind of look to tie into the
older New Orleans look of our film. There was a police station set that
another film had used and we expanded and added to it. It was housed in
an old historic building in the quarter that was closed down while its new
use was to be determined. We almost did not get to film there. The
building was now in a soup of local politics being fought over by the city
and state governments as well as the local preservationists who didn't
want film people to touch it. One of my draftsmen had happened to run
into an architect involved in the preservation, and happened to mention
that we would be shooting at the building. This guy's reply was, "Oh no
you're not." Well, you don't know what we went through. We just barely
got the scene on film. The preservationists had their crew erect a construction scaffold outside one of the windows of our set, deliberately trying to hamper our filming. Lucky they didn't manage to put up any more
until we finished there, but you will notice that one window has the
blinds closed to hide the scaffold [fax to author].

John Woo differs from many directors in one important respect. He
works very easily with actors. He does not see actors as pawns in the midst
of elaborate stunts, nor as images to be manipulated à la Sternberg. An
evaluation often made of Woo is that he "isn't much on dialogue." It is
true that intricate dialogue is not his forté, but nevertheless his use of dialogue and his emphasis on character relationships are quite underrated.

In speaking with many of the actors from Woo's *Hard Target*, I
gained a very unified sense of Woo as a working director. The consistent
response to my questions about Woo and his "handling" of actors was that
he works very well, in a very intuitive and empathetic manner, with his
cast. South African–born Arnold Vosloo (Pik) stated that Woo allows his
cast a great deal of interpretive independence, within the limits of the

script outlines. He referred to a moment in the film mentioned also by Lance Henriksen (Fouchon), when Pik and Fouchon threaten Randal Poe (Eliott Keener). Vosloo invented the sadistic and memorable line "If I come back, I cut me a steak" (alluding maliciously to Poe's bulk).

Vosloo told me that once Woo came to trust an actor, he let him have his head in the role: "And that comes from John, [he] really said, you know, go for it, you guys [Arnold and Lance] go off and find out who these guys are. He allowed us that freedom and the luxury of doing that" (Vosloo, telephone interview, 18 December 1995). Eliott Keener also commented that he took a hand in designing his character: "Well, you know, seeing the film, everybody always talks about the cigar. I happen to enjoy a cigar. I saw the character as a cigar-smoker. You try to tap into what facets of yourself there [are] in the character. And I just remember particularly I've had more people say something about the cigar falling out of my mouth. Apparently it was a good bit." Keener, a teacher of film and a frequently seen character actor, also noted that Woo was "very good about letting the actor create" (Keener, telephone interview). Lance Henriksen chose his wardrobe and had some memorable ad-libs. And Willie Carpenter added some important realism to his character, Elijah Roper:

> There was one thing I really remember, as an audience member myself, people do things in a movie, and if they don't make sense, you check out. There was one thing in the movie that wasn't in the script, and it was that meeting when I first met the bad guys, Arnold and Lance, their characters—where they make this proposal to me, and I've got to decide what I'm going to do here. And there was no scene where he saw the money. Now here's a guy, he's not a bum, he's just trying to get through, and he's not stupid, he's a decorated veteran, and there was no scene where they make the proposal to him, and initially he just accepts it and goes off. But I told them, in order for this guy to take this deal here, he's got to see the money. So I said, "This guy, he's got to be smarter than that. At this point, he's out here on this train yard, and they're going to kill him anyway." So they put in a scene where I actually see the money, he flashes the money. As I said, it's just a little moment; it's a tiny thing, but it's a big thing [telephone interview].

Woo is authoritative but not authoritarian with his actors. Yancy Butler (Natasha) noted some examples of this attitude; for instance, she wondered during the filming about why she should throw the gun to Van Damme during a fight scene: "I said, 'Why wouldn't I just shoot him, instead of throwing somebody a gun?' And [Woo] said, 'Well, you're aiding his movements,' and it was very interesting. He did have to convince me to do that" (Butler, telephone interview). Woo did not simply reply, "I'm the director, you do what I say." He patiently explained to Butler the rationale behind his position. This patient approach is mentioned repeatedly by personnel connected with Woo's films.

While it was always clear who was the director—that is, where the authority lay—Woo had a way of making all the participants feel included in the creative process. Much of this effect had to do with his quiet and friendly style of working on the set.[15] Woo would guide his cast and crew in the direction he wanted them to go rather than order them about; or, in some cases, when an effect was not technically feasible or dramatically workable, he would offer an agreeable, "Okay, let's do it your way."

One factor that should have caused trouble on *Hard Target* was the language barrier. Woo's English skills have gradually improved since his move to the States, but he is not readily fluent and often speaks hesitantly. As with language learners in general at a certain stage of their acquisition, his listening skills have far exceeded his speaking ability. So he had little difficulty understanding questions or suggestions from cast, crew or producers, but his active communication skills were limited in comparison to a bilingual or to a native English speaker.

Woo's methods of communicating his wishes during a shoot are thus often intuitive, visual and very economical. He would sometimes, on the Vancouver set of *Once a Thief*, physically demonstrate what he wanted from a stuntperson or actor. The *Hard Target* cast members (and those from other Woo projects) whom I interviewed all said that they never had communication problems with Woo; he seemed to sense the questions they had, and was able himself to get his points across by facial expressions, gestures, or by a very few words.

On the other hand, Woo experienced serious difficulties with Van Damme because of the actor's limited English-language ability, his tendency to show himself off, and his interference with shooting decisions. This case, however, was the only outstanding example of such problems. Woo established a good working relationship with his cast and crew; he learned quickly about the American system of moviemaking and began to adjust himself to it.

One of the major differences between the Hollywood and the Hong Kong systems is that of directorial authority. As Phil Dagort observed, Woo was not accustomed to government by committee. In Hong Kong the director is much more of a boss than he is in the complicated political system in Hollywood. Woo was often importuned and interfered with by production, and he sometimes did not understand the differences between the two systems (Dagort, telephone interview).

For example, when Woo wanted to use documentary footage of big game hunting in a montage of Fouchon playing the *Appassionata*,[16] he was told, as Eliott Keener put it, "You can't do that." Woo, according to this account, was simply taken aback, surprised that such an issue would be made about what was for him an artistic question:

> Universal said, "You can't do that." And John said, "Well, but that's what this is all about." And they said, "Yeah, but you can't do that." He said, "Why not?" and they said, "Because the picture's too John Woo." He said, "Well, if you didn't want John Woo, why did you hire John Woo?" And that's kind of how that went down [Keener, telephone interview].

Lance Henriksen commented that this incident of studio interference was most unfortunate, as it directly affected the portrayal of his character in depth: "It really bugged me [that the montage was cut]. I mean, it really did. Because it was an inspired idea. It literally cinematically puts you right into the mindset of this man" (Henriksen, telephone interview). Such sentiments were echoed by other participants, including Chuck Pfarrer.

Similarly, Woo perhaps did not at first totally understand, as Dagort noted, that stuntwork was different here in terms of safety limitations than in Hong Kong:

> John screened a couple of his movies for us because some of us had not yet known his work. We were startled by the stunt work. We had doubts that we could get away with doing this Hong Kong style in a U.S. film. I remember John saying to us [in his characteristic whisper and accent], "My actors,... they die for me." I don't think he was kidding. The production company played it pretty safe from the beginning. We only had one incident, and thankfully no one was hurt. I do regret that we did not film a boat-helicopter chase sequence that John wanted to do (it ended up on horseback!). The production company wouldn't let him do it. I'm glad to see that he finally got to film it in *Face/Off*, and it was more amazing than it would ever have been in *Hard Target* [fax to author].

But these adjustment problems did not cause Woo to give up on the system, nor did they interfere noticeably with his ability to "reach" his actors and crew in a remarkable way. (Phil Dagort commented: "Working with John was great. He trusted you to give him what he needed. He has an amazing way of choreographing the camera, and a marvelous visual sense. What else could a production designer ask for?" [fax to author]). Again, Woo is not often thought of as an "actor's director." In fact, though, he has consistently drawn interesting performances from supporting as well as lead actors. *Hard Target* is no masterpiece, but it does contain, at least, nice performances even in the smaller roles. Kasi Lemmons (Carmine) and especially Willie Carpenter (Roper) turned in expressive performances in roles that could have been merely perfunctory. These actors and others appear to have responded to something in John Woo which led them to draw particularly deeply from their resources. The same might have been said of Marco St. John's role as Dr. Morton if so much of it had not been cut; and Eliott Keener, always accomplished, here out-does himself as the sleazy Randal Poe.

In the larger roles, Woo also touched something in his performers. Jean-Claude Van Damme has never been known for his acting talent, but in Woo's film he passes muster at least generally. He even reaches the level of emotional connection with the viewer in some scenes.

More can and should be said of Yancy Butler, who was unfairly sav-aged for her work here. If her performance is indeed limited in range and depth, still it is at the least adequate for the part. Woo contributed to her impact by using one of her most expressive features, her large slate-grey eyes, to great effect, as in the scene at the beginning of the film when Chance beats off her attackers near the Half-Moon Restaurant. The role itself was limiting and "difficult," as she said, "because there's only so much you can do being the damsel in distress" (telephone interview). Thus, her effectiveness must be judged within a limited range of responses; in fact, by how well she limits herself and does *not* step out of the role. She explained that this was quite challenging, since "it's a little hard to be the damsel in distress and be so convincing. My personality is to take the bull by the horns, and it was a bit of a stretch for me, I guess."

But in some fashion probably intuitive, Woo's collaboration with Butler, and with other actors in the cast, produced effective moments. One such is the scene in the bayou when Chance kills a snake that is out of the viewer's field of vision, behind Natasha. The shot widens to reveal the snake, and Butler is asked to pretend that she thinks Chance is about to kiss her (he asks her to shut her eyes). After he kills the snake, her eyes widen incredulously. Butler commented on the scene, highlighting Woo's positive input and his ingrained knowledge of how a scene will read:

> That day—the shoot was very difficult for everybody, and I was extremely tired, and I was telling [Woo] that I didn't know if I could give him the reaction that he needed. And he said, "Do not worry about it, do not worry about it. Just do exactly what you did. It'll read, believe me." And I heard the clicking of the slo-mo. I don't actually know, [but] I don't think he told me it was going to be in slow motion. And he loved it. And I turned to him and I said, "I didn't feel like I did anything." And he went, "No, it was fantastic." I had given him the element of pretending that Chance was going to kiss me. And I'm so glad he was pleased.

In this instance, apparently the combination of Butler's talent, her real fear of snakes ("For the record," she told me, "snakes are my absolute worst fear, and this thing [the mechanical snake] was so real, it was unbelievable"), and Woo's understanding of how to elicit emotional responses by quiet communication and patience resulted in a very effective scene.

Generally, we might say that Woo's relationship with his actors on *Hard Target* was based on mutual respect. This was nowhere more true than with Lance Henriksen, who related to me a revealing anecdote about his first meeting with Woo:

> When I met him, I unconsciously shook his hand and bowed. It was one of those moments of absolute respect for each other. He somehow understood immediately that I had a great respect for his work. When we started working on the film it was everything I had hoped for. Very emotional kind of contact with the man that I had [Henriksen, telephone interview].

This rapport certainly contributed to the quality of Henriksen's work, as he was willing to do stunts that he wouldn't have done for anyone else (the "burning coat" scene) and was given much leeway in interpreting his role. As already mentioned, he chose his own wardrobe; he told me how this came about in an account amusingly revelatory of his rapport with Woo and of Woo's basic shyness:

> There is no language barrier between people when it comes down to real feelings. One of the first things that happened to us, we had a wardrobe designer on the movie [who] was, I thought, quite bad. She made me look like Fred Astaire in a herringbone checkered suit. I hated it. Actors in Hong Kong always sort of wear suits in the movies. So I put the suit on and went to lunch and sat across from John and he looked at me. So I said, "John, do you like this suit?" He looked back at me and he went, "Do you like it?" "Yeah, I sort of like it"—and it took us five minutes to admit that both of us hated the fuckin' suit. You know what I mean? We were trying to be so tender with each other's feelings. And that was the way it always was with John. When I would come up with an idea he would relish it and support it.

In an earlier cut of the film, Fouchon can clearly be seen imitating Napoleon after the attack on Douvee's cabin. Although the pose is very rapidly shown in the final cut, vitiating the original intent, the idea was Henriksen's and would probably have remained at greater length if Woo had had greater control over the finished film. Also, Henriksen ad-libbed rather readily, and sometimes his ad-libs were retained:

> There was a line I came up with, it was an improvised line. I screamed, "You're a bunch of fucking buffalo." That came from running behind those guys. They were like buffalo, and the ground was shaking. I was

laughing so hard I had to turn away from the camera [Henriksen, telephone interview].

This ad-lib takes place when Fouchon restrains his men from shooting
Douvee as he flees on his horse after the destruction of his cabin. Arnold
Vosloo explained the context to me:

> [The hunters] were just kind of stomping all over the scene, which we
> call stuntmen acting, and basically running around dazed and confused,
> and I guess Lance was trying to cover up his own humor at all this, and
> not wanting to be caught out by the camera. He just kind of ad-libbed; he
> felt like if he didn't say something at this point, he was going to burst out
> laughing at these guys, so he turned it around and used it [Vosloo, tele-
> phone interview, 18 December 1995].[17]

As noted above, Henriksen and Vosloo had a great deal of liberty,
based on Woo's trust in them, to interpret their roles. Vosloo told me:

> He really allowed us to develop a back story for both our characters. The
> first two weeks of the shoot or so, Lance and I would get together and sit
> in a bar and just talk about who we think these guys were, and where
> they've been and what they've done, and it was really nice. One of the
> executives at Universal, when they saw one of the first previews, said what
> he really liked best about the movie was Lance and I, and our relation-
> ship. He said it was tangible, he really felt like these guys had been
> together for a while. Which I thought was a real compliment, because
> that just means that we did our part. And that comes from John; [he]
> really said, go for it, you guys go off and find out who these guys are
> [Vosloo, telephone interview, 18 December 1995].

Such rapport based on trust and respect has resulted in Woo's gain-
ing ardent defenders when his work on *Hard Target* is criticized. For
example, Arnold Vosloo—who struck me always as a fair-minded and
intelligent man who is not chary about speaking his piece—severely criticized Van Damme's interference in the film and maintained that Woo's
authority as a director should have gone unquestioned because of his cre-
dentials:

> I can say this—and I can only say this because I was there—in John's
> defense. The entire *Hard Target*, the fact that it turned out like it turned
> out is a miracle, considering the restraint that was put on John, not just
> creatively, but also in terms of finance—and quite frankly by Jean-Claude
> Van Damme. I will go on the record as saying that the fact that Jean-
> Claude was the star hurt John more than it helped him. I really believe
> that, I really absolutely believe that. If he had somebody that was more
> willing to be a player as opposed to a star, it would have been a far better
> film—but Jean-Claude really hurt John. [He] caused a lot of problems

simply by arriving on set after John had already set shots and then questioning John on his shots. Now, when you have who is in my opinion the greatest pure action director of all time, you don't walk in and say why are you shooting like this, and let's do it like this. You shut the fuck up and you hit your mark and you just do it, because you are in very capable good hands. But unfortunately Jean-Claude did not see it that way. And I really believe that that hurt John [Vosloo, telephone interview, 18 December 1995].

Other cast and crew members expressed similar sentiments and emphasized the unfortunate results of front-office interference in creative decisions.

Woo, incidentally, did not always oppose such meddling openly. Rather, he employed indirection: His English would get worse. "The most interesting thing was to watch John play dumb sometimes. Because he spoke more English—he kind of used it as a shelter, too. I remember sitting down with him and trying to get the feeling he wanted, that took lots of sessions, there was a lot of stuff, and a lot of the time I think I exhausted him" (Dagort, telephone interview). In confrontations with the production office, Woo preferred to go along to get along, but lamentably his accommodating manner led to his agreeing to some adulteration of his filmic vision.

Every director working within a system has experienced the pressure to compromise, but John Woo had been fortunate in this regard before coming to Hollywood. Leaving aside his career before *A Better Tomorrow* (1986), he had been given a great measure of autonomy, including much control over final cut. The major exception to this state of affairs was *A Better Tomorrow II*, but in this case it might well be argued that Woo's extravagance brought some of the misery down on his own head.

When he got to Hollywood, Woo soon learned, as we know, that the director had not often been king since Orson Welles was given his "train set" on *Citizen Kane*. As we have seen, there were many "cooks" on *Hard Target*, and as an earlier version of the film shows, much that was "John Woo" did not stay in the final release.

In some cases the "Woo" material removed was very significant, like the big-game scene; in others, it was less egregious in its absence, if still regrettably lost. One instance of the latter comprises a very few moments of film, but would have added an unmistakable John Woo signature to this movie. When Pik is trying to track Chance and Natasha, he is left alone by Fouchon and the hunters. In the finished film, we see only Pik kneeling down under the railroad bridge, near the point at which the two must have jumped from the train that was their means of escape. Then we see a cut to the two running through the bayou. But in the earlier cut,

Pik stares, and as we follow his eye-line, we see ghostly images of Chance and Natasha running along by the bridge. This establishes Pik as an intuitive, indeed extrasensorial, tracker, and lands us fully in the middle of John Woo's world, in which appearances mask inner realities and people, good and bad, are subtly aided by external forces. And, of course, we are left with the clear implication of Pik as somehow a *doppelgänger* of Chance (and, perhaps, of his *anima* Natasha), since he sees his "shadow" running away from him. The image also connects directly into John Woo's own film language, for cognoscenti would immediately recall Tequila, in *Hard Boiled*, stepping into the footsteps of his double Alan after Alan has carried out his library hit on the traitor Jimmy.

Such subtleties, though, were thought by some of the producers on *Hard Target* to elude the understanding or the patience of the American filmgoer. Other cuts were less noticeable but still unfortunate. Most involved a lessening of the degree of violence. Zenan's body does not now flop when Fouchon shoots him, as it did originally, as Jim Jacks noted; some of the impact hits on Binder's body have been excised. These cuts, and the ones already mentioned, add up to a cumulative detraction from the John Woo effect of the film. Woo's films *work* on the viewer; the emotional "bang" is additive and often gradual in its final effect, and to tinker with this effect by subtracting too many elements from his films is to risk vitiating the entire outcome.

Some cuts adversely affected narrative plausibility or coherence. One such was the entire deleted (but filmed) scene which showed Natasha and Chance in Chance's flop, kissing and obviously working towards an intimate liaison. At least some of the criticism about the lack of depth in the two characters could have been avoided if they had been shown as romantically involved. The film now seems unmotivated at times, as Yancy Butler pointed out:

> So as it stands now—when Willie Carpenter is shot to death, and I end up kissing him [Chance] on the cheek, and it's such an intimate thing without the love scene that we did shoot that people went, oh—well, I guess *they're* sleeping together. So it was *very* weird losing that. Because it was such an intimate moment for two people who aren't intimate yet in the film, and we had been [intimate] in the original, it came off as very strange [telephone interview].

Fortunately, though, enough of Woo's touches survived to make the film something other than standard Hollywood product. Russell Carpenter alluded to some of Woo's transitions having been lost, and commented on the importance of this trope for Woo:

I know the transitions are a signature for John. For him, the end shot or shots of one sequence to the beginning shots of the next sequence were very, very important. And I think he had a rhythm, a pacing, a system of transitions all worked out in his head. During the editing period, those wonderful transitions were some of the first things to go. And this is completely third-hand, but what I heard was that the studio kept telling John, "American audiences aren't going to understand that." So, this is totally as a bystander, but I felt that what happened in the editing process was that John was forced to part with significantly John Woo signatures and it became more of an American film [Carpenter, personal interview].

Again, fortunately for the viewer, a few of Woo's masterful transitions remained.

One of these occurs quite early in the film, when Natasha goes to file a missing persons report on her father and meets Detective Carmine Mitchell, the duty officer (Kasi Lemmons).[18] In a typically Woo moment, we see Carmine putting away her own birthday cake in embarrassment (probably at having to celebrate it alone), taking the report from Natasha, and then, when Natasha has left, suddenly remembering that she had put the cake, with a lit candle, in her desk drawer. She opens the drawer, now filled with smoke, lifts the cake with its single candle, says, "Happy birthday to me," closes her eyes, and blows out the candle. Then the shot dissolves, amidst the smoke, into a beautiful long shot of the New Orleans skyline. The contrast between the loneliness of the detective, alone in her drab enclosed space (with the additional subtle hint of the synechdochic cake's enclosure in the desk drawer), and the bustle of New Orleans could be no clearer.

If *Hard Target* does not realize its potential, still it was not totally an unpromising start for Woo in the United States. He had at the very least made some friends in the Hollywood community and had begun to learn how to survive in the complicated and sinuous Hollywood system. And for some Woo viewers, *Hard Target*, despite its obvious flaws, is yet a film that contains enough Woo signatures and an ambience somehow exotic enough to stand out from the usual run of Hollywood action films. The film's highlighting of social inequities, as Tony Williams has noted ("From Hong Kong" 41), and its sometimes intriguing twists on the action formula make it a not entirely fruitless detour in Woo's career; it may even be viewed as a necessary stepping-stone of which Woo made the most.

Broken Arrow

After completing *Hard Target*, Woo turned to *Tears of the Sun*, a film set in the Amazon with Brad Pitt in the lead. The project did not work out; after several months of development, Pitt withdrew and the film was shelved. Casting around for another project, Woo was shown the script for *Broken Arrow* and convinced the studio, 20th Century–Fox, that he could do the special-effects adventure film even though it was not exactly in his line (Chang, personal interview, 4 November 1995).

The film did well at the box-office, but it was not a critical success. It was certainly a disappointment for those devoted to Woo's style. Thin on plot, symbolism, and character development, it even lacked, for the most part, strong action sequences. *Broken Arrow* seemed rather a perfunctory exercise in mechanical Hollywood action filmmaking. Perhaps, as Woo and Terence Chang have sometimes said, Woo was trying to prove he could make a straight action picture like the usual Hollywood product. Perhaps—but he did suffer again from studio interference, and the result was a picture that contained precious little of his signature. Nevertheless, it served to establish him as a marketable director who could deliver a big hit, and thus it prepared him for the legitimate artistic success of *Face/Off*.

As Zigelstein and Williams have both noted (Williams, "From Hong Kong" 41; Zigelstein 10), *Broken Arrow* awakens early optimism in the seasoned Woo viewer. We see two men, Deakins (John Travolta) and Hale (Christian Slater), engaged in a boxing match, a metaphor for their competition during the film. Deakins reveals his aggressive, take-no-prisoners attitude during the fight. The match is innovatively and excitingly filmed, with a visually striking intrusion by the title "Directed by John Woo." The viewer of the film may be optimistic at this point that Woo has very interesting things in store (this writer certainly was).

But this optimism is soon deflated as we see that Woo's control of stylistic choices is vitiated. The first marked sign of this occurs a few minutes into the film when Deakins is shown in hazy, heat-waved slo-mo coming into the frame from the desert, accompanied by Hans Zimmer's apt little theme. This is a clear allusion to Leone's *Once upon a Time in the West*, which has a similar (but recurring) shot. Here, it appears that Woo's intentions were to hold the shot for much longer, and this is what the seasoned Woo viewer expects. Regrettably, however, the shot ends after a few seconds. The effect is to tantalize and disappoint. Furthermore, the shot falls far short of its model in terms of thematic importance. In the Leone film, the blurriness of the image expressionistically depicts the blurriness of the memory of the man experiencing it; and so the image recurs at strategic points during the film, with more information gradually added until we come to the final, climactic encounter between the two adversaries Frank (Henry Fonda) and Harmonica

(Charles Bronson). Perhaps Woo would have liked to do something similar but did not have the freedom to do so. In any case, from this point (at least) the film becomes more and more compromised.[19]

Another disappointment for many viewers was the inadequacy, or the lack of "sparks," in the adversarial relationship between the erstwhile friends Deakins and Hale. Perhaps Travolta is not the ideal actor for a villainous role; perhaps the casting should have been reversed, with Slater playing the psycho Deakins. Travolta certainly seems less than convincing (or convinced) in his role as bad guy; he appears to treat many of his lines as throwaways. Whether or not this is conscious,[20] the result is that what should be a cynosure of the film, Deakins, becomes a soft center, leaving Hale really very little to react against.

The gunfights, stunts, and so forth, with few exceptions, are also remarkably tame for a Woo film. The gunfight in the tunnel is rather exciting but certainly does not measure up either to similar confrontations in *Face/Off*, or, *a fortiori*, in *The Killer* or *Hard Boiled*. Again, the effect of such thinning out of Woo's style was to vitiate the impact of the film for Woo connoisseurs and for perceptive reviewers.

The film also had continuity problems, at least one of which was quite noticeable even on a first viewing. Near the end of the film, Terry (Samantha Mathis) hides in a boat at the last minute when Deakins and his men show up and leave in it. The difficulty here is that we never see her get out of the boat, and she suddenly shows up dry after presumably having been wetted by the spray. Faith Conroy, the script supervisor, explained what happened:

> Samantha's character was supposed to be hiding when the bad guys walk up to the boat. There was a piece taken out there. We filmed a shot where you see the corner of her coat being yanked inside a white storage cabinet so you know that's where she's hiding when Travolta pulls back the tarp and she's not there. I'm not sure why that was taken out. The next time you see her she's hiding in some bushes and she runs and jumps onto the back of a moving truck. It was felt that the audience would make the story leap and realize she sneaked off the boat and hitched a ride on the back of the truck, where they obviously had transferred the nukes. Then she shows up on the train, which is where the nukes are presumably unloaded from the truck.... I know John had other shots in mind for that sequence but we ran out of time. That piece with the truck was shot at the end of our last day of filming. We were on location and we literally ran out of time and couldn't shoot anymore [Conroy, fax to author, 23 March 1998].

Despite such problems and the thinness of the film's text and texture, *Broken Arrow* is still a rather entertaining example of Hollywood action fare. It should be regarded as another stepping-stone in Woo's access to Hollywood, a piece of journeyman work needed to gain entrance to Hollywood's list of top directors. Certainly it prepared Woo for his great success with *Face/Off*, and it also gave him more exposure to the Hollywood system of studio politics than he had experienced on the lower-budget and lower-profile *Hard Target*. On *Face/Off*, Woo was to enjoy much more freedom and much more creative control than during his previous work in Hollywood, and the results were accordingly much more positive.

Face/Off

Face/Off (Paramount) marks a high point for Woo in Hollywood, at least to the present. This 1997 film bears many of Woo's "signatures," but it also advances from Woo's Hong Kong films to a newly explicit concern with family as a theme. Woo has said that "*Face/Off* mainly was about family—where a man sees his family almost falling apart and he fights to get them back" ("Hong Kong and Vine"). Curiously, in *Face/Off*, a film with much horror and mayhem, so-called "family values" are privileged in an emotionally direct manner.

The emotive quality of this film may threaten to tip over into self-parody, but Woo was intentionally front-loading his pathos here. From the opening scene, the audience is made aware that Sean Archer (John Travolta) is not a typical "shoot-em-up" action hero. He is a bereaved father with a score to settle with Castor Troy (Nicolas Cage), who killed his son Michael in an attempt to kill Archer. Like Detective Dave Bannion (Glenn Ford) in Fritz Lang's *The Big Heat* (1951), who became an obsessed pursuer of the killers of his wife, Archer will pursue Castor with little regard for the cost to himself or to his family. Archer will even assume his enemy's identity in order to stop him.

The actors were advised by Woo to perform naturally, that is, to work in an unfettered manner. This kind of acting perhaps seems "over the top" to Western audiences (and actors) but not necessarily to Asian ones. Audiences brought up on Peking Opera, which though stylized can be excessive and melodramatic, and on *wuxia pian* and samurai films, would understand overstated and unrestrained performances. In any case, Woo appears to imply that the actors' training was interfering with their natural responses, and that things improved after they "got out of their own way":

At first, they were playing the emotional scenes a little more subtle—the traditional American way. But they really wanted to do something a little more real. So, after the first day, I said, "Let's try it another way: my way. You want to cry—just cry; you want to laugh—just laugh. You want to hit the wall—do it. You want to smash the table—smash the table. You want to sit down—just sit down. Just do it exactly how you feel." Wow! That opened everyone up. It made John [Travolta] and Joan Allen and Nick Cage very happy, so we tried it that way. Some people think that's maybe too over the top, but it gives the actors a lot of room to explore themselves.

So we only do one or two takes for each setup. And then that was it. And everyone felt great, because all the emotions were real.

The result was, as Woo's interviewer noted, that in *Face/Off* the actors' "intensity" recalled his Hong Kong movies (Woo, "Hong Kong and Vine").[21]

A very cooperative relationship existed between Woo and his screenwriters, Michael Colleary and Mike Werb.[22] The script itself, including the basic concept, had been in development since 1990 and was the

Woo demonstrates a stance for "Castor (Archer)" (Nicolas Cage) before the big shoot out at Castor's pad in *Face/Off* (1997). (Photograph by Stephen Vaughan; courtesy John Woo.)

creation of Colleary and Werb. But the concept, and its treatment, had undergone some crucial transformations in the process of script development, first for Warner Bros., then at Paramount prior to Woo's direct involvement (Colleary and Werb, telephone interview).[23]

The film was originally conceived as a huge action picture. The script had become less ambitious but was still more futuristic than the final version approved for shooting by Woo and the studio. Woo had seen the script in 1992 but was not too interested in it, according to Colleary and Werb, because of its very futuristic quality. Gradually, as the script was rewritten, it became less of a science-fiction and more of a psychological film, centering on the Archer-Castor duality and especially on the conflicts in the Archer family.

By the time Woo read the script again in 1995, it had taken on a form similar to the final version. Woo was very interested but was committed to do *Broken Arrow* for Fox. When he finished his commitment, he signed to film the script, which had again become available. Woo told the screenwriters, "This is the best script I ever read" (Colleary and Werb, telephone interview).

Colleary and Werb saw their screenplay for Woo as a drama about family relationships and not primarily as an action piece. They became convinced that Woo was on the same wavelength when he told them that the ending must include Adam (Sasha's son by Castor). Other directors had not understood this point. Marco Bandella (*Demolition Man*), one of the directors on the project prior to Woo, had wanted a big set piece shootout to end the film. But Woo understood instinctively that the core of the screenplay was the struggle by Archer to regain his moorings after the murder of his son, and that the only way to restore wholeness to his and his family's lives would be, as Werb put it, to embrace his enemy's son (Colleary and Werb, telephone interview).

The emphasis here on the screenplay's importance is not meant to downplay Woo's contribution to the film; on the contrary, it highlights the importance of a sensitive director like Woo who can appropriate the qualities of a script that seems promising for his talents and can then develop it to its artistic endpoint. Most of Woo's mature work has gained in importance because he has also written the stories; in this case, he was fortunate to find two writers who thought along lines similar to his own. As they commented, the highest compliment that Woo could pay them was to ask them back to write the script for his upcoming project designed for Chow Yun-fat, *King's Ransom*.

With a workable script for *Face/Off* and considerable leeway from the studio, Woo became able to put an unusual stamp on his Hollywood film.

He is not remaking or rehashing his Hong Kong work, but extending its bases and actually translating it into an American ambience. Travolta and Cage, particularly, function rather like overlays on a Hong Kong mold, as if former Woo characters and actors inform their moves, emotions, and mannerisms. That is, Woo appears to have successfully grafted American filmmaking style—blunter, with broader strokes—onto Hong Kong's look, based on quick cutting, symbolic juxtapositions, and cultural, traditional allusiveness. For the first time in a stateside film, the trademark elements of Woo's style have been placed at the service of a more straight-ahead mode which is now surprisingly complex. A sure signal that Woo has begun to master his new milieu is the presence of his own brand of peculiar, sometimes perverse humor, as if he felt relaxed enough to begin to poke fun at himself and to bring the audience into some comic relief in the midst of an actually quite serious film.

The seriousness in *Face/Off* relates to its subtext, the importance of the family unit. While critics might fashionably deplore or ridicule such a "conservative" defense of the nuclear family, little has been offered to take its place. In any event, while it is certainly true that Woo privileges the Archers over the dysfunctional Sasha-Castor liaison that produced Adam (now being raised by Sasha because of Castor's desertion) and also against the undoubtedly close brother-sister relationship between Sasha and Dietrich, we must not overlook the fact of the narrative's patent sympathy for these characters.

This empathetic stance is particularly pronounced regarding Sasha (Gina Gershon), who is first presented when under arrest by Archer. He tries to interrogate her about Castor and threatens to take Adam away from her. Despite some of her less attractive qualities—she is obviously a mean, tough, streetsy woman, as well as the associate of a notorious criminal—Sasha reacts very maternally to this threat. We next see her after Archer has "become" Castor. Her resentment towards him, mixed with passion, is highlighted, but we also see her protectiveness towards Adam when he comes into the room carrying Castor's .45 (*Face/Off* laserdisc ch. 27). If there is any criticism here of the mother-son relationship, it is clearly aimed at their environment, perceived as dangerous because of the constant presence of firearms and shady and unpredictable people. So the implied comparison between the Archers' domesticity and Sasha's home with Adam boils down to a critique of environmental conditions, not of "better" or "worse" parents.

We find, actually, that Sasha has done everything within her power to provide for Adam. He is well-dressed and healthy and has comforts such as a Walkman on which he listens to family-oriented music—not,

Before the final showdown on the beach in *Face/Off* **Woo confers with Nicolas Cage (as "Castor [Archer]," left) and John Travolta (as "Archer [Castor]," right) while cast and crew members look on. (Photograph by Stephen Vaughan; courtesy John Woo.)**

as one might expect, violent or corrosive, but instead the score of *The Wizard of Oz*. Clearly this is not a boy who has been abused, neglected, or corrupted. Sasha, and her brother, are the more praiseworthy for their care of him given their own negative lifestyles. And when Sasha dies protecting Castor (Archer), she asks him to promise to have Adam cared for so that he will not be "like us." He has already promised her that no matter what happens, Archer won't bother her any more; this is to be fulfilled when she dies, though not in the way he intended. But he will keep his promise to her about Adam by adopting him into his family at the end of the film.

Castor is also treated with more complexity than first impressions might indicate. As commentators on the film (for example, the two reviewers for "He Said, She Said" on CNN's *Showbiz Today*) have noted, Cage's character is humanized by little touches that are typical of John Woo. When we first see Castor in his threatening garb, with his tough henchmen, we also see him bend down solicitously to tie his kid brother

Pollux's shoe. Earlier in the setup scene for the film, when he tries to kill Archer and accidentally kills his son Michael, Woo shows us an expression on Castor's face that mixes disappointment and consternation, even horror, at what has happened. We are led to see that perhaps even this evil man is not totally inhuman.

Furthermore, Castor fits almost too easily into Archer's home life when he takes his place as "Archer." It is too simple to say, as does Zigelstein, that Castor is only playing at being Archer for cynical reasons. If that is so, how are we to read scenes like his candlelight dinner with Eve, or his genuine anger at the young man who tries to take advantage of his "daughter" Jamie (Dominique Swain)? Is he just being manipulative, or is there another dynamic here? He does not need to go to such lengths for a mere deception. He clearly attempts to replace Archer—actually, to improve on Archer, whom he terms a "loser" because of his inability to relate to his family. Castor does not simply parody the conduct of a true father; he becomes more of a father to Jamie than Archer has been, rescuing her from a potential date-rape and teaching her to defend herself with a blade. Now, we may not approve of some of his fatherly advice here, but the fact is that he tries to fit into the family, and we must wonder why he seems to take his role so seriously.

Perhaps the answer lies in his own background, a level of narrative omitted from the finished film but present in an earlier version of the script. According to the screenwriters, the script once included an overnight visit by Archer (as Castor) to Castor's mother, where he sees firsthand the life Castor had when growing up. Castor's mother, Helen, is very disheveled and living in squalor. Werb and Colleary were influenced in the creation of Castor and his mother by the Cody Jarrett character incarnated so unforgettably by James Cagney in *White Heat* (Raoul Walsh, 1949), whose mother (played by Margaret Wycherly) was a Ma Barker type leading a dysfunctional "family" of robbers for whom killing was justified and normal. Some of the mother-domination over Cody was transferred by Colleary and Werb into the symbiotic Castor-Pollux relationship.[24] Although Castor is the elder, it is perhaps most accurate to say that the power relationship is dominated by the manipulative, and more intelligent, Pollux; in any case, Castor reacts very strongly when Pollux is killed and will attempt revenge on Archer and his family. Similarly, Cody goes berserk when he learns of his mother's murder. And Cage appears to interpret the Castor role (or rather, Cage as Archer within Castor's body parodies Castor) as an exaggerated, histrionic, Cagney-like performance. His mugging and jerky physical movements seem like an impressionist's take on Cagney as Cody Jarrett (which role was itself an exaggerated, parodic version of Cagney's signature role as Tom Powers in *Public Enemy* [William Wellman, 1931]).[25]

Woo clearly enjoyed making this film. He is evidently pleased with his material and with the talent afforded him to convert that material into screen reality. Not only does he work in some of his best signature mode, but he surpasses his previous work in scenes such as the Walsh Clinic sequence, when the faces are exchanged. The line between grotesque, creepy horror and repulsiveness is never crossed: that is, Woo keeps the audience right on the edge but never lets us "fall off" and become so disgusted at the physical horror involved in actually removing someone's face that we simply turn away and turn off.

Chapter 10

The End of the Beginning

*A cultivated style would be like a mask. Everybody knows
it's a mask, and sooner or later you must show yourself—or
at least, you show yourself as someone who could not afford
to show himself, and so created something to hide
behind.... You do not create a style. You work, and develop
yourself; your style is an emanation from your own being.*
—Katherine Anne Porter,
Interview
(in *Writers at Work* [*Second Series*],
ed. George Plimpton, 1963)

*There is an electric fire in human nature tending to purify—
so that among these human creatures there is continually
some birth of new heroism. The pity is that we must wonder
at it, as we should at finding a pearl in rubbish.*
—John Keats,
Letter, 14 February-3 May 1819,
to his brother and sister-in-law
George and Georgiana Keats
(published in *Letters of John Keats*
no. 123, ed. Frederick Page, 1954)

*"To give style" to one's character—a great and rare art! He
exercises it who surveys all that his nature presents in
strength and weakness and then moulds it to an artistic
plan until everything appears as art and reason, and even
the weaknesses delight the eye.*
—Friedrich Nietzsche,
The Gay Science (rev. ed., 1887),
aph. 290[1]

John Woo has been one of several Hong Kong filmmakers to come to Hollywood. He has been the most successful of these directors—Ringo Lam, Tsui Hark, Ronny Yu, Kirk Wong—in translating a personal style of filmmaking into the Hollywood context. After a tentative beginning with *Hard Target*, Woo made a flashy, but not uncritically accepted,

Woo in 1997. (Photograph by Stephen Vaughan; courtesy John Woo.)

entrance into the big publicity wars of Hollywood with *Broken Arrow*. He has experimented with television, a medium in which he had not worked as director, and has shown his usual thoroughgoing concern with style on his two projects for the small screen, *Once a Thief* (1996; a free remake of his 1991 film) and *Black Jack* (1998). And Woo's performance with *Face/Off* reassured those who were concerned about his losing that unique style which brought him to critical attention beginning with *The Killer*.

Woo has exercised a great deal of influence on Hollywood filmmakers. Most of this influence is unfortunately of a superficial nature. Young directors, particularly, or directors with little individual style of their own are likely to be interested in those aspects of Woo's style that seem easily imitated: two-handed gunning, flashy cutting in action scenes, and gunmen flying through the air while the camera changes speed. Imitation is a sincere form of flattery, but all too often these directors miss the "heart" in Woo's style. Additionally, the complexity in Woo's gunfights is missing in such efforts—most directors mistake a few shots of two-handed gunplay for "Hong Kong" or "John Woo" style. One of the keys to Woo's style, his complex montage constructions on the Eisenstein model, with symbolic implications arising from the combination of shots, and with flash editing that operates subliminally on the viewer, is missing in such examples as well. And finally, the "John Woo standoff" becomes mere caricature unless first underpinned by strong character relationship and development such as the nexus between Li and John or between Tequila and Alan. Robert Rodriguez, Walter Hill and Quentin Tarantino have all drawn from Woo, and their work is the best example of creative imitation; at least these directors have their own established style within which to fit their borrowings (although Tarantino often fails to assimilate his borrowings and parodies). But below this level are a raft of directors who clearly do not understand the subtext below Woo's surface style: for style is much more than surface.

So John Woo has arrived in Hollywood and is well-established as a marketable director. The period from *Hard Target* to *Face/Off* may well be "the end of the beginning" for Woo. Since he has demonstrated that he can work within the Hollywood system without "selling himself," as *Face/Off* clearly proves, he should be freer to explore new techniques and new stylistic combinations in his filmmaking. Woo does not wish to be identified as an "action director," and it is certainly an error to put his style into a pigeonhole inhabited only by *The Killer* and *Hard Boiled*. Woo appears to be breaking away from the restrictions inherent in the "action film" and broadening his vision, if we are to judge from the varied emphasis of some of the scenes in *Face/Off*. His current interests, in filming *King's Ransom* and in developing the adaptation of *The Devil Soldier*, are further evidence of this. It is only to be hoped that Woo's recent success with *Face/Off* will lead to his having the freedom necessary to develop such projects and thus to grow even further as an artist and filmmaker.

Filmography

I am indebted to the Hong Kong Movie Database, formerly at website www.mdstud.chalmers.se/hkmovie/hkdatabase, now at http://egret0.stanford.edu/hk, for the Chinese equivalents of these titles and for their chronology. I have had frequent recourse to this database for assistance with information about Hong Kong films and film personnel. Other useful sites for me were as follows: Red on White John Woo website, formerly at http://www.geocities.com/Hollywood/4588/animate.js; The Bullet in the Web website at www.johnwoo.com; and the Hard Boiled/cinema of John Woo website at http://userpage.fu-berlin,de/owib/HardBoiled/.

The publicity release for Broken Arrow, prepared by David Chute, was also of much assistance.

In the listing below, the American release title is followed by the Chinese title given first in Cantonese and then in Mandarin. In parentheses, the literal English translation of the Chinese title is given, if it differs from the English release title.

Young Dragons. *Tit hon yau ching/Tie han rou quing* (Young Dragons/Farewell Buddy.) Golden Harvest, 1973/75.

The Dragon Tamers, aka **Belles of Taekwondo.** *Nui ji toi kuen kwan ying wooi/Nu zi tai quan qun ying hui* (Female Trample Fist Crowd Hero Meeting). Golden Harvest, 1974.

Hand of Death, aka **Countdown in Kung Fu.** *Siu lam moon/Shaolin Men* (Shaolin Gate). Golden Harvest, 1976.

Princess Chang Ping. *Dai Nui Fa/Dinu Hua* (Princess Flower). Golden Harvest, 1976.

Follow the Star. *Daai saat sing yue siu mooi tau/Dasha xingyu xiaomei tou.* Golden Harvest, 1977.

Money Crazy. *Faat chin hon/Fa qian han.* Golden Harvest, 1977.

Last Hurrah for Chivalry. *Ho hap/Hao xia.* Golden Harvest, 1978.

Hello, Late Homecomers. *Haluo yeguiren.* (Moonlighters). One episode by Woo. Golden Harvest, 1978.

From Riches to Rags. *Chin jok gwaai/Qian zuo guai* (Money Make Strange). Golden Harvest, 1979.

Laughing Times. *Waat kai si doi/Hua ji shi dai* (Comical Times). Cinema City, 1981.

To Hell with the Devil. *Moh dang tin si/Mo deng tian shi* (Modern Sky Master). Golden Harvest, 1982.

Plain Jane to the Rescue. *Baat choi Lam A Jan/Ba cai Lin Ya Zhen* (Eight Variety Lam Ah Chun). Golden Harvest, 1982.

Run Tiger Run. *Leung ji lo foo/Liangzhi lao hu*. Cinema City, 1986.

The Time You Need a Friend. *Siu jeung/Xiao jiang*. Cinema City, 1986.

The Sunset Warrior, aka **Heroes Shed No Tears.** *Ying hung mo lui/Yingxiong wu lei*. Golden Harvest, 1986.

A Better Tomorrow. *Ying hung boon sik/Yingxiong bense* (True Colors of a Hero). Film Workshop/Cinema City/Golden Princess, 1986.

A Better Tomorrow II. *Ying hung boon sik 2/Yingxiong bense 2* (True Colors of a Hero 2). Film Workshop/Cinema City/Golden Princess, 1987.

The Killer. *Dip huet seung hung/Diexue shuang xiong* (A Pair of Blood-Splattering Heroes). Film Workshop/Magnum/Cinema City/Golden Princess, 1989.

Just Heroes, aka **Tragic Heroes.** *Yi daam kwan ying/Yi dan qun ying* (Righteous Courage Group of Heroes). Magnum/Golden Princess, 1990.

Bullet in the Head. *Dip huet gaai tau/Diexue jietou* (Blood-Splattered Streets). Milestone Films/Golden Princess, 1990)

Once a Thief. *Jung waang sei hoi/Zongsheng sihai* (Criss Cross over Four Seas). Milestone Films/Golden Princess, 1991.

Hard Boiled. *Laat sau san taam/Lashou shentan* (Hot-Handed Supercop). Milestone Films/Golden Princess, 1992.

Hard Target. Alphaville-Renaissance/Universal, 1993.

Broken Arrow. 20th Century–Fox, 1996.

Once a Thief. Alliance Productions/WCG; television; 1996.

Face/Off. Paramount, 1997.

Black Jack. Alliance Productions/WCG; television; 1998.

Notes

Introduction

1. These quotations, and the epigraphs in subsequent chapters, unless otherwise indicated, are derived from the CD-ROM encyclopedia *Microsoft Bookshelf '94*, s.v. "hero," "heroes."

2. Woo explained this connection in an interview with Mark Savage: "I wanted to make an uplifting film to highlight the lost traditional values, including the values of family, friendship, tolerance, etc. So I decided to remake a sixties film (*True Colors of a Hero*, directed by Lung Kong) and that became *A Better Tomorrow*" (Woo, interview with Mark Savage 1).

3. The literal translation of the Chinese title for *A Better Tomorrow* is "True Colors of a Hero" ("Ying hung boon sik"). For films made in Hong Kong, where Cantonese is spoken, I also provide, following the Cantonese title, the Mandarin or pinyin versions of the titles, in this case, "Yingxiong bense." (Pinyin is the system for romanizing, or transliterating, Chinese characters which is used by the government in Beijing, where Mandarin is the official language.) Cantonese (that is, Hong Kong) audiences, would know this film as "Ying hung boon sik." Woo's film starred veteran actor Ti Lung (as Ho); Leslie Cheung, a popular singer turned actor (as Kit); Chow Yun-fat, a television and (at that time) occasional movie actor (as Mark); and Waise Lee Chi-hung (as Shing).

4. In "Traditional Heroes in Chinese Popular Fiction" Robert Ruhlmann provides the following information about traditional heroes in China:

> The Chinese equivalents for "hero" include *ying-hsiung* ("male," "outstanding man"), the archaic phrase *ta-chang-fu* ("great man"), and the plebian *hao-han* ("good fellow"); also widely used in fiction texts are the term *fei-ch'ang jen* ("extraordinary man") and the epithet *ch'i* ("remarkable," "strange"). These words most often connote unusual physical or moral strength, energy and purposefulness, devotion to a great cause—good or bad—unconventional behavior, and sometimes striking traits of physiognomy and stature [150].

The term commonly used in Hong Kong films is "ying hung," that is, the Cantonese equivalent of Mandarin "ying-hsiung."

5. This film is not to be confused with its relatively loose TV remake, shot by Woo in Vancouver in 1996.

6. This character is also called "Alan" in the film. The name "Alan" is his pseudonym, or cover name, for his activities in the Triad. "Tony" is apparently his real name. In this book, I will use "Alan" in contexts appropriate to his "cover," that is, during the earlier parts of the film, when he carries out activities related to his work in the criminal organizations, and "Tony" in his police context, or in the latter parts of the film.

7. I provide the actor's name in this form in order to distinguish him from Tony Leung Ka-fai, who has appeared in many films such as Kirk Wong's *Gunmen*, Tsui

Hark's *A Better Tomorrow III* and the French film *The Lovers*. In Hong Kong, people often adopt an English given name. Thus, the actor and singer Leslie Cheung is actually named Cheung Kwok-wing. His name may sometimes appear, therefore, as Leslie Cheung Kwok-wing. (The draft *Supplements Text* for *The Killer*, Criterion-Voyager Laserdisc, helped to clarify this question for me, in the chapter "The Name Game.")

8. In *Hara-kiri*, a samurai (Tatsuya Nakadai) dies avenging the death of his son; the Nakadai character, after fighting against impossible odds, commits suicide before he can be killed. In *Rebellion*, the samurai hero, played by Toshiro Mifune, dies protecting his grandson from those who wish to exterminate the clan line.

9. Woo, personal interview, 8 November 1995. (All interviews with the author have been edited for content and fluidity. Ellipses are not indicated.) Woo seems to be conflating the historical, or semi-historical, account of Ching K'o in *Shih chi* 86, by Ssu-ma Ch'ien (*Records of the Historian: Chapters from the Shih chi* 55-67), and the adventures of the hero in Chang Cheh's *One-Armed Swordsman*. In any case, Woo's narrative is quite revealing of his perspective on heroism. (I am indebted to Lori Tilkin, assistant to Terence Chang, for the source of the Ching K'o story.)

10. The remarks in this sentence are based on two points in McDonagh's essay (47). I differ from McDonagh in her rather severe criticism of such "rough spots," a point upon which I will later elaborate.

11. Woo may get his chance. According to Lori Tilkin, Terence Chang's assistant, a film of Caleb Carr's biography *The Devil Soldier* is now "under development." The biography details an American mercenary's unusual role in the Tai-ping Rebellion. Woo mentioned his interest in filming the Carr book to me in November 1995 but apparently had no definite plans.

12. For a good summary of Hong Kong movie history, see Paul Fonoroff, "A Brief History of Hong Kong Cinema," *Renditions* 29-30 (1988): 293-308.

13. Both Ringo Lam and Kirk Wong are now working in Hollywood, as are directors Tsui Hark, Ronny Yu and actors Chow Yun-fat and Michelle Yeoh.

14. In Cantonese, Woo has also been known as Ng Yu Sum.

15. Although Canton is the older romanization for this city, I provide the form most well known to English speakers, instead of the modern pinyin form "Guangdong."

16. The following biographical information is derived from "Woo in Interview" (25).

17. Shaw Brothers was one of the most important film studios in Hong Kong during the 1960s and 1970s. It was especially known for colorful period epics, showcasing stylized martial arts and swordplay.

18. This studio, "founded in 1970 by one-time Shaw employee Raymond Chow," became "Hong Kong's largest and most consistently successful company for most of the last twenty years" (Fore 41). Fore comments (41) that "the legendary Shaw Brothers studio effectively ceased movie production in 1986 and has reentered the market only recently."

19. This studio was founded in the early 1980s by Karl Maka, Dean Shek and Raymond Wong.

20. Hoberman (33), writing on *The Killer*, states: "Originally dedicated to Jean-Pierre Melville and Martin Scorsese, *The Killer* evokes all manner of disreputable genre maestros: Sergio Leone, Douglas Sirk, Brian De Palma." While agreeing with the thrust of Hoberman's evaluation, I should note that Woo had apparently never seen any films by Douglas Sirk when he made *The Killer*. He told me that he only saw *Magnificent Obsession* after making *The Killer* (personal interview, 7 November

1995). Terence Chang, Woo's business partner, also confirmed this (personal interview, 4 November 1995).

21. Malcolm Dome presents the career of Chang Cheh in "Chang-Shaw Massacre" (see Bibliography, below). Chang is a major influence in Hong Kong filmmaking, having set a style for swordplay and martial arts films at the famous Shaw Brothers Studios. His important films include *One-Armed Swordsman* (1967), *The Girl with the Thunderbolt Kick* (aka *Golden Swallow*) (1968), *Vengeance* (1970), and *Five Deadly Venoms* (1975).

22. King Hu (1931-97) was a very influential stylist who specialized in semi-historical period pieces, among them *Come Drink with Me* (1965), *Dragon Gate Inn* (1966), *A Touch of Zen* (1969) and *The Fate of Lee Khan* (1972).

23. Ephraim Katz, in his *The Film Encyclopedia*, describes American director Lester (b. 1946) as a "[l]ow-budget, violent action specialist." His films include *Truck Stop Women* (1974), *Commando* (1985) and *Showdown in Little Tokyo* (1991) (Katz 820). His most recent release is *The Ex* (1997), with Yancy Butler (Natasha in Woo's *Hard Target*).

24. For a brief, sensible discussion of Woo's special qualities as a director of action films, see Feerick, especially 56.

25. McDonagh (49) also notes Woo's use of the triangle.

26. Both films, directed by Akira Kurosawa, starred Toshiro Mifune as the nameless samurai who served as the model for Clint Eastwood's Man with No Name in films such as *A Fistful of Dollars* (1964) and *For a Few Dollars More* (1965), both directed by Sergio Leone.

27. See his *Confessions of a Cultist* (1970) and "The Auteur Theory Revisited" (1977), listed in the Bibliography below.

28. All citations from *Hard Boiled* in the text refer to chapter numbers from the Criterion Laserdisc release, in CAV format (ch.). The audio commentary is heard on Analog track 2.

29. See Williams' sensible discussion of this issue concerning Woo ("To Live and Die" 44).

30. See Kapsis, *Hitchcock: The Making of a Reputation*, in the Bibliography below.

31. All citations from *The Killer* in the text refer to chapter numbers from the Criterion Laserdisc release, in CAV format (ch.). The audio commentary is heard on Analog track 2. Individual frames are indicated by the chapter number, colon, and the frame number.

32. The traditional Chinese emphasis on ethics, or morality, is quite pronounced. In the words of one commentator on Chinese cultural history,

> In my study of Chinese history I have often observed that our humanistic thinking, more than anything else, has been the determining factor in our way of life. Name anything Chinese, chances are that it is more or less linked with our moral conceptions. In politics, we like to talk about the importance of virtue in the art of government instead of the technique of promoting administrative efficiency. In military science, our thoughts revolve around brotherly love, faithfulness and mutual trust as superior weapons to heavy armament and trained warriors.... Regarding literature, we judge its merits by the moral lessons it contributes.... It seems that everything concerning China is somehow connected with either the meaning of life or the purpose of life [Wang 4].

33. For a balanced and informative study of Lawrence, see Malcolm Brown and Julia Cave, *A Touch of Genius: The Life of T. E. Lawrence* (London: J. M. Dent, 1988).

34. For example, when I asked him in 1996 about the Romantics he had in mind, he mentioned Françoise Sagan—certainly French, and very neo-romantic, but not exactly a Romantic in the usual sense (personal interview, 2 March 1996).

Chapter 1

1. Chandler, the author of the novels and stories starring cynical detective Philip Marlowe, has often been treated as a neo-chivalric writer.

2. *Romance of the Three Kingdoms*, though "compiled" by Lo Kuan-chung (c. 1330-1400), was heavily influenced by earlier tales and poems about its major characters (Hsia, *Classic Chinese Novel* 35). Hsia comments that "[b]y and large it is a sober drama of political and military contentions of about a hundred years' duration (A.D. 168-265) among rival power groups bidding for control of the Chinese empire" (35). *Water Margin* went through several versions; a much-read edition of 100 chapters was published about 1550 (Hsia 77). Hsia summarizes the novel as follows: "*Shui hu chuan* tells of Sung Chiang and his band of outlaws who flourished briefly during the reign of Hui-tsung of the Northern Sung dynasty.... They surrendered in 1121 and, according to some sources, they were enlisted in the government campaign against a rebel of far greater historical significance, Fang La" (Hsia 76).

3. "The same people who most looked down on these novels, namely, the members of the scholar-official class, wrote them and also avidly read them" (v).

4. Strong female characters were often to be found in Hong Kong films of the 1960s and 1970s. Angela Mao Ying was a dynamic presence in films such as *When Taekwondo Strikes* (1973) and *Broken Oath* (1977).

5. The dynastic chronologies are taken from Charles O. Hucker, *China's Imperial Past* 435; the chronological reference to drama and novel from C. T. Hsia, *The Classic Chinese Novel* 10-12. The *wuxia pian* genre owes much to a parallel genre, or subgenre, of the Chinese novel, referred to by C. T. Hsia in his presentation of the classic swordsman hero (the *chien-hsia*): "In Hong Kong and Taiwan, new novels and stories about swordsmen (*wu-hsia* [*wuxia*] *hsiao-shuo*) are being continually published and avidly read" (*Classic Chinese Novel* 30).

6. Tales of chivalry are not to be confused with

> popularizations of history such as the famous *Romance of the Three Kingdoms*.... Although the two kinds of fiction may overlap in subject matter, certain differences between them exist. In chivalric tales the knights-errant act as individuals and usually fight single-handed; in historical romances the heroes are professional warriors who lead armies to battle. In the former our attention is focused on the personal courage and loyalty of the knights; in the latter the main interest lies in battles and stratagems [Liu 81-82].

Liu classifies *Water Margin* as "a chivalric romance": "Some chivalric tales told orally centered round certain groups of heroes. When these tales were joined together, they formed the bases of long prose romances" (108).

7. Lent 115, referring to a 1980 *Asiaweek* article:

> In the 1950s-early 1960s swordplay films, the Confucian code dominated. Plots revolved around filial ties, destruction of which led to violence and revenge, and the master-pupil relationship was important. During the following decade, with directors Chang Cheh and King Hu dominating, martial arts films changed. They were now more action-oriented, the moralistic overtones were replaced by men fighting their way to fame and fortune with deadly weapons, and the aesthetics of kung fu, almost dance-like, prevailed.

One might differ with the characterization of Chang Cheh, given films like *One-Armed Swordsman* and *Vengeance*, but the emphasis on the shift from Confucian values to more "modern" concerns is useful. In this context, *A Better Tomorrow* seems even more like "a swordplay film in modern dress," given its emphasis on filial duty and vertical loyalty relationships.

8. Or, at least, a Confucian would assent to violence only after the failure of moral suasion. This is exactly the role of Wong Fei-hong as played by Kwan Tak-hing in films like *The Skyhawk*, according to Tony Williams ("Kwan Tak-hing" 3).

9. He told me, "I hate to be established as an action director—my action sequences [have] so much else besides action" (Woo, personal interview, 8 November 1995).

10. Robert Ruhlmann specifies two "types of loyalties" in the Confucian system, "*vertical*" and "*horizontal*" (original emphasis). The vertical applies "between prince and subject, lord and vassal, father and son"; the horizontal between brothers and peers (170). Both are present in Ho's family, and, as we shall see, in Ho's Triad, although their violation in both cases leads to the disaster in the film.

11. Kirk Wong has emphasized this theme in his films *Crime Story* (1993; with Jackie Chan and Kent Cheng), *Organized Crime and Triad Bureau* (1994; with Danny Lee and Anthony Wong Chau-sang) and *Rock 'N' Roll Cop* (1994; with Anthony Wong and Yu Rong-guang).

12. Teo (175-76) discusses *A Better Tomorrow* in terms of *yi* (the Chinese concept of loyalty and obligation). For more on *yi*, see the discussion of knightly virtues later in the chapter.

13. The *bushido* code, though similar in broad outlines to the Chinese knightly ideal, differs markedly in other respects.

14. Although the authorship of this history is traditionally attributed solely to Ssu-ma Ch'ien (c. 145-c. 86 B.C.), the work was actually the product of more than one compiler, probably of at least three (Loewe, Introduction, *Cambridge History* 3-4).

15. Woo says of *The Killer* that "[m]y killer is not very contemporary: he's a killer from several centuries ago, when they killed for a reason" ("Woo in Interview" 25).

16. For a compact, well-written treatment of the code, see Nitobe, *Bushido*, in the Bibliography.

17. See Chapter 6 for a discussion of the parallels between this film and *The Killer*.

18. Woo has commented on his debt to the *bushido* code on several occasions; for example, "I always worshipped the chivalrous behavior of ancient knights, the loyalty of the Samurai spirit and the French romantics" (Woo, Interview by Jillian Sandall, 39).

19. The similarity to *Duel in the Sun* (1946; with Jennifer Jones and Gregory Peck) has been noted, but the subtext here is quite different from that film's. And Woo apparently has not even seen this film. I am thus understandably reluctant to regard it as a source for him.

20. As my colleague Michael Anderegg pointed out, such demonstrations would not have been permitted in South Vietnam. So Woo takes some liberties with history here, but his point about the inhumanity of tyrannies is still forcefully driven home.

21. This incident occurred on February 1, 1968, in Saigon, in the early hours of the Tet Offensive:

> General Nguyen Ngoc Loan, chief of South Vietnam's national police, was the crude cop who had brutally crushed the dissident Buddhist movement in Hué two years earlier. Now his mood was even fiercer: Communist invaders had killed several of his men, including one gunned down with his wife and children in their house...
> That morning, Eddie Adams ... and Vo Suu [two press photographers] had

been cruising around the shattered town. Near the An Quang temple, they spotted a patrol of government troops with a captive in tow.... The soldiers marched him up to Loan, who drew his revolver and waved the bystanders away. Without hesitation, Loan stretched out his right arm, placed the short snout of the weapon against the prisoner's head and squeezed the trigger. The man grimaced—then, almost in slow motion, his legs crumpled beneath him as he seemed to sit down backward, blood gushing from his head as it hit the pavement.... [Karnow 542].

My colleague Richard Beringer, from the History Department at the University of North Dakota, informs me that Loan commented, "Buddha will understand." See also Braestrup 1:460-62 and *Dictionary of the Vietnam War* 310-11.

22. Woo says that this *Pietà* group was fashioned by his production designer, and that he wished to set up a contrast like the one mentioned here:

I just told the production designer I wanted a statue like that on the wall. It looks tender for love, you know, so when the young man got shot, I wanted to refocus to the statue as a montage to emphasize the cruelty [Woo, personal interview, 7 November 1995].

23. Woo contextualizes his Pilate reference into the general religious symbolism in his films:

As a Protestant, I am strongly influenced by Christian beliefs about love, sin, redemption. I designed the final scene of *The Killer* in a church because for the protagonist it is the only peaceful place in the world. I spent a lot of money to make the perfect Virgin Mary statue: when it is shot to pieces, truth is destroyed by evil, and with it the spirit of chivalry displayed by ancient warriors. In *A Better Tomorrow*, when Chow Yun-Fat [Mark] is beaten up, the villain takes his scarf and wipes his hand; when Christ was crucified, Pilate washed his hands ["Woo in Interview" 25].

24. The film's production designer, Phil Dagort, noted that his crew actually designed some of the crypts and built the cemetery gates seen in the film. Dagort also went to some lengths (perhaps somewhat inspired by Woo's intuitive use of symbols, but in any case by a sense of accuracy and artistic dedication) to make the gates iconographically precise: "I did a lot of research on the symbols that are in the ironwork of the cemeteries. Particularly there are arrows that point down, that's one of the symbols of death, you know, an arrow pointing down." Unfortunately, these symbolic touches cannot be seen too well in the finished film (Dagort, telephone interview).

25. Terence Chang noted that the use of the paper cranes was not Woo's idea (Chang, personal interview, 4 November 1995). But Woo certainly put the idea to very creative and meaningful use.

26. Kwan Yi (Kuan Yü) was an important military figure from the Three Kingdoms period (A.D. 220-80):

The military adventures of Liu Pei and his sworn brothers, Chang Fei and Kuan Yü (both d. 219), originally as lieutenants of [Han General] Ts'ao Ts'ao and then as his most dedicated antagonists, became one of the great epic legends of China and the inspiration for much later fiction and drama [for instance, *Romance of the Three Kingdoms*]. Kuan, in fact, was eventually canonized as China's god of war [Hucker 133-34, 434].

Ruhlmann notes that, in the Chinese tradition, "[n]ames of great men readily turn into common names, synonymous with specific attributes or virtues.... Kuan Yü [becomes] the symbol of unwavering fidelity to his lord" (149).

27. As Richard James Havis and Alexandra A. Seno comment, "These days Hollywood has claimed Woo as one of its own—and U.S. reviewers like to spot such

all-American influences. The fact is, however, Woo is very much an Asian auteur who started out making kung-fu movies" (Havis and Seno).

28. The image of the dragon's eye is a masterful synecdoche. It hints at the "bullseye" in John's sights and establishes a Pudovkinesque link to Tony's dead eye, shown staring after he is shot in, additionally, a clear reference to Marion Crane's death in *Psycho*. Alternatively, the red circle in the dragon's eye refers to Jean-Pierre Melville's *Le Cercle rouge*, in which a marksman (Yves Montand) shoots out a red security lock (a red circle) in a freestanding, "from the hip" rifle shot reprised here by John and by Tequila in *Hard Boiled*.

Chapter 2

1. The epigraphs in this chapter were derived from Version 1.0 of *Correct Quotes* software (Novato, CA: WordStar International, 1990-92).

2. I have relied here on the credits listing in Garnham, *Samuel Fuller* (162-76).

3. This was recently echoed in *The Professional* (Luc Besson, 1995).

4. For a discussion of the indebtedness of *The Killer* to the "knightly" tradition in China, see the enlightening M.A. thesis by Lori Tilkin, "The Journey of the Knight-Errant from Past to Present," Washington University (1997). Tilkin, who is Terence Chang's assistant, has benefitted in her careful work not only from fluency in Mandarin but also from close working contact with Woo, who commented usefully for her in the thesis.

5. I am indebted to Michael Anderegg for highlighting for me this aspect of John's development as a character.

6. On one occasion early in the film, Pentangeli wants the Rosato brothers hit because they sell drugs in their own neighborhood, that is, they violate the old code.

7. One is reminded, in yet a different sense, of the scene in the police station from *The Terminator* (James Cameron, 1984) when the Terminator passes unharmed down corridors through a gauntlet of police who pop out of doors only to be dispatched.

8. *American Film Genres: Approaches to a Critical Theory of Popular Film*, Chapter 10. The term "pods" is important to *Invasion* but is extended by Kaminsky to cover Siegel's thematics of individualism.

9. David Wu was music editor on *The Killer* and the 1991 *Once a Thief*. He edited the television pilot for *Once a Thief* (1996), directed by Woo, and has directed episodes of the television series.

10. In an interview with the author on November 7, 1995, Woo said:

> The way Hitchcock shoots the movie [*Strangers on a Train*], he makes it differently from how he usually does; the suspense, the thrill and even the rhythm are all different. *Strangers on a Train* seems to be like an orchestra—the whole movie from the beginning to the end—everything moves so smoothly and is always happening, keeps happening, keeps surprising you. [Hitchcock has] no need to do what he usually does: take a long time to build up the scene as in *The Birds*, [where he takes] half the movie to build up all the suspense. So in that movie [*Strangers*] you can follow the character, from beginning to end, it's very anxious and suspenseful to watch what's happening, what's he going to do.

11. Or so it seemed to this writer. But the film's screenwriters told me that this scene was always in the script, even before Woo became involved, and that this was not their intent (Werb and Colleary, telephone interview).

12. See the illuminating defense of Peckinpah against such charges in his *Peckinpah: The Western Films*, especially 97-100.

13. Williams, "From Hong Kong to Hollywood," has noted Woo's use of Eisensteinian techniques, remarking, "Ivan Muricy has commented on Woo's development of Eisenstein's editing techniques, seeing them as evidence of a deliberate strategy in undermining and delaying the process of classical Hollywood linear time techniques" (46 n. 13). Eisenstein's influence, and Pudovkin's too, I might add, is felt in Woo's films not only at the textual level but importantly at the level of construction. Woo's reliance on editing has often been noted (for instance, by the script supervisor for his first two Hollywood films, Faith Conroy [telephone interview]). Russell Carpenter commented, "What John's doing is, he's designing his sequences so that he can come out of one rather quick action sequence with many pieces of usable film and each piece of film adds to and amplifies another piece of film" (telephone interview, 8 January 1996). This practice sounds remarkably like that of the Russian Formalist directors and in fact connects such technique, in Woo's case, with Chinese poetic theory (see Lau Shing-hon, "Three Modes of Poetic Expression in Martial Arts Films," especially the discussion of *bi-xing* mode).

14. Incidentally, Woo underscores both the theme of loyalty and his criticism of bureaucracy or totalitarian organization by panning past a group of Japanese junior executives bowing to their boss and promising to take care of things for him while he is away. The camera (that is, Li) at first mistakes this man for John because of some physical similarity.

15. I am indebted to Tony Williams for this last connection to Chang Cheh.

16. Tony Williams notes Woo's "fail[ure] to make Josephine Shiao an acceptable knightly heroine in *Plain Jane to the Rescue*" ("Space" 73).

Chapter 3

1. I am referring here to Borges' memorable short story "El milagro secreto" [The secret miracle], in which a Czech playwright about to be executed by the Nazis is granted, by divine action, the psychic time necessary to finish his play. The actual time transpiring is the split second needed for the bullets to reach him.

2. Teo (179) notes the "Leone-esque" quality of *The Killer*, with its emphasis on close-ups. To his assertion that Leone's *Once Upon a Time in America*, more than his Westerns, was "seminal" (n. 5) to Hong Kong filmmakers, I would add the important qualification that Leone's masterpiece *Once Upon a Time in the West* was at least as influential on Woo, and, according to David Wu, on other film artists in Hong Kong.

3. For the geometric style of *Rio Bravo*, see Guillermo Cabrera Infante, *A Twentieth Century Job* 272.

4. Faith Conroy, script supervisor for *Hard Target* and *Broken Arrow*, commented on her experience with Woo's camera setups on *Hard Target*:

> ...[Woo's camera] takes on a life of its own, and it moves like a snake. It's just got a drama all of its own.
>
> It would take me three inches of notebook paper to describe one camera move. One camera move. And there were usually six of them per shot.
>
> The camera people would play games with me. I called it "Find the Cameras." They wouldn't tell me how many were out. I would have to go looking for them. They would laugh and eventually say, "Okay, we'll give you a hint. There are six."

So I would run around like I was on an Easter egg hunt looking for these cameras... [fax to author].

5. For Chapman's style, see Schafer and Salvato, chapter 5.

6. Lance Henriksen pointed this out in a telephone interview with the author. Russell Carpenter also distinguished between Peckinpah's technique and Woo's: "John is different from Peckinpah in that [in] Sam Peckinpah's shots, I think, the camera was static. [John is] constantly moving his camera and he'll do it even in slow-motion shots. John's sequences are like ballet" (telephone interview, 8 January 1996).

7. For a fuller discussion of these analogies, see Chapter 1.

8. See the works by Keppler and Hallam, in the Bibliography, for presentation and discussion of these ideas.

9. Or at least this is what the film in its present form concludes; but see Terence Chang's comments in Chapter 8.

10. Although one must remember that Woo's Romantic influence is of the popular variety (through decidedly watered-down, or if one prefers, bastardized samples like works by Françoise Sagan), nevertheless even popular Romanticism, including *film noir*, can trace its ancestry back to Hoffmann, Poe and Shelley.

11. See Rothman for Hitchcock's camerawork, especially as relating to *Murder*. I am indebted to Michael Anderegg for suggesting Hitchcock as a possible source for this kind of camera work.

12. Julian Stringer is the rare critic who has noted the textured layering of music in Woo's films. See his comments in "Your Tender Smiles," especially 30 n. 5.

13. The Latin phrase is Horace's, meaning that a poem is like a picture. Hazard Adams comments that

> The idea that the poem is like a picture, attributed to Horace ... is not original with him but apparently traceable back to Simonides, a Greek poet of the fifth century B. C.... Horace says that poetry is like painting in that some works will be more effective viewed up close, others farther off. He uses this analogy to emphasize the variety of poetry rather than to limit it to the effects of painting in words. Though Horace does see similarities between the poem and painting and tends to think of the poem in spatial terms, he can hardly be held responsible for the tendency of later critics of neoclassical [and Romantic] persuasion to extend the analogy [*Critical Theory since Plato* 67].

14. Woo's insistence on keeping the part about John and the contract at the beginning of the film was crucial, since the early scenes prepare us for the presence of the musical leitmotifs for characters.

15. See especially the latter Lake Tahoe scenes of *The Godfather Part II* and the opening scene of *The Godfather Part III*.

16. Its narratively apt lyrics include the following lines: "No regrets, no remorse. Let bygones be bygones.... Just set me free from this reverie, / For the pain lingers."

17. Williams also notes this connection ("To Live" 47).

18. Certainly Lowell Lo was inspired by Morricone's work; he noted, "I got some of the ideas from *Once Upon a Time in America*. I use bottle blower a lot as it gives me a haunting effect" (fax to author). And David Wu, music editor for the film and contributor of some of its music as well, confirmed that the harmonica music in Westerns generally and in Leone films in particular has much importance for his own work and for that of other Hong Kong filmmakers (telephone conversation with author).

19. I am indebted to Gene DuBois for this source.

20. Note, for example, the frequent musical references in *Water Margin*.

21. I am indebted to Gene DuBois for pointing out this musical allusion.

Chapter 4

1. Siao, or "Fong Fong," as she is familiarly known, has made a stunning comeback in the 1990s, beginning with her scene-stealing (and nearly show-stealing) performance in Corey Yuen Kwei's *Fong Sai Yuk* (1990) (Chute, publicity release, *Broken Arrow* 44).

2. I will use the English name for the character Lam Ah Chun for purposes of convenience.

3. Hui is one of an extremely talented trio of brothers, the other two being Michael (a true comic genius) and Sam (a very talented singer as well as a gifted comic and action performer).

4. In his essay *Laughter* (1900), Henri Bergson formulated an influential theory of the comic that emphasized the comedy of the mechanical: "*The attitudes, gestures and movements of the human body are laughable in exact proportion as that body reminds us of a mere machine*" (Bergson 79; original emphasis). Wylie Sypher comments in his introduction to Bergson's work:

> To Bergson's notion, a comic impasse occurs wherever a human being ceases to behave like a human being—that is, whenever he "resembles a piece of clockwork wound up once for all and capable of working automatically," but is incapable of *living*. The instant this automatic figure ... appears under the glare of our intelligence, he looks ridiculous, particularly when he is caught at an intersection of events where his automatic response is seen to be inadequate. Then he is *isolated*, in all his mechanical idiocy, facing unexpected demands; and we behold him as if he were set, like a type displayed, on a stage where he forfeits our sympathy [Sypher xii].

Much the same can be said of Lam Ah Chun in several situations.

5. Tsui Hark's *Once Upon a Time in China* series revolves, in a generally serious fashion, around precisely this opposition. See Lo Kwai-chung, "*Once Upon a Time*: Technology Comes to Presence in China."

6. For an illuminating if somewhat canted presentation of Legalism and its effects in China, see Amaury de Riencourt, *The Soul of China*. Its author claims that the present regime in mainland China is nothing more than a modern recasting of Legalist tendencies. If we accept this characterization, the contrast between Legalism and classical Confucianism can be seen to have relevance for Woo's films, given his anti-totalitarian and generally pro–Confucian stance.

7. The second Lam Ah Chun film (Woo's was the third) appeared in 1979, and was directed by Wong Wah-kei. It was called *Lam Ah Chun Blunders Again*.

8. My point here only reinforces Woo's assertion (above) that he pioneered the use of visual humor in Cantonese comedy.

9. In the Supplements text for the Criterion laserdisc edition of *The Killer*, the actor playing Kao is incorrectly identified as Wei Pai. Wei Pai is actually the lead actor here ("Magic Sword"), while Kao is played by Lau Kong, also seen in films such as Ringo Lam's *City on Fire* (1987). (The entries at the *Hong Kong Movie Database* assisted me in this piece of cast untanglement.)

Chapter 5

1. Woo explicitly links the two films, stating that Chow's character in *A Better Tomorrow* and the knight called "Green" in *Last Hurrah* are "the same character" (Woo, commentary, *The Killer* ch. 30).

2. Terence Chang observed about the film that:

John at that time talked to Tsui Hark a lot and Tsui Hark asked him to put all of his emotions into the characters. So I think this film is so strikingly different from his previous works. He's entered another phase, he's taken the first step toward maturity as an artist. Then it became history—a huge hit and so forth [personal interview, 2 March 1996].

3. Stephen Teo discusses Lung Kong's career in his *Hong Kong Cinema* (138–39). The Lung Kong film remade by Woo is also known as *The Story of a Discharged Prisoner*. Despite lamenting that Lung Kong has not received his deserved critical attention, Teo notes Woo's "tribute" to Lung Kong's film in remaking it (138).

4. The family name is Sung. Ho's full name is given in the film as Ho Sung-tse.

5. His father is played by Tien Feng, one of the finest stars of Shaw Brothers films. He had played such memorable roles as Lee Khan in King Hu's *The Fate of Lee Khan* (1972) and Kang's *sifu* (master) in Chang Cheh's *The One-Armed Swordsman* (1969). Not only is this nice casting, it is suggestive, because Tien had often played fatherly or leader-like roles for Shaw Brothers, while Ti Lung had often played young, hot-blooded action roles (as in Chang Cheh's *Vengeance* [1970] and *Ci Ma [Blood Brothers]* [1973; Assistant Director, John Woo]). More recently, Tien played the grandfather of Hueyin (Maggie Cheung Man-yuk) in Ann Hui On-wah's *Song of the Exile* (1990), in which he transmitted Confucian, imperial traditions to Hueyin as a child.

6. Kit's ignorance of Ho's *métier* brings to mind *Public Enemy* (1931), in which James Cagney, as the younger brother Tom in the Powers family and the "public enemy," resents his elder brother Mike (Donald Cook), who as the "straight" brother tries to protect their ailing mother from learning about Tom's career. The irony is that Mike is not unfriendly with the mob. He appears rather well-acquainted with Tom's boss and takes his orders a little too readily.

7. These fatherly criminal figures are common in Woo's films. We will see a particularly ill-fated example in *Hard Boiled* (Mr. Hui), but Woo also included one in his 1996 TV pilot *Once a Thief* (the Godfather, played by Robert Ito).

8. Or, at least, its younger members' ethic, since Yiu represents a more old-fashioned and, in this context, more ethical kind of leadership. Julian Stringer, commenting on "family relationships and obligations" in this film, insightfully notes that "*A Better Tomorrow* is all about the disaster that can strike if that Chinese network of interpersonal relationships is severed" (31).

9. This was the big "break" for Chow, who had appeared in many television shows and some films previously. Chow attained immediate fame, upstaging the leads in the film, and became both a close friend and a brilliant collaborator, as actor, for John Woo.

10. Woo has a small but important role as the Taiwanese policeman who follows Ho's case.

11. The boss is played by Kenneth Tsang, an often-seen actor with several important roles in Woo's films, including *The Killer* and *Once a Thief* (Hong Kong version). He most recently appeared as the villainous Mr. Wei in *Replacement Killers* (Antoine Fuqua, 1998; with Chow Yun-fat and Mira Sorvino).

12. We might well see parallels here between the boss and the Pat O'Brien character of films such as *Angels with Dirty Faces* (1938). This is the obvious reference or parallel; but perhaps we could also think of the bandits' "lair" in *Water Margin* (*Shui hu chuan*), which serves as a kind of hospice and employment source for all sorts of

men on the run, from common criminals to political refugees. *Water Margin* has been very influential in shaping Woo's world view; see above, Chapter 1.

13. The trenchcoat and shades worn by Mark were a deliberate homage to Alain Delon's costume in *Le Samouraï*, one of Woo's formative films. After providing this information, David Chute notes, "The style of designer shades that Chow wore constantly in the role—Alain Delon's signature brand imported from France—sold out in the colony the week after *A Better Tomorrow* opened. The French actor sent the Hong Kong actor a card thanking him for his inadvertent promotional effort" (Chute, "Woo's on First," *Hard Boiled* ch. 51). Delon's own trenchcoat is evocative of the *film noir* and gangster genres, recalling the trenchcoated protagonists of such films as *Out of the Past* (Jacques Tourneur, 1947; with Robert Mitchum) and the seminal *This Gun for Hire* (Frank Tuttle, 1942; with Alan Ladd).

14. Woo, discussing early audience reaction to his *Hard Target* (1993), referred to the perception of genre by the viewing public and its reluctance to embrace experimentation that entailed the mixing of elements from different genres, as in his own films:

> It seems to me that in older times, the Asian audience would hardly accept anything. You used to see movies in a certain way—like the American film nowadays, the audience [has] certain ways of understanding it. The action movie is for action. You can't put any drama element in the action. The comedy is a comedy. The drama is drama. A serious drama is drama—you can't put any action element or comic element in it. So when you tried to mix up something, you tried to do something special ... or change the style, most audiences [in Hong Kong] would laugh (Woo, personal interview, 8 November 1995).

15. One is reminded here of a similar scene in *Bullitt*, when Bullitt visits his girlfriend (Jacqueline Bisset) and is bemused and mystified at her work on tubing for an art project she is making. The contrast between worlds is the point here; Bullitt is a mature and competent policeman.

16. Faith Conroy, the script supervisor for *Hard Target* and *Broken Arrow*, commented on Woo's intuitive working methods, which nonetheless result in a surprisingly coherent product: "[T]his man knows exactly what he's doing. The thing is cutting in his mind as he's shooting it. He sees every angle before he shoots it" (telephone interview, 24 February 1996).

17. According to Terence Chang, it earned $34 million HK, a very large sum at the time (personal interview, 2 March 1996).

18. A good example would be the brief duel at the beginning of *Seven Samurai*, when the skilled swordsman is forced to kill an insistent braggart. Williams ("Space" 84 n. 34) also notes the connection between the Chong and Mad Dog characters.

19. Woo explains: "You remember the scene in the middle with the old man, he's using Chow Yun-fat to draw a comic book. We had a story for him [the old man] but it was too long and got cut out" (Woo, personal interview, 8 November 1995).

20. A fine example of such treatment comes from Miguel de Cervantes' *Don Quixote* (1605–15), in which Don Quixote and Sancho Panza eventually read about their own adventures and have occasion to lament the inaccuracies in the stories about themselves.

Chapter 6

1. As Terence Chang explained, "John was toying with two projects, one was *Bullet in the Head*. He wanted Chow Yun-fat for *Bullet in the Head*. And the other

was *Once a Thief.*" But Woo could not use Chow for these films due to Chow's contractual obligations. "So without Chow he couldn't do *Bullet in the Head.*" [As Chang commented further, "Before *The Killer*, John wanted to do *Bullet in the Head* and that got turned down."] (Chang, personal interview, 2 March 1996). Unless otherwise indicated, all comments in this chapter by Terence Chang are taken from this interview.

   2. Lee, also a director and producer, has appeared in many films, including *The Law with Two Phases, Dr. Lamb, City on Fire, Red Shield, Organized Crime and Triad Bureau* and *The Asian Connection.*

   3. Some of the deleted material can be viewed on the Criterion laserdisc of *The Killer.*

   4. The Cantonese title, *Dip huet seung hung*, is quite evocative but loses in translation, meaning literally "A Pair of Blood-Splattering Heroes." Despite its clumsy-sounding literalness in English, though, the title does indicate some crucial points about the film: we will see a pair of heroes, not one villain, as "The Killer" would suggest, and they will "splatter blood" like Chang Cheh's or Kobayashi's sword-wielding heroes.

   5. John is called Jeff in the VHS release of the film, but for the Criterion laser release, Woo restored the name to his original intention: as a kind of character surrogate for his persona.

   6. I am referring, of course, to the English titles, which are quite far from the original Chinese ones. One might question the relevance of a translated title. But the fact remains that these are the titles by which the films are commonly known, Woo presumably having approved their use, and that many in the Hong Kong audience would have enough familiarity with English to interpret them.

   7. Again, we might point out that the Chinese title translates literally as "A Pair of Blood-Splattering Heroes."

   8. It is important to note here that the opening of the film was not Woo's originally intended one (before shooting began). He wanted the film to begin with John and Jenny performing together at the bar, that is, already knowing each other. This is a rare case of a producer's wishes being right (for the wrong reason: the producer, Tsui Hark, claimed that Hong Kong viewers would not appreciate jazz [Chang, personal interview, 2 March 1996])—the opening as it stands is much more evocative than Woo's might have been. Accidental or no, John's first vision of Jenny confirms his outsider status and sets the tone for the film. Apparently Woo made much the best of an enforced decision and gave his work resonances that it might not have had otherwise.

   9. *Laura* (1944) was directed by Otto Preminger and starred Dana Andrews, Gene Tierney and Clifton Webb. *Portrait of Jennie* (1948) starred Joseph Cotten and Jennifer Jones. In both films, the male protagonist falls in love with a portrait, much as John becomes fascinated less with Jenny, at first, than with her visual image and the sound of her voice.

   10. The music was changed during planning for the film from jazz to Cantopop songs.

   11. The film originally called for John to have known Jenny from his visits to the jazz bar where she sings. But, according to Woo and to Terence Chang (Woo, commentary, *The Killer*; Chang, personal interview, 2 March 1996), Tsui Hark objected to this opening, claiming that audiences in Hong Kong would not understand jazz (see n. 8, above). So, the opening was cut and rearranged. Later, after the film was finally cut, according to Terence Chang, Tsui wanted the film to open with

Danny Lee, eliminating the lead-in scene with John and Sidney in the church or limiting this to a flashback. Woo and film editor David Wu argued for the introductory scene as it stands, maintaining that it was necessary for a true understanding of the film—and rightly so, for the film would be quite another without this evocative and revelatory opening. The planned jazz opening was later used in *Hard Boiled*, with, of course, a different emphasis.

12. Dave Kehr discusses this point in the commentary text for *Hard Boiled* (chs. 26–27).

13. Woo, in fact, denied specific influence from *Bullitt*. Still, the similarities are often difficult to ignore, even if they are coincidental (as in the airport scene and also in Mad Dog's murder of Foxy; both these scenes reminded me, and still do, of similar scenes from *Bullitt*).

A good example of such coincidental similarity is a scene in *Hard Boiled*, when Alan (Tony Leung) walks into the hospital where the stoolie Foxy is hospitalized, ostensibly to kill him. He is carrying a rose bouquet which conceals his pistol. This scene would appear to be a direct allusion to *Terminator 2: Judgment Day* (James Cameron, 1991), which contains a masterfully chilling shot of Arnold Schwarzenegger carrying a bouquet of red roses that conceals a shotgun. But Woo said that this was merely coincidental, although he is quite aware of the similarity (personal interview, 2 March 1996).

14. McDonagh is closer to the mark when she says that "[h]e's an unabashed appropriationist, but without the baggage of postmodern attitude" (47).

15. As we have seen in Chapter 1, some of these values are also associated with Confucianism and with the Chinese heroic tradition.

16. Part of the voluminous novel was filmed recently as *All Men Are Brothers—Blood of the Leopard* (Billy Chan Wui-ngai, 1992), starring Tony Leung Ka-fai, Joey Wong and Elvis Tsui Kam-kong. Woo was assistant director to Chang Cheh on a 1972 version of excerpts from the novel, *Seven Blows of the Dragon*, with David Chiang and Ti Lung.

17. See Chapter 1 "The Chinese Chivalric Hero," for further discussion of this novel.

18. *Ronin* were formerly employed samurai who became masterless as a result of clan upheavals. The heroes of Kurosawa's and Kobayashi's famous swordplay films are *ronin*.

19. The Neo-Confucian movement began "toward the latter half" of the T'ang dynasty, when "the *Tao Hsüeh Chia*, or 'School of the Study of the Tao,' ... had a revival and grew into Neo-Confucianism, with certain Buddhist and Taoist ideas permeating Confucian thought" (Day 183–84). Although the Neo-Confucian movement was hardly uniform, according to Day, he paraphrases a study by Leonard Tomkinson, "Sung and Ming Philosophers on Character Culture," which advances "certain propositions on which there was general agreement among Neo-Confucians, even though belonging to different schools of thought. They agreed, for example, that individual character-influence was a prime factor in perfecting the social order; that the example of a perfect ruler could cause his people to delight in righteousness. All agreed, therefore, on the cultivation of good personal character as the *sine qua non* of any system of education; furthermore, that this end would be accomplished best by achieving *sincerity* in each individual" (Day 228).

20. With the assistance of Prof. Keiko Iwai McDonald and of Toei Studios, I was able to determine the title of this film, not currently available in the United States. It is *Narazumono* (1964), directed by Teruo Ishii for Toei Company and starring Ken Takakura and Tetsuro Tamba.

21. Another important allusion to this film will be examined in the discussion of *Hard Boiled* in Chapter 8.

22. Linda Hutcheon argues convincingly that the traditional "definition of parody as the conservative ridiculing of artistic fashion's extremes" should be expanded:

> What I do want to suggest is that we must broaden the concept of parody to fit the needs of the art of our century—an art that implies another and somewhat different concept of textual appropriation. Certainly new directors like Robert Benton and Brian De Palma are not attempting to ridicule Hitchcock in films such as *Still of the Night* and *Blowout* [sic] [11].

Hutcheon could just as well have mentioned Woo, who is definitely "not attempting to ridicule" Scorsese, Peckinpah, or Chang Cheh by "appropriating" their imagery or elements of their style.

23. The method used by cinematographer Wong Wing-hang is explained by him: "First I shot Chow Yun-fat's upper body against a white screen and then the backdrop was handpainted animation. After that, there was a composite and masking shot" (Wong, fax).

24. *Spy vs. Spy*, a feature that began in *Mad* magazine in January 1961, was a comic strip parody of the James Bond spy craze. It featured two characters, a black and a white bird, in witty cloak-and-dagger rivalry.

25. Woo ties this scene from *Hard Boiled* also to *Le Cercle rouge* (commentary, *Hard Boiled* ch. 30).

26. As Michael Anderegg pointed out to me in conversation, the little girl becomes John's camera. I am indebted to Anderegg for the specific observation about the 180-degree rule.

27. The scene reminds this viewer of the quick move by Borrachón (Dean Martin) in *Rio Bravo* (one of Woo's favorite films) to kill an ambusher in the town saloon. Having previously wounded a man who was running from a murder, he notices blood dripping into a beer glass on the bar. Seeming indifferent, he takes a couple of steps forward and suddenly kneels and fires at the second-floor balcony, drilling the assailant who is perched there with a rifle.

28. The two names are childhood nicknames. "Ah B" means, more or less, "baby" or "kid." "Ha Tau," literally, "Shrimp Head," has also the connotation of "baby" or "kid," in our English sense of "little shrimp" (Win Lee, telephone conversation, 21 March 1998). But they are ultimately, as Terence Chang says, impossible to translate (personal interview, 4 November 1995). So, the different English versions (dubbed or subtitled) of *The Killer* attempt to come up with equivalents, in one case, "Mickey Mouse" (for Li) and "Dumbo" (for John) and in another, "Numbnuts" (for Li) and "Butthead" (for John) (*The Killer*, supplements text).

29. Perhaps Woo was inspired here by Coppola's similar device in *The Godfather Part II*, when the organ music for Anthony Corleone's baptism is the "Godfather theme" composed by Nino Rota.

30. This was the concept, expressed in works such as *Dialogues of Love* by humanist León Hebreo (d. 1535), that the soul expresses itself through the visual faculty; therefore, love "enters" through the eyes. I would like to thank Gene DuBois, a medieval and Renaissance specialist, for consulting with me on this subject.

31. Similarly, the innocent Adam in *Face/Off* is symbolically closed off from the destruction around him, and is vouchsafed the promise of a new life, by listening to "Somewhere Over the Rainbow" with his Walkman earphones. Thus, in an odd way, he is sensorially cut off from the world around him and is thereby protected.

Chapter 7

1. Chang, personal interview, 2 March 1996. Unless otherwise indicated, all comments by Terence Chang in this chapter are taken from this interview.

2. According to Terence Chang, actor Mark Cheng (who appeared most memorably in Tsui Hark's *Gunmen* [1988], as one of the crimefighting heroes and in his *Peking Opera Blues* [1986], as a courageous opponent of the warlords) was considered for the Mark Lee part in *A Better Tomorrow* which was to make Chow Yun-fat famous. The role was, according to Chang, "a supporting part, but you know, John used Chow Yon-fat instead and he became a star because of that supporting part [as Mark Lee]. Nobody looked at it as a supporting part. They thought he was the star of the film." The sequel question was a difficult one, since "[Chow] totally overshadowed the other actors, [but] since he's killed in the film, how do you do a sequel?"

3. This is an interesting concern, given the fact that John Woo had been largely responsible for Chow's having such star power, since he had hired him, over skeptical opposition, for *A Better Tomorrow*. Now the studio that had seen such spectacular box office returns due in large part to a creative decision by Woo was maintaining that he could not make money for them without the star whom he had helped to create. Of course, one would not wish to downplay the tremendous contribution of Chow to film and to John's own career—the point is simply that the studio was mistrusting the goose that had laid a golden egg for them, in fact was cracking the egg over his head.

4. I owe this view of *Coriolanus* to Prof. Richard Hosley of the University of Arizona.

5. Triangular setups like this are a favorite device of Woo's; he was still very consciously employing them (although not in exactly the same form as here) in his 1996 TV pilot *Once a Thief*.

6. Woo appears in a very brief cameo as a policeman who inquires of Jane regarding Ben's whereabouts.

7. This statement, of course, does not apply precisely to Paul, who acts out of greed or fearful obsessiveness.

8. Woo also explicitly connects the film to 1960s French film culture by showing a photo of Catherine Deneuve on the wall in Luke's room. The photo is later shown splashed with blood. Woo told me that he got this idea from John Huston's *The Life and Times of Judge Roy Bean* (1972), which has a similar image with a picture of singer Lily Langtry (with whom Roy Bean [Paul Newman] is comically infatuated) (Woo, personal interview, 7 November 1995).

9. In this connection, consider David Bordwell's observations about the "New Hollywood," written in 1983:

> Nor were the lessons of art-cinema narration lost on filmmakers. The wheel turned almost full circle: classical Hollywood influenced the art film (often negatively); the art film influenced the "New Hollywood" of the 1960s and the 1970s. Everything from freeze frames and slow motion to conventions of gapping and ambiguity has been exploited.... Like its European "New Wave" forebears, the New Hollywood took up an explicit intertextuality.... More broadly, art-cinema devices have been selectively applied to films which remain firmly grounded in classical genres....
> [T]he Hollywood cinema absorbed those aspects of art-cinema narration which fitted generic functions [*Narration* 232].

10. Additionally, the film implies the need for HK people to be united in the face of opposition and to help other HK people when abroad, as in the case with Sally.

Woo, discussing his plans to make *The Devil Soldier*, expressed such sentiments to me about the Chinese in general:

> I think for Chinese society now we also have the same situation as the *Romance of the Three Kingdoms*. We are so separate, in four parts, one is mainland China, one is Taiwan, one is Hong Kong, they all hate each other—they never forgive each other—and I always ask why? Especially here [in the United States]. Chinese people, when they walk on the street and they see each other, they just walk away, they don't even nod or smile—they only say hello to the Americans. And why are the Chinese like a ball of sand? That's a phrase from Chinese—like a ball of sand, [meaning] all separate. That's why I made up my mind to make this story, to try to use the oldtime story to let the people know that if you want us to be strong, if you want our country to be stronger, we have to unite, we have to stick together and not fight any more. A fight will only hurt each other [Woo, personal interview, 8 November 1995].

11. Paul's character owes more than a little to Fred C. Dobbs, Bogart's gold-corrupted prospector in *The Treasure of the Sierra Madre* (John Huston, 1948).

12. McDonagh comments that "Woo's spin on Cimino's Russian roulette scenes is infinitely crueler and more morally compromising" (48).

13. This final scene was cut from the original release print and then restored (Chang).

14. Microsoft Bookshelf '98 CD-ROM, s.v. "friendship."

15. David Wu, the music editor for the film, plays the auctioneer.

Chapter 8

1. A similar dynamic is perceptible in *The Killer* between Li and John.

2. For the *jidai-geki*, or "period film," see Richie, Films, 3d ed., 97.

3. The teahouse scene, where Tequila kills the "undercover cop," or, as the Chief later calls him, "my best witness," always seemed very confusing to me. I wondered why an undercover cop would wantonly shoot innocents, as the man killed by Tequila does. I asked Terence Chang about this problem, and he responded as follows:

> I'm glad you brought it up—because nobody else did. Because there were scenes left from the earlier story. So, none of that makes sense. The only link that we have is that one of the bad guys got killed in a shootout. We added a little bit of the inspector saluting him like he's an undercover cop. But that was added later. That was basically the opening scene for a previous story. Actually we shot that in a week because the teahouse was going to be demolished. And we rented [it to] do what we wanted with it, to destroy it. And then we stopped the production for one month so we could come up with another story. I mean, it was never explained. You don't know who's shooting whom.... He [the man Tequila shot] was not supposed to be a cop. He was even killing innocent bystanders. How could an undercover cop do that? I'm glad you noticed that [personal interview, 4 November 1995].

Notwithstanding the difficulties with the script doctoring, the effect on Tequila's conscience is indisputable and makes for an unforgettable moment later in the film when Tony does kill a real cop.

As an additional point about the early planning for the film, music editor David Wu told me that originally a big shoot-out was planned in a supermarket, complete with slipping and sliding in broken jars of peanut oil. Tequila's partner was to be played by Michelle Yeoh. As the script concept changed to an emphasis on the opposed characters Tequila and Tony, the *dramatis personae* simply became too cluttered, and Yeoh's character was (unfortunately for this author) dropped (Wu, telephone interview, 19 January 1998).

4. But this will have its cost: Tony accidentally shoots one of the policemen. We notice, though, that Tequila's reaction to this indicates his growth. He tells Tony that he must put this behind him in order to be effective, in fact in order to go on living. Williams ("Space" n. 34) refers to the "ironic rebirth" of Tequila in his exit from the morgue, citing an essay by Mike Robins.

5. We could also mention the *Once a Thief* films here, with Cherie Chung or Sandrine Holt as female additions to the mix.

6. David Wu also commented that, since Woo already wanted to move to Hollywood, Terence Chang was concerned that American audiences seeing *Hard Boiled* would react negatively to a story with children being killed (Wu, telephone interview, 19 January 1998).

7. Philip Kwok confirmed that the character of Mad Dog was "John Woo's creation.... John Woo also did not want him to kill the patients in the hospital. He didn't want him to be a cold-blooded murderer but a killer with a conscience.... And I agree with him totally" (fax response to author).

8. The scene in question is Li's first appearance, in a shot paired by transition with John's visit to Jenny's flat. See Chapter 6.

9. Originally, Wu said, Woo had chosen Barbra Streisand's "On a Clear Day You Can See Forever," but the selections were later changed (telephone interview).

Chapter 9

1. Jacks, personal interview, 6 November 1995. All commentary by Jacks cited in this chapter is taken from this interview.

2. Jacks noted that Davis drops little homages to *Hard Target* into his films:

> Andy both in *Under Siege* and in *The Fugitive* makes references to *Hard Target*. At the beginning of *Under Siege* [Seagal's character] starts talking about Boudreaux the Cajun. And, well, that's the character, Seagal's friend, Boudreaux the Cajun. And of course, in *The Fugitive*—"We are on a 'hard target' search."

According to Chuck Pfarrer, a "hard target" is a military term for a well-protected objective (as opposed to a "soft target").

3. Van Damme declined to be interviewed for this book.

4. All chapter citations of *Hard Target* in the text refer to the laserdisc release.

5. When I pointed this out to Chuck Pfarrer, he confirmed the association: "I wanted to hark into that a little bit. I deliberately put castles in there, you connect these two guys, especially Pik, the Evil Lord and his Prince Master, so I'm glad that connected, it was kind of a toss-off line" (telephone interview, 8 December 1995). Williams ("John Woo and His Discontents" 43) also connects the Eastern Europe remark to the recent problems there.

6. This is actually part of a series of lines, cut from the final film, that Fouchon shouts at Chance during their last battle. The lines appear to cast Fouchon as a Satanic presence, or perhaps as a war god, who is omnipresent when battle is joined: "There isn't a country in the world I haven't fired a bullet in! You can't kill me. I'm on every battlefield" (*Hard Target*, First Complete Version).

7. Although Pik's shaved head seems to hint at some sort of Skinhead affilia-
tion, Arnold Vosloo, in answer to my question to that effect, responded: "No! The
shaved head is a sign of economy. Pik is all about economy" (Vosloo, fax to author).

8. Pfarrer informed me that these two characters were named for small towns.
Pik's full name is Van Cleaf; originally, says Pfarrer, he named the character "Van
Cleave" after a small town north of Biloxi, Mississippi (Pfarrer's original home),
but the name had to be changed because "the fact-checkers on the movie found
somebody in the phone book with the same name and they said you're going to
have to change the name" (telephone interview, 2 February 1996). The "Pik" came
from Pik Botha. Fouchon was also named for a small town, this one in South
Louisiana.

9. Terence Chang explained that he and Woo had control over choosing the
crew:

> For the key crew members, I think we met with three or four people, and then
> chose one, because it was a non-union film and we didn't have a lot of money to
> spend. And we tended to go for people who were talented, but who hadn't got a
> chance to do a film of that scale. I mean, maybe people who had worked in 6-mil-
> lion dollar range movies. This is their first big break, a 20 million [budget]. That
> was how we picked the cinematographer and the production designer [personal
> interview, 4 November 1995].

10. Personal interview, 7 November 1995. Unless otherwise indicated, all commentary by Galotti is derived from this interview.

11. Thus, characters used weapons including the following, according to Galotti:
"We had Mossberg 12-gauge, we had a Winchester Defender 12-gauge, we had a
Street Sweeper shotgun. Of course, the Contender, Glock, MP5K, MP583, there's
lots of those, because they're great weapons. Super-reliable."

12. Steve Melton, the property master and armorer (Galotti was the wrangler
on this film, according to Melton, but did not provide the arms) came across the idea
for using the pneumatic gun in a magazine that he was reading on the plane to New
Orleans. The script called for a bow and arrow but not a pneumatic arrow gun. Melton
said that when he showed the picture of the gun to Woo, Woo insisted on getting it
(Melton, telephone interview).

13. A Contender, Galotti explained, is a versatile handgun, made by Thomp-
son Arms, with interchangeable barrels: "It's a single-shot weapon that you can change
the barrels on. You can put everything from a .22 on it up to a .45-.70, which is what
we had on *Hard Target.*"

A similar approach was taken in *Broken Arrow* with the choice of a weapon for John
Travolta's character, Deakins. Galotti recounted, "We [Woo and Galotti] couldn't
find something for Travolta that we both liked. And then suddenly I just sat one day
in my house, and I was thinking about different police departments. What are different
police departments in the country using, because they've got good weapons. And I
thought, hey, the U.S. Marshals use a Ruger AC556F, it's a little 13-inch barrel full
automatic, an M14 basically [but a .223, not a .308]. Big ol' fire. Travolta looked at
it and said, 'It's nice,' he said, 'I really like the wood on it, it's really good for my character.'"

14. This set appears in the rough cut of the film but was severely cut for the final
version.

15. I can attest to all these characteristics of Woo's working methods as being
present on the set of his television-movie *Once a Thief*, which I visited in Vancouver
in 1996.

16. This scene, and also the scene showing Mr. Zenan coming to hire Fouchon and Pik for the hunt of Roper, were, despite the studio interference, good examples of the creative use of the locale's richness. Phil Dagort, following Woo's insistence on a spacious set for Fouchon's home, found some pictures in his book on Louisiana plantation homes, and showed them to Woo, who quickly noticed the ballroom for a particular home. The plantation home that was rented for the shoot is the Nottoway Plantation, about an hour's drive from New Orleans. It was completed in 1859 and, according to its web page, is "the largest surviving plantation home in the South." It also has a chivalrous bit of history:

> The mansion owes its survival to Mrs. Randolph, the wife of John Randolph who built the mansion. During the war, a Union gun boat on the Mississippi fired at the house. When Mrs. Randolph appeared on the front gallery, the young captain recognized both her and the house. He had been a guest there before the war. He came ashore and offered her his protection [Nottoway web page].

17. Bob Murawski, the film's editor, regretted the loss of another catchy line, when one of the hunters has just fallen prey to a trap set by Chance (a snake bites him). Murawski said that Fouchon's line (surely an ad-lib), which appears in earlier cuts of the film, "You guys are as dumb as a sack of hammers," did not make the final film because of studio reluctance: the line was thought too insulting! (Murawski, telephone interview).

18. This character is based on a real-life detective of the same name. The screenwriter, Chuck Pfarrer, explains:

> I rode around for a week with a female detective, and she was in the PA Department, Public Affairs, but she had been a working detective, she wasn't one of those people that never made it, she had been a working detective in New Orleans, and I needed somebody to be the police connection in this story, but I hadn't decided it would be a woman, until I spent some time with this woman whose name was Carmine Mitchell. I just changed it [a real-life arrest of a fugitive by Mitchell], I based the whole character on this one incident—this isn't Starsky and Hutch, so she called for backup [at the man's house]. [S]he snuck up to the guy's car and flattened two of his tires. That's it [I decided]—that's the woman right there [Pfarrer, telephone interview, 8 December 1995].

19. Faith Conroy said of the Woo shot, "Oh, isn't that a great shot? It didn't play like I thought it would though. It was shot at several different angles, there were many cameras moving, and very tight, very ominous...." She also agreed that the shot could have been longer:

> I don't know what happened there. With my understanding of John's style, I thought you would have seen a lot more because that was the moment of showing the demon. It could have been so dramatic, so much more than what you saw.
> People may not realize there are a lot of people involved in the final version of any film. It's hard to say what happens during the editing process, what decisions are made and who makes them. That's why it's always fun to see a director's cut of a film because you get to see what the director intended. I don't know that John has had that kind of freedom here in Hollywood [Conroy, fax to author].

20. In "John Woo and His Discontents," Tony Williams advances the interesting theory that Travolta was overacting because of lack of faith in the role and ultimately in the film—not in John Woo, but in what the project had become. Referring to comments by former student Ivan Muricy, he notes that "He [Muricy] has ... suggested that Woo and Travolta decided to treat *Broken Arrow* as a joke with director allowing star to overact similar to Scorsese and De Niro's attitude to *Cape Fear*"

(46 n. 13). Possible support for this notion is offered by Travolta himself, who at least implies that he contributed to exaggerating the character's mannerisms. In response to my faxed question, "Did you contribute any ideas to the film about your character or about any other aspects of the script or shooting?", he responded: "The war monger attributes. The bigger-than-life quality" (Travolta, fax to author). Muricy's suggestion is intriguing and would certainly help to explain Travolta's curious decision to underplay and to ham, alternately, and even within scenes, as if he were walking through his role.

21. As on other Woo projects, the actors were put at ease by Woo's graciousness and openness. Joan Allen told of a nice moment from rehearsal:

> [A]t one point during the process of rehearsing it, it seemed like from where the camera was, it would help if I moved across the room a little differently. And so I mentioned it to John. And he said, "No, no, no, no. We will move the camera. You don't move for the camera. The camera moves for you." And I thought, my God, this is from a man whose camerawork and the kinds of things he accomplishes on camera—I was so moved that his concern was that I shouldn't move—I shouldn't have to change anything, the camera would change for me. And that John was so concerned about the actors and accommodating them as well as his work, was just an incredible thing to me. I was so touched by that and impressed with his perspective on his work. I just thought it was so wonderful [telephone interview].

22. Werb appears in a cameo in the film as the father of an injury patient. Incidentally, Laurence Walsh, Woo's assistant, appears briefly as the assistant to Dr. Walsh, who performs the face-removal surgery on Archer.

23. See Rupert Howe, "Doubles All Round," for details on the progressive paring down of the screenplay. Colleary and Werb explained this process to me in some detail in a telephone interview. Quite clearly, the screenplay only came to full fruition as a result of the creative interaction between the screenwriters and Woo; in fact, Colleary and Werb stated to me that when they first saw *The Killer*, they realized that Woo should be the man to direct their script. According to Colleary and Werb, the script went through some 38 rewrites before reaching its present version.

24. The screenplay also featured more back story on the two brothers that "explained" their psychological twists as due to a broken home, alcoholic mother, etc. This is the story that Archer (as Castor) would have learned about from Pollux in Erewhon Prison if the scene had stayed in the finished film (Werb and Colleary). Additionally, the concept of the cop who becomes the killer was inspired by the Edmond O'Brien character in *White Heat*, a cop who goes undercover as a prisoner, becoming Cody's cellmate and eventually shooting him at the end of the film (Colleary and Werb, telephone interview).

25. In *White Heat*, the Edmond O'Brien character enters prison to get close to Cody Jarrett and nearly becomes trapped in his role. He shoots Jarrett in the famous ending atop a giant oil tank, where Jarrett dies amid a fiery explosion, which he starts by shooting an oil tank, screaming, "Made it, Ma! Top of the world!"

Chapter 10

1. Microsoft *Bookshelf '98* CD-ROM, s.v. "human nature," "style."

Bibliography

Abbas, Ackbar. *Hong Kong: Culture and the Politics of Disappearance.* Public Worlds 2. Minneapolis: University of Minnesota Press, 1997.

All Men Are Brothers [Shui hu chuan]. Trans. by Pearl S. Buck. 2 vols. First published 1937; reprint, New York: John Day, 1968.

Arnold, Edwin T., and Eugene L. Miller. *The Films and Career of Robert Aldrich.* Knoxville: University of Tennessee Press, 1986.

Avary, Roger. "Commentary." *Hard Boiled.* Dir. John Woo. With Chow Yun-fat and Tony Leung. Barry Wong, screenwriter. Criterion-Voyager, 1994.

Bate, Walter Jackson. *From Classic to Romantic: Premises of Taste in Eighteenth-Century England.* First published 1946; reprint, New York: Harper Torchbooks/ Academy Library–Harper, 1961.

Bazin, André. *Orson Welles: A Critical View.* Trans. Jonathan Rosenbaum, Foreword by François Truffaut. New York: Harper and Row, 1978. 74–82.

_____ *What Is Cinema?* Ed. and trans. by Hugh Gray. Berkeley: University of California Press, 1967.

Belton, John. *Cinema Stylists.* Filmmakers 2. Metuchen, N.J.: Scarecrow, 1983.

Benedict, Ruth. *The Chrysanthemum and the Sword: Patterns of Japanese Culture.* Foreword by Ezra F. Vogel. First published 1967; reprint, Boston: Houghton Mifflin, 1989.

Bergson, Henri, and George Meredith. *Comedy: "Laughter" and "An Essay on Comedy."* Appendix and introd. by Wylie Sypher. Garden City, N.Y.: Doubleday, 1956.

Bordwell, David. *Narration in the Fiction Film.* Madison: University of Wisconsin Press, 1985.

Braestrup, Peter. *Big Story: How the American Press and Television Reported and Interpreted the Crisis of Tet 1968 in Vietnam and Washington.* Introd. by Leonard R. Sussman. Boulder: Westview, 1977. 2 vols.

Brown, Malcolm, and Julia Cave. *A Touch of Genius: The Life of T. E. Lawrence.* London: J. M. Dent, 1988.

Cabrera Infante, G[uillermo]. *A Twentieth Century Job.* Trans. of *Un oficio del siglo 20: G. Caín 1954-60.* (La Habana: Ediciones R, 1963.) Trans. by Kenneth Hall with the author. London: Faber, 1991.

Chang, Pe-chin. *Chinese Opera and Painted Face.* Taiwan: n.p.; New York: DBS, 1969.

Chang, Terence. "Commentary." *The Killer.* Dir. John Woo. With Chow Yun-fat and Danny Lee. John Woo, screenwriter. Criterion-Voyager, 1993.

_____. E-mail to the author. 2 February 1999.

Chown, Jeffrey. *Hollywood Auteur: Francis Coppola.* New York: Praeger-Greenwood, 1988.

Chute, David. Publicity release for *Broken Arrow.* WCG Entertainment, 1995.

_____. "Supplements Text." *The Killer.* Criterion-Voyager, 1993.

_____. "Woo's on First." *Hard Boiled.* Dir. John Woo. With Chow Yun-fat and Tony Leung. Barry Wong, screenwriter. Criterion-Voyager, 1994.

Ciecko, Anne T. "Transnational Action: John Woo, Hong Kong, Hollywood." In

Transnational Chinese Cinemas: Identity, Nationhood, Gender, by Sheldon Hsiao-peng Lu. Honolulu: University of Hawaii Press, 1997. 221–37.

Cirlot, J. E. *A Dictionary of Symbols.* Trans. by Jack Sage. Foreword by Herbert Read. First published 1962; reprint, New York: Philosophical Library, 1962.

Connell, Richard. "The Most Dangerous Game." In *Great Tales of Action and Adventure.* Ed. George Bennett. New York: Laurel-Dell, 1959. 71–94. 1924.

Cowie, Peter. *Coppola.* New York: Scribner's-Macmillan, 1989, 1990.

Critical Theory since Plato. Ed. by Hazard Adams. New York: Harcourt, 1971.

Dannen, Fredric, and Barry Long. *Hong Kong Babylon: An Insider's Guide to the Hollywood of the East.* New York: Miramax-Hyperion, 1997.

Day, Clarence Burton. *The Philosophers of China: Classical and Contemporary.* New York: Philosophical Library, 1962.

Dictionary of the Vietnam War. Ed. by James S. Olson. New York: Greenwood, 1988.

Dome, Malcolm. "Chang-Shaw Massacre." *Eastern Heroes* 2 (1994): 17–22.

Feerick, Lisa. "John Woo: Spaghetti Easterns." *Film Threat Video Guide* 6 (1992): 52–57.

Fonoroff, Paul. "A Brief History of Hong Kong Cinema." *Renditions* 29-30 (1988): 293-308.

Fore, Steve. "Golden Harvest Films and the Hong Kong Movie Industry in the Realm of Globalization." *Velvet Light Trap* 34 (Fall 1994): 40-58.

Frayling, Christopher. *Spaghetti Westerns: Cowboys and Europeans from Karl May to Sergio Leone.* London: Routledge, 1981.

Frye, Northrop. *Anatomy of Criticism: Four Essays.* Princeton: Princeton University Press, 1971.

Fuchs, Cynthia J. "The Buddy Politic." *Screening* 194-210.

Garnham, Nicholas. *Samuel Fuller.* New York: Viking, 1971.

Gorbman, Claudia. *Unheard Melodies: Narrative Film Music.* London and Bloomington: BFI/Indiana University Press, 1987.

Hallam, Clifford. "The Double as Incomplete Self: Toward a Definition of Doppelgänger." In *Fearful Symmetry: Doubles and Doubling in Literature and Film.* Florida State University Conference on Literature and Film, 1980. Ed. and introd. by Eugene J. Crook. Tallahassee: University Press of Florida, 1981. 1-31.

Hammond, Stefan, and Mike Wilkins. *Sex and Zen and a Bullet in the Head: The Essential Guide to Hong Kong's Mind-Bending Films.* Foreword by Jackie Chan. New York: Fireside-Simon, 1996.

Havis, Richard James, and Alexandra A. Seno. "The Road to Hollywood." *Asiaweek On-Line.* 29 Aug. 1997. http://www.pathfinder.com/Asiaweek/97/0829/cs1.html.

Hoberman, J. "Hong Kong Blood and Guts." *Premiere* Aug. 1990, 33+.

Hong Kong Movie Database. Comp. by Lars-Erik Holmquist et al. http://egret0.stanford.edu.

Honig, Edwin. *Dark Conceit: The Making of Allegory.* Evanston, Ill: Northwestern University Press, 1959.

Howe, Rupert. "Doubles All Round." *Neon* Dec. 1997: 48-55.

Hsia, C. T. *The Classic Chinese Novel: A Critical Introduction.* New York and London: Columbia University Press, 1968.

_____. "The Military Romance: A Genre of Chinese Fiction." In *Studies in Chinese Literary Genres,* ed. by Cyril Birch. Berkeley: University of California Press, 1974. 339-90.

Hsiung-ping, Chiao. "The Distinct Taiwanese and Hong Kong Cinemas." In *Perspectives on Chinese Cinema,* ed. by Chris Berry. London: British Film Institute, 1991. 155-65.

Hucker, Charles O. *China's Imperial Past: An Introduction to Chinese History and Culture.* Stanford: Stanford University Press, 1975.

Hutcheon, Linda. *A Theory of Parody: The Teachings of Twentieth-Century Art Forms.* New York: Methuen, 1985.

Internet Movie Database. http://www.imdb.com.

Ishii, Teruo, dir. *Narazumono* [An Outlaw]. With Ken Takakura and Tetsuro Tamba. Toei, 1964.

Kaminsky, Stuart M. *American Film Genres: Approaches to a Critical Theory of Popular Film.* N.p.: Pflaum Publishing, 1974.

Kapsis, Robert E. *Hitchcock: The Making of a Reputation.* Chicago: University of Chicago Press, 1992.

Karnow, Stanley. *Vietnam: A History.* 2d rev. ed. New York: Penguin, 1997.

Katz, Ephraim. *The Film Encyclopedia.* 2d ed. New York: HarperCollins, 1994.

Kehr, Dave. "Commentary." *Hard Boiled.* Dir. John Woo. With Chow Yun-fat and Tony Leung. Barry Wong, screenwriter. Criterion-Voyager, 1994.

Keppler, C. F. *The Literature of the Second Self.* Tucson: University of Arizona Press, 1972.

Klein, Andy. "Hong Kong and Vine: Facing Off with *Face/Off* Director John Woo." *Phoenix New Times* 26 June–2 July 1997, n. p.

Lau, Shing-hon. "Three Modes of Poetic Expression in Martial Arts Films." In *A Study of the Hong Kong Swordplay Film,* ed. by Shing-hon Lau. Hong Kong: Urban Council, 1981. 117-26.

Lent, John A. *The Asian Film Industry.* Texas Film Studies Series. Austin: University of Texas Press, 1990.

_____. "Recent Publications on Asian Cinema." *Asian Cinema* 7.1 (1995): 30–47.

Leonard Maltin's TV Movies and Video Guide: 1998 Edition. Ed. by Leonard Maltin. New York: Signet, 1998.

Li, Cheuk-to. "The Return of the Father: Hong Kong New Wave and Its Chinese Context in the 1980s." In *New Chinese Cinemas: Forms, Identities, Politics,* ed. by Nick Browne et al. Cambridge: Cambridge University Press, 1994. 160-79.

Liu, James J. Y. *The Chinese Knight-Errant.* Chicago: University of Chicago Press, 1967.

Lo, Kwai-cheung. "*Once Upon a Time*: Technology Comes to Presence in China." *Modern Chinese Literature* 7.2 (1993): 79-96.

Loewe, Michael. Introduction to *The Ch'in and Han Empires, 221 BC-AD 220,* ed. by Denis Twitchett and Michael Loewe. Cambridge: Cambridge University Press, 1986. (Vol. 1 of *The Cambridge History of China.* 15 vols. to date. 1978- .) 1-19.

Logan, Bey. *Hong Kong Action Cinema.* Woodstock, N.Y.: Overlook, 1995.

MacCambridge, Michael. "Gore and More in Woo's 'The Killer'" (Review of *The Killer.*) *Austin American-Statesman* 19 Apr. 1991: 7.

McDonagh, Maitland. "Action Painter: John Woo." *Film Comment* (Sept.-Oct. 1993): 46-49.

Meglin, Nick. Interview. *All Things Considered.* National Public Radio. 26 February 1998.

Mellen, Joan. *Voices from the Japanese Cinema.* New York: Liveright, 1975.

_____. *The Waves at Genji's Door: Japan through Its Cinema.* New York: Pantheon, 1976.

Miller, Roy Andrew. Introduction to *Romance of the Three Kingdoms* by Kuan-Chung Lo. Trans. by C. H. Brewitt-Taylor. 2nd ed. Vol. 1. First published Shanghai: Kelly and Walsh, 1925; reprint, Rutland, Vt.: Tuttle, 1959. 2 vols. v-xii.

Mishima, Yukio. *Runaway Horses.* Trans. by Michael Gallagher. New York: Knopf, 1973. Vol. 2 of *The Sea of Fertility.* 4 vols.

Nitobe, Inazo. *Bushido: The Soul of Japan.* Introd. by William Elliot Griffis. Rev. ed. Rutland, Vt.: Tuttle, 1969.

Nottoway Plantations. 9 Mar. 1998. http://www.louisianatravel.com/nottoway/.
The Oxford History of World Cinema. Ed. by Geoffrey Nowell-Smith. Oxford: Oxford University Press, 1996.
Pfarrer, Chuck, screenwriter. *Hard Target*. Filmscript. Final version, Nov. 19, 1992. MCA-Universal, 1993.
Puzo, Mario. *The Godfather*. New York: Putnams, 1969.
Rayns, Tony. "Chivalry's Last Hurrah—John Woo." *Monthly Film Bulletin (London)* (Sept. 1990): 276.
_____. "Hard Boiled." *Sight and Sound* (Aug. 1992): 20-23.
Reed, Walter L. *Meditations on the Hero: A Study of the Romantic Hero in Nineteenth-Century Fiction*. New Haven: Yale University Press, 1974.
Reynauld, Beatrice. "John Woo's Art Action Movie." *Sight and Sound* 3.5 (1993): 23.
Richie, Donald. *The Films of Akira Kurosawa*. 3d ed. With additional material by Joan Mellen. Berkeley: University of California Press, 1996.
_____. *The Films of Akira Kurosawa*. 2d ed. Berkeley: University of California Press, 1973.
Riencourt, Amaury de. *The Soul of China*. New York: Coward-McCann, 1958.
Rothman, William. *Hitchcock—the Murderous Gaze*. Cambridge, Mass.: Harvard University Press, 1982.
Rowland, Beryl. *Birds with Human Souls: A Guide to Bird Symbolism*. Knoxville: University of Tennessee Press, 1978.
Ruhlmann, Robert. "Traditional Heroes in Chinese Popular Fiction." In *The Confucian Persuasion*, ed. by A. F. Wright. Stanford: Stanford University Press, 1960. 141-76.
Sarris, Andrew. "The Auteur Theory Revisited." *American Film* 2.9 (1977): 49-53.
_____. *Confessions of a Cultist: On the Cinema, 1955-1969*. New York: Simon and Schuster, 1970.
Schaefer, Dennis, and Larry Salvato. *Masters of Light: Conversations with Contemporary Cinematographers*. Berkeley: University of California Press, 1984.
Scharres, Barbara. "The Hard Road to *Hard Target*." *American Cinematographer* (Sept. 1993): 62-73.
Screening the Male: Exploring Masculinities in Hollywood Cinema. Ed. by Steven Cohan and Ina Rae Hark. London and New York: Routledge, 1993.
Seydor, Paul. *Peckinpah: The Western Films*. Urbana: University of Illinois Press, 1980.
Singer, Kurt. *Mirror, Sword and Jewel: A Study of Japanese Characteristics*. Introd. by Richard Storry. New York: Braziller, 1973.
Smith, D. Howard. *Confucius*. New York: Scribner's, 1973.
Ssu-ma, Ch'ien. *Records of the Historian: Chapters from the Shih Chi of Ssu-ma Ch'ien*. Trans. by Burton Watson. New York: Columbia University Press, 1969.
Stringer, Julian. "'Your Tender Smiles Give Me Strength': Paradigms of Masculinity in John Woo's *A Better Tomorrow* and *The Killer*." *Screen* 38.1 (1997): 25-41.
Sypher, Wylie. Introduction to *Comedy: "Laughter" and "An Essay on Comedy"* by Henri Bergson and George Meredith. Garden City, N.Y.: Doubleday, 1956. vii-xvi.
Tan, Patrick. "East/West Politics." *CineACTION* 42 (Feb. 1997): 47-49.
Tasker, Yvonne. "Dumb Movies for Dumb People: Masculinity, the Body, and the Voice in Contemporary Action Cinema." *Screening* 230-44.
_____. *Spectacular Bodies: Gender, Genre and the Action Cinema*. New York: Routledge, 1993.
Teo, Stephen. *Hong Kong Cinema: The Extra Dimensions*. London: British Film Institute, 1997.
Tilkin, Lori Sue. "The Journey of the Knight-Errant from Past to Present." M. A. thesis, Washington University, 1997.

Wang, Gung-hsing. *The Chinese Mind.* First published [New York:] Doubleday, 1946; reprint, New York: Greenwood, 1968.

Watson, Burton. *Ssu-ma Ch'ien, Grand Historian of China.* New York: Columbia University Press, 1958.

Weisser, Thomas. *Asian Cult Cinema.* Introd. by Max Allan Collins. New York: Boulevard-Berkley, 1997.

Williams, C[harles] A[lfred] S[peed]. *Encyclopedia of Chinese Symbolism and Art Motives. An Alphabetical Compendium of Legends and Beliefs as Reflected in the Manners and Customs of the Chinese Throughout History.* Rev. ed. New York: Julian, 1960.

Williams, Tony. "From Hong Kong to Hollywood: John Woo and His Discontents." *CineACTION* 42 (Feb. 1997): 40-45.

_____. "Kwan Tak-hing and the New Generation." Unpublished paper. Asian Cinema Studies Society, Trent University, Peterborough, Ontario. 21 Aug. 1997.

_____. "Space, Place, and Spectacle: The Crisis Cinema of John Woo." *Cinema Journal* 36.2 (1997): 67-84.

_____. "To Live and Die in Hong Kong: The Crisis Cinema of John Woo." *CineACTION* 36 (1995): 42-52.

_____. "Woo's Most Dangerous Game: Another Look at *Hard Target.*" Unpublished paper. 1996.

Wolcott, James. "Blood Test." *New Yorker* (Aug. 1993): 62-68.

Woo, John. "Chinese Poetry in Motion." *Sight and Sound* 4.7 (1994): 61.

_____. "Commentary." *The Killer.* Dir. John Woo. With Chow Yun-fat and Danny Lee. John Woo, screenwriter. Criterion-Voyager, 1993.

_____. Interview. By Accomando, Beth. *Hong Kong Film Magazine* 3 (Spring 1995): 26-32.

_____. Interview. By Chang, Terence. *The Killer* (video). Criterion-Voyager, 1995.

_____. Interview. By Martin, John, with occasional interjections by Terence Chang. In "Paint It Red: Two Interviews with John Woo." *Asian Trash Cinema* 1.5 (1993): 38-39, 40.

_____. Interview. By Sandell, Jillian. *Bright Lights Film Journal* 1.3 (1994): 36-39.

_____. Interview. By Savage, Mark, with the assistance of Frank Bren and Terence Chang. In "Paint It Red: Two Interviews with John Woo." *Asian Trash Cinema* 1.5. (1993): 38, 41-42.

_____. Onstage appearance. Seattle Art Museum. 6 July 1996. http://www.projectionmag.com. (24 Feb. 1998.)

_____. "Woo in Interview." With Berenice Reynaud. Trans. by Terence Chang. *Sight and Sound* 3.5 (1993): 23-25.

Yost, Graham, screenwriter. *Broken Arrow.* Revised by William Wisher. Los Angeles: 20th Century-Fox, 1995.

Zigelstein, Jesse. "Staying Alive in the 90's: Travolta as Star and the Performance of Masculinity." *Cineaction* 44 (1997): 2-11.

Interviews Conducted by Author

IN PERSON

Russell Carpenter, 8 Nov. 1995, Los Angeles.
Terence Chang, 4 Nov. 1995, Los Angeles.
Terence Chang, 2 Mar. 1996, Vancouver.
Chow Yun-fat, 6 Nov. 1995, Los Angeles.
Rock Galotti, 7 Nov. 1995, Los Angeles.
Sandrine Holt, 2 Mar. 1996, Vancouver.
Jim Jacks, 6 Nov. 1995, Los Angeles.
Bill Laurin and Glenn Davis, 1 Mar. 1996, Vancouver.
Nicholas Lea, 1 Mar. 1996, Vancouver.
Ivan Sergei, 1 Mar. 1996, Vancouver.
John Woo, 7 Nov. 1995, Los Angeles.
John Woo, 8 Nov. 1995, Los Angeles.
John Woo, 2 Mar. 1996, Vancouver.
David Wu and Terence Chang, 1 Mar. 1996, Vancouver.

BY TELEPHONE

Joan Allen, 26 Jan. 1998.
Yancy Butler, 18 Jan. 1996.
Russell Carpenter, 8 Jan. 1996.
Willie Carpenter, 14 Dec. 1995.
Faith Conroy, 24 Feb. 1996 (with corrections and changes by fax from Conroy to author, 23 Mar. 1998).

Phil Dagort, 21 Feb. 1996 (with corrections and changes by fax from Dagort to author, 16 Nov. 1998).
Rock Galotti, 29 June 1997.
Lance Henriksen, 14 Dec. 1995.
Eliott Keener, 15 Dec. 1995.
Danny Lee, 4 Jan. 1996.
Kasi Lemmons, 21 Nov. 1995.
Samantha Mathis, 27 Nov. 1995.
Bob Murawski, 1 June 1997.
Chuck Pfarrer, 8 Dec. 1995.
Chuck Pfarrer, 2 Feb. 1996.
Michelle Poulik, 23 Feb. 1996.
Marco St. John, 14 Dec. 1995.
Kurtwood Smith, 6 Mar. 1996.
Arnold Vosloo, 18 Dec. 1995.
Arnold Vosloo, 7 Jan. 1996.
David Wu, 19 Jan. 1998.
Graham Yost, 8 Jan. 1996.

RESPONSES TO FAXED QUESTIONS:

Philip Kwok (trans. by Lori Tilkin), 1996.
Lowell Lo, 12 June 1996.
Lowell Lo, 13 June 1996.
Christian Slater, 11 Dec. 1995.
John Travolta, 16 Apr. 1996.
Arnold Vosloo, 16 Nov. 1995.
Wong Wing-hang (trans. by Lori Tilkin), 13 May 1996.

Index

Numerals in boldface refer to illustrations in the text.